For Larry,
The pride of the Loyola
Econ. department,

Best wishes,

Tom DiLorenzo

UNHEALTHY CHARITIES

Unhealthy Charities

HAZARDOUS TO YOUR HEALTH AND WEALTH

James T. Bennett

and

Thomas J. DiLorenzo

BasicBooks
A Division of HarperCollins*Publishers*

Designed by Joan Greenfield

LIBRARY OF CONGRESS CATALOGING-IN-PUBLICATION DATA

Bennett, James T.
    Unhealthy charities : hazardous to your health and wealth / by
James T. Bennett and Thomas J. DiLorenzo
    p. cm.
    Includes bibliographical references and index.
    ISBN 0–465–02910–8
    1. Charities, Medical—United States—Finance. 2. Fund raising—
United States—Finance. 3. Voluntary health agencies—United States—
Finance. I. DiLorenzo, Thomas J. II. Title.
HV687.5.U5B45   1994
362.1'0425'094—dc20   94–6191
                                                                  CIP

94 95 96 97 ❖/HC 9 8 7 6 5 4 3 2 1

CONTENTS

TABLES

PREFACE AND
ACKNOWLEDGMENTS

For the past decade, our research has focused on the economics of nonmarket institutions, such as government and nonprofit organizations, including labor unions. Our first book dealing specifically with nonprofits was *Destroying Democracy: How Government Funds Partisan Politics* (1985), which explored the phenomenon of government-financed lobbying by nonprofit political activist organizations. *Unfair Competition: The Profits of Nonprofits* (1989) investigated the causes and consequences of the commercialization of the nonprofit sector— for-profit businesses operated by nonprofit entities in competition with taxpaying, for-profit firms.

Each of us has also authored or coauthored dozens of articles in professional journals and elsewhere on the economics and politics of nonprofits. This book is an extension of these earlier efforts and is motivated, in part, by personal tragedy: The sister-in-law of one of the authors was diagnosed with ovarian cancer. After repeated surgery and months of chemotherapy and radiation treatments, which caused almost as much trauma as the disease, she was pronounced "cured." But less than six months later, the cancer reappeared and, after many more months of debilitating chemotherapy and radiation treatments, she died.

This tragic event stimulated our thinking: Just what have the American Cancer Society and other health charities been doing all these years? For decades the public has been told in fund-raising appeals that major breakthroughs in disease research were imminent—if only there was enough money to support the research. We have also been told that lifestyle changes would greatly reduce the risk of disease and that the health charities were doing much to help disease victims.

To our surprise, no objective, book-length study of these and other claims made by the so-called voluntary health agencies had been pub-

lished for at least fifteen years. The only recent book on health charities is the American Cancer Society's *Crusade: The Official History of
the American Cancer Society* (1987), a self-published book that can hardly
be considered objective.

Our past research taught us that the world of philanthropy is
rapidly changing, so there is a need to fill this information vacuum
about health charities, which are among the largest (in terms of revenues) of all American charities. Such research is especially important
in light of accumulating evidence of the abuse of charity by those who
control and manage the organizations.

There has always been a degree of mismanagement in all types of
organizations, but the 1992 United Way of America scandal shocked
the nation because of the egregious nature of the conduct at one of the
nation's oldest, largest, and most respected charitable organizations. Is
it possible that the United Way of America scandal is just the tip of the
iceberg? This is a major question we address in this book.

Typically, any organization considered "charitable" is viewed almost as a sacred cow largely immune from careful scrutiny by
researchers, the media, and the public. With their well-funded public-
relations operations, the larger charities have been able to create an atmosphere in which questioning the activities, expenditures, and objectives of a charity is interpreted as an attack on charitable activities
themselves, if not on the poor, the sick, or other recipients of charity.
This is an absurd notion—implying, for example, that the national
uproar over the United Way of America was the result of a grand
conspiracy against those in need of United Way's assistance—but it
nevertheless prevails. Such a mind-set serves only those who would
abuse and misuse charity.

As we delved into the financial and annual reports of some of the
major health charities in the course of our research, we were shocked
by what we found: Health charities plead for money for programs to
aid those in need while at the same time holding millions of dollars in
cash, stocks, bonds, real estate, and automobiles. They claim to be volunteer organizations but, in many cases, salaries, fringe benefits, and
payroll taxes account for half or more of their expenditures. Many implicitly allude to helping disease victims while admitting that they do
absolutely nothing in terms of direct assistance. Instead, tens of millions of dollars are spent annually to educate high-income health professionals about disease while the poor are largely ignored. Most of the

lifestyle advice given through "public education" programs is so simplistic that it's worthless or, worse, misleading and incorrect.

Much of the research spending by health charities is not aimed directly at finding the causes of and cures for disease, but at helping favored researchers obtain government grants. There is nothing inherently wrong with such seed grants, but donors are given the impression that their contributions are used for original research, not as a researcher's means for getting more money from taxpayers. Health charities play only a minor role in financing disease research and, as we argue in this book, their efforts may actually hinder rather than help progress in the war against disease.

All too often, there is a chasm between fund-raising rhetoric and the reality of health-charity programs. A case can be made that the primary beneficiaries of these organizations are their executives and staffs and members of the medical establishment, not disease victims, their families and friends, or the general public.

As emphasized throughout this book, we begin with the assumption that health charities do a great deal of good. We are convinced, however, that far more good could be done if they stressed health instead of wealth; stopped subsidizing high-income health professionals; reduced spending on dubious public education programs; directed their energies toward helping the poor; and made far better use of their volunteers.

The major health charities must return to their charitable roots, and we offer an effective prescription to achieve this goal: "sunshine laws" requiring charities to open their books to anyone interested in investigating their spending and activities. The mere existence of such laws, we believe, will put enormous pressure on charity managers to spend their funds more wisely. As things now stand, neither the pressures of the marketplace nor the rigors of electoral politics place effective constraints on the behavior of those who control nonprofit organizations. Moreover, we show that the charity watchdog groups and the auditing firms that the public has relied on for decades to monitor and evaluate charities are not effective, and they may do more harm than good.

We are grateful to many who helped make this work possible. Financial support was provided by the Earhart and the Sunmark foundations. We also appreciate the support given by our respective institutions, George Mason University and Loyola College in Maryland.

Michael D. Killian of the George Mason University Library left no database untapped in our search for information. Capable research assistance was provided by Joshua David, John Furey, Christopher Laukaitis, Don Ratcliffe, Kenneth Rubb, David Spage, Ed Spriggs, and Andy Writer. Special thanks for efforts well beyond the call of duty are due Christopher A. Farris, now 2d Lieutenant Farris, U.S. Marine Corps, who was always "gung ho."

UNHEALTHY CHARITIES

GREAT PHILOSOPHERS

1

INTRODUCTION: ARE HEALTH CHARITIES AILING?

Most nonprofit institutions were founded by philanthropic people to take care of the poor. But I'm afraid the old Brahmins would be rolling over in their graves if they could see some of these . . . today.
—Representative Brian J. Donnelly (D-Mass.), 1993

Charity and voluntarism are deeply ingrained in the American psyche and play a much larger role in the United States than in other advanced nations. The commitment of Americans to aid their fellows was so pervasive that it made a lasting impression on Alexis de Tocqueville, the astute observer of Americans and their attitudes in the nation's formative years. In *Democracy in America,* he observed that

> Americans of all ages, all conditions, and all dispositions, constantly form associations. . . . Not only commercial and manufacturing companies in which all take part, but associations of a thousand other kinds . . . to give entertainments, to found establishments for education, to build inns, to construct churches, to diffuse books, to send missionaries to the antipodes; and in this manner they found hospitals, prisons, and schools. I have often admired the extreme skill with which the inhabitants of the United States succeed in proposing a common object to the exertions of a great many men, and in getting them voluntarily to pursue it.
>
> Nothing . . . is more deserving of our attention than this sector. . . . The health of a democratic society may be measured by the quality of the functions performed by private citizens.[1]

The historical record of America's voluntary accomplishments is nothing short of phenomenal. For example, at the end of the nineteenth and well into the twentieth century, millions of immigrants arrived in the United States with little more than the clothes they were wearing and a powerful conviction that a better life could be made for themselves and their families in their adopted nation. Despite their poverty, language difficulties, culture shock, and myriad other disadvantages, the immigrants adjusted quickly to their new surroundings and were rapidly submerged in the melting pot. All of this was accomplished by private, voluntary efforts, for federal, state, and local governments largely practiced "benign neglect" toward the needy. Food stamps, housing subsidies, medical assistance, disability and unemployment payments, and all the other forms of government assistance currently available to the needy did not exist then.[2]

American charitable institutions are held in high regard by the public and have been granted many special privileges by government to encourage their activities and to provide subsidies that lower their operating costs. These privileges include exemptions from taxation and from numerous regulations regarding bonds, franchises, and inspections that burden for-profit or commercial entities; subsidized postal rates; and special treatment with regard to antitrust, copyright, minimum wage, and other federal and state regulations. The primary justifications for this special treatment are that charitable organizations benefit the public and perform functions that neither government nor the for-profit sector can do effectively.

Evidence that many Americans still believe that private philanthropy has an important role to play is provided by their willingness to give generously to a host of different causes. According to U.S. Department of Commerce statistics (see table 1.1), total contributions to charitable causes from all sources—including individuals, corporations, and foundations—exceeded $120 billion in 1990. Tens of billions of dollars are donated each year to numerous domestic causes as well as to foreign-relief initiatives. If donors' concerns are accurately reflected in the volume of their contributions, apparently their first priority is to save their own and others' souls: Far and away, contributions to religious causes account for the lion's share of donations. Great store is also placed in educational activities and institutions and in human services, such as feeding the hungry and helping the poor, each of which receives about 10 percent of all charitable contributions.

Health-related causes rank fourth in contributions from all sources; clearly, the conquest of disease and aid to its victims are a major social concern. Private foundations, for instance, contributed $752 million to health-related causes in 1990, a figure second only to their donations to education ($1.15 billion). That same year, corporations gave $481 million to health-related charities; as with foundations, this amount was second only to that for education ($700 million). The average house-

TABLE 1.1
*Contributions to Private Philanthropy in
1990 by Type of Activity*

Purpose	Donations ($ billions)
Religion	$65.8
Education	12.4
Human Services	11.8
Health	9.9
Arts and Culture	7.9
International Relief	5.3
General Public Benefit	4.9
Environment	2.3

Source: U.S. Bureau of the Census, *Statistical Abstract
of the United States, 1992* (Washington, D.C.: Government Printing Office, 1992), p. 375.

hold contributed $143 in that year to health causes, which ranked sixth
in priority after religion, education, human services, arts and culture,
and international relief efforts.[3]

For the most part, charity begins—and stays—at home. Many
social problems addressed by charitable institutions, such as hunger,
disease, illiteracy, and homelessness, are far more severe in underdevel-
oped nations than in the United States. Yet in 1990 American contributions for international relief to alleviate such problems accounted for
less than 5 cents of each dollar donated.

This book focuses on health charities that emphasize specific diseases, also known as voluntary health agencies (VHAs). No one knows
how many health charities there are, but they clearly number in the
thousands and new ones are constantly being formed. The *Encyclopedia of Associations* lists more than two thousand active organizations in
the health and medical field.[4] And, as shown in table 1.1, Americans
give generously to these organizations. Health charities are big business
in America.

Many health charities are household names and have reputations
that most for-profit firms would envy. The high regard that Americans
have for health charities is partly attributable to their mission: The
conquest of disease and assistance to disease victims strike a responsive
chord, since every family has been or eventually will be affected by
disease. In addition, health charities have widespread name recognition

TABLE 1.2
Twenty of the Largest Health Charities

American Cancer Society	Muscular Dystrophy Association
American Diabetes Association	National Association for Retarded Citizens
American Foundation for the Blind	
American Heart Association	National Easter Seal Society
American Lung Association	National Hemophilia Foundation
Arthritis Foundation	National Kidney Foundation
Cystic Fibrosis Association	National Multiple Sclerosis Society
Epilepsy Foundation	National Society to Prevent Blindness
Leukemia Society	
March of Dimes	Planned Parenthood
Mental Health Association	United Cerebral Palsy Association

Source: Carl Bakal, *Charity, U.S.A.* (New York: Times Books, 1979), p. 29.

because, outside of religious organizations, they are among the nation's oldest charitable institutions. The first health charity in the United States was formed more than a century ago: In 1892, Lawrence F. Flick, a physician suffering from tuberculosis, formed the Pennsylvania Society for the Prevention of Tuberculosis, the forerunner of today's American Lung Association. Most of the largest and best-known health charities (see table 1.2) have operated for a half-century or more. Health charities have thus withstood the test of time.

The sterling reputations enjoyed by most health charities have, in many ways, been created by the charities themselves. Fund-raising activities offer excellent opportunities to promote the good works of these organizations; public service announcements on television and radio and in the print media call attention to these organizations and their programs. Direct-mail solicitations result in tens of millions of appeals—along with self-promotional materials—being sent each year to potential contributors. Other fund-raising functions, such as charity balls, walkathons, and tournaments, are widely publicized by the media anxious to do their part in the battle against disease. In addition, health charities often obtain widespread publicity by providing advice to the public about how to avoid or reduce health risks.

By and large, then, Americans donate generously to health charities not because of their knowledge of what health charities actually do, but because of what the health charities say they do. Finding the causes of and cures for disease, educating the public, assisting patients, and providing services to the community—together, the ostensible raison d'être of most health charities—are universally supported. Our focus in this book is not on their self-professed good intentions, however, but on their actual performance. How effective are they in achieving their objectives? Is their fund-raising rhetoric an accurate description of what they really do? Are the billions of dollars donated to them well spent? Are they finding cures for diseases, as some have been promising for decades? Who controls these multimillion-dollar organizations, and what kinds of incentives guide their behavior? What mechanisms or checks and balances, if any, assure that charity dollars are well spent on one of the most emotional of all issues—suffering caused by disease? Can the efficiency and accountability of these institutions be improved?

Our research on these and many other issues related to health charities is motivated by a skepticism about organizations that are judged more on the basis of their purported good intentions than by objective criteria. After all, there is a long history of failed or counterproductive government programs that also have noble, well-meaning, and widely acclaimed aims, such as ending poverty, improving education, expanding housing for the poor, and cleaning up the environment. If there is anything we should have learned from the past half-century of government social experiments, it is that good intentions do not guarantee good results.

As with so many of these failed government programs, most of what health charities do (and what all charities do, for that matter) is also judged more by intentions than by results. This assertion doesn't mean that the charities are necessarily ineffective, nor would a similar complaint mean that no government program is effective. Rather, it means that there is a real need to examine closely the operations and activities of health charities and to assess their performances—a task that very few scholars, to our knowledge, have attempted.

This information vacuum is unfortunate, for these uniquely American institutions—which have at their disposal billions of dollars in annual donations and millions of dedicated volunteers—are in a position to do a great deal of good. And we recognize that these organizations undoubtedly *do* do a great deal of good. But the important questions are: How much good do they really do? and, Could they do even more good if they shifted their spending patterns among programs?

WHY SO LITTLE INTEREST IN HEALTH CHARITIES?

Health charities number in the thousands, receive billions of dollars annually in contributions, mobilize millions of volunteers, engage in massive national educational and public-relations campaigns, employ tens of thousands of people, and often pay their top executives salary and benefit packages valued well into the six figures. And yet health charities have received very little attention in the scholarly or popular literature.

One reason for this apparent neglect may be that there is no central data source on charitable organizations in general, let alone health charities. To researchers accustomed to readily available data, this means that health charities are not a very profitable area of inquiry because gathering basic data is a costly, time-consuming task.

A second reason is a widely held but misguided belief that to criticize the operations of individual charities is to criticize the act of charity itself. Senator Orrin Hatch (R-Utah) noted this attitude at a Senate investigation of certain nonprofits that are partially funded by the federal Legal Services Corporation (LSC). The LSC distributes grants to hundreds of nonprofit legal service organizations, which ostensibly assist the poor with their civil legal problems. For a U.S. senator or anyone else to question the activities of these grantees, however, is

> politically disadvantageous. One is led to believe that the nobility of the [Legal Services] Corporation's purpose makes any question as to the propriety of some of its activities nothing less than a vicious attack on the poor themselves. This misinformed, oversimplified presumption has scared away much needed review and has provided the Corporation with a congressional carte blanche to operate without oversight, without review, and without criticism.[5]

The LSC has had a controversial history,[6] with Senate investigators discovering that hundreds of millions of dollars earmarked by Congress for legal services for the poor had been diverted to many questionable uses having little to do with aiding the poor.[7] Yet those who deprived the needy of funds apparently convinced the public that criticism of this diversion is nothing less than a direct attack on the poor.

Just as oversight of nonprofit legal services organizations can make it more likely that resources intended for charitable purposes are in fact used for those purposes, we believe that there is an urgent need for more effective oversight of health and other charities that solicit funds from the general public.

As we discuss in chapter 2, charities in general and health charities in particular are only weakly influenced by either the market forces that regulate the behavior of for-profit firms or the political pressures that keep government enterprises in check. Charities' public support is based almost entirely on trust, and that trust is sometimes abused. As discussed in later chapters, health charities are not always forthcoming and truthful to the public about their expenditures and operations. The public needs to know more about these organizations so that they—the donors—can become more confident that their contributions are being wisely spent.

THE BIG THREE

There are thousands of health charities, with very diverse characteristics—many are small and recently formed, while others are old and well established, with substantial revenues—and different objectives and programs. There is no such thing as a "typical" health charity, and it would be impossible even to attempt any kind of comprehensive analysis of the whole universe of health charities in the United States. To keep a comprehensive analysis manageable, one would have to aggregate the data to such an extent that much of the important information about the health charities' operations would be irretrievably lost. Most of this book thus focuses on what we call the Big Three health charities: the American Lung Association (ALA), the American Cancer Society (ACS), and the American Heart Association (AHA). The ALA is the oldest health charity in the United States, and the other two are also older than most other health charities. Although it is not the largest in terms of revenues, the ACS is the best known of all health charities due to its mammoth public-relations machine and door-to-door fund-raising crusades.[8] The AHA is also among the best known health charities, and heart disease is the nation's number-one killer.

Moreover, many other health charities model themselves after the Big Three. Indeed, such imitation has so infuriated the Big Three that in 1989 they convinced a few members of Congress to conduct an investigation of "look-alike" health charities. We believe that by analyzing in depth a small, manageable number of health charities that are well known and among the oldest and best established, we will minimize suspicion that our analysis is based on the aberrant behavior of organizations chosen to support a preconceived bias. Virtually all health charities have the same basic organizational structure as the Big Three's, so an analysis of the Big Three should apply to the health-charity category as a whole.

WHO'S MINDING THE CHARITIES?

Chapter 2 also examines the structure and incentives of nonprofits in general, and health charities in particular, in order to make some generalizations about behavior in the nonprofit health-charity sector. All nonprofits are largely insulated from the competitive pressures of the marketplace because there is no bottom line, or profit motive. There are no shareholders who have a financial stake that might be threatened if the organization were poorly managed. Furthermore, the "customers" of health charities are not their principal source of revenue, as is the case with for-profit firms. Donors typically do not receive the services of the charities to which they contribute, and contributions are often given for purely emotional reasons.

Consequently, health charities often have much more latitude to engage in self-serving behavior than private, competitive businesses do, and the potential for the misuse and abuse of funds is far greater.

Nonprofit organizations have accountability standards that, in many ways, are even weaker than those of government decision makers. At least with regard to government enterprises, elected representatives at some point have to answer to the voters. And, at the federal level and for many states as well, freedom of information and "sunshine" legislation make it relatively easy for interested parties to obtain detailed information about the expenditures, programs, and activities of public enterprises. But nonprofit organizations are self-perpetuating entities that are insulated from the competitive forces of the marketplace and from the political pressures of government. Ultimately, nonprofits are accountable only to themselves; their sole obligation to those who wish to investigate their operations is to release their most recent tax returns.

Boards of directors of health charities typically consist of medical professionals and lay people; in fact, many health charities were established by physicians whose medical specialty was the disease with which the charity is concerned. Board members without medical expertise are chosen with an eye toward enhancing the health charity's prestige and fund-raising abilities. All serve without compensation on a part-time basis, so there is little incentive for members to delve deeply into the health charity's policies and programs. Thus, the boards tend to be dominated by a small clique of activists, many of whom are health professionals. Consequently, supervision of the management of health charities by boards of directors tends to be weak and ineffective, leaving the professional staff, along with a small segment of the board (usually medical professionals), free to run the health charity with few constraints. This absence of accountability and constraints is the root cause of the abuse, or the inefficient use, of charitable donations that has plagued the health-charity sector for decades.

To a large extent, most of the major health charities are effectively controlled by the medical establishment. This is not necessarily a bad thing; medical expertise is a necessary ingredient of success for health charities. But at the same time, as we point out often in this book, the financial interests of the medical establishment too often seem to take precedence over programs that benefit the public. Under the halo of "charity," health charities can engage in activities that benefit the medical establishment without arousing public suspicion—the health charities permit the self-interests of the medical establishment to be cloaked in the garb of "doing good" for the public.

Also discussed in chapter 2 are the close links among the medical profession, the health charities, and the National Institutes of Health (NIH). By controling most major health charities, which in turn exert great influence over NIH funding priorities, a relatively small clique of medical professionals controls disease research, defining what is and what is not appropriate. Later, we show that this arrangement can easily impede major breakthroughs in finding the causes of and cures for disease.

In chapter 3, the 1992 United Way of America (UWA) scandal dramatically illustrates how charitable contributions can be misused and abused with relative impunity because of the unique organizational structure and incentives prevalent among nonprofits. The question is not whether mismanagement will occur, but how severe it will be and how long it will take to be discovered. A report to the UWA board of governors revealed that, for years, the organization's past national president, William Aramony, used charitable donations to support his lavish lifestyle; to engage in blatant cronyism, patronage, and nepotism; and to finance highly questionable business deals (at this writing, the Internal Revenue Service and the Federal Bureau of Investigation are still investigating). Unfortunately, similar behavior also occurs, though not on such a grand scale, in many health charities and in other health-related nonprofit organizations, including Blue Cross–Blue

Shield, local affiliates of the American Heart Association, nonprofit hospitals, and the nonprofit medical-care industry.

The UWA episode is especially worrisome because the two external checks and balances that the public relies on to prevent (or at least strictly limit) this type of behavior—independent auditors and charity-rating services—failed to uncover Aramony's gross abuse over a long period of time. Year after year, the UWA's finances were routinely reviewed by Arthur Andersen & Company, the National Charities Information Bureau, and the Philanthropic Advisory Service of the Better Business Bureau. These organizations on which the public relies for unbiased assessments of charitable operations failed to uncover, let alone prevent, a major scandal.

If the public cannot rely on independent auditors or respected rating services to ensure that their donations are used wisely and to separate the "good" charities from the "bad" or indifferent ones, there seems to be no effective external checks to prevent the abuse and misuse of contributions. An important issue addressed in chapter 4 is why the auditors and ratings services cannot be counted on to root out mismanagement; in the final chapter, we propose a solution to this problem.

CREATIVE ACCOUNTING

Chapters 4 through 6 examine in depth how health charities—primarily the Big Three—spend the tens of millions of dollars they receive from the public each year. In chapter 4, we ask a simple question: Where does the money go? There we examine the Byzantine world of nonprofit accounting—described by an Internal Revenue Service (IRS) official as of "third world" quality—and attempt to interpret and make sense of it.

Health-charity financial statements, even though they conform to standard accounting practices, hide as much as they reveal. Donors are interested in how much of their contribution reaches the needy, but under current accounting practices, this information is impossible to obtain. One problem is that *the cost of providing a service is counted as part of the service itself.* So a highly inefficient charity that spends most of its donations on salaries rather than on services can report that most of its expenditures benefit the public, when in fact the primary beneficiaries are its executives and staff.

A second difficulty is that the allocation of costs to such activities as fund-raising, public education, and community services is basically arbitrary. Thus, fund-raising costs may be hidden as "public education" expenses simply because the fund-raising appeal purports to "educate" the public about the disease for which the solicitation is made. The accounting firms that audit health charities have less incentive to conduct a stringent review of their finances than they do in reviewing private firms, and the IRS is reluctant to apply the same oversight standards to health charities as it does to private businesses and individual taxpayers. The problem is not a lack of accounting expertise, however, for even the nation's finest certified public accountants cannot determine from financial statements alone whether a given charity is providing the most for its money.

The financial statements of the Big Three unequivocally reveal that the accumulation of wealth has high priority. Most donors would be surprised by the vast hoards of cash, stocks, bonds, and certificates of deposit held by the Big Three. Their relentless fund-raising activities, which suggest a critical need for funds for programs, are very different from the reality of health-charity wealth, which has increased steadily over the past decade. In addition to financial holdings, large sums are also diverted to the acquisition of physical property—land, buildings, and automobiles. There are urgent needs for services, but how do stocks, bonds, real estate, land, and other assets ease the suffering of disease victims or help find the causes of and cures for various maladies? We examine why wealth accumulation takes place and who benefits from these asset holdings.

Charity watchdog organizations, such as the highly regarded National Charity Information Bureau, have barks much worse than their bites when it comes to protecting the public. Health charities are so numerous that the charity-rating services are overwhelmed by an impossible task. The data that the rating services analyze are the audited financial statements provided by the charities themselves. Despite their good intentions, the watchdogs are no different from anyone else in that they cannot discern from this source alone how the funds are actually being spent. Moreover, mistakes are inevitable. For these and other reasons, charity watchdogs may cause more problems than they cure. If nothing else, they favor large, national, long-established charities over newly formed and local groups. At best, the advice of charity-rating services should be viewed with considerable skepticism.

WHAT DO CHARITIES DO?

To understand what health charities actually do, it is necessary to examine in detail their various programs and activities, most of which are carried out not by the national headquarters but by state and local units spread across the nation. Thus, it is essential to investigate the annual reports and financial statements of health-charity subunits. Typically, these are issued annually by state divisions that are responsible for fund-raising and for mobilizing volunteers. By convention, health charities report their activities in five functional categories: public education, professional education, research, patient services, and community services. Few health charities, however, engage in all five activities; most concentrate their programs in three or at most four categories.

Public Education

Virtually all health charities spend significant sums to inform us about the causes of disease and the lifestyle changes that may reduce the likelihood of contracting a particular illness. As shown in chapter 5, however, public education seems inherently contradictory: The health charities stress the importance of research funds because so little is known about the causes of and cures for various maladies. How can they educate the public when so little is known? Moreover, because of the medical profession's lack of understanding of the root causes of most illnesses, much of the lifestyle advice offered by health charities is so simplistic that it is worthless, or so contradictory and misleading that it may even be hazardous to our health. Finally, the health charities report such enormous numbers of persons they "educated" each year that one might reasonably ask whether they shouldn't reduce spending on public education and use those funds for more important purposes.

Put into perspective, a persuasive case can be made that "public education" is little more than thinly disguised fund-raising activity and that the category was created so that fund-raising expenses could be written off as educational activities. In addition, a highly consistent theme appears in most public education messages: See your physician for regular checkups. The health charities can admonish the public to increase their consumption of medical services under the halo of charity, but if the American Medical Association were to promote the same message, the specters of self-interest and greed would arise.

The most important and enduring myth uncovered by our analysis of health charities is that they direct their programs and services to the poor and the needy. Conventional wisdom has long held that charity, by definition, exists to aid those who cannot help themselves and are less fortunate than those who are able to donate their time and money.

But many health charities give only token assistance, if any at all, to disease victims. Among the Big Three, the AHA spends nothing on heart-disease sufferers and the ALA spends only a fraction of 1 percent of its funds on lung-disease patients; only the ACS has numerous programs to aid cancer victims. Yet the ACS has issued a report showing that cancer education for the poor is often irrelevant and insensitive, that the poor suffer disproportionately from cancer, and that the poor are not being adequately served.[9]

Professional Education and Research

Although the health charities spend only minimal sums to aid the needy, the Big Three devote huge sums each year to subsidize the professional education of high-income health professionals, as discussed in chapter 6. Although every patient has a right to expect his or her physician to be knowledgeable about the latest procedures, tests, and treatments, is professional education an appropriate activity for the health charities, given the unmet needs of the indigent? After all, other professionals pay for their own continuing professional education. Health professionals are the primary beneficiaries of the education, which enhances their careers and incomes. Professional education is also a tax-deductible business expense. What's happened to the notion that those who reap the benefits should also bear the costs?

There is also a fairness issue: Is it fair to solicit donations from lower- and middle-income Americans to subsidize the education of some of America's highest-paid individuals—medical professionals? When funds are used to educate doctors, dentists, nurses, and allied health personnel, that money is not available to assist needy heart, lung, and cancer patients. Would the public be as generous to health charities if it knew that its contributions were being used to subsidize high-income health professionals?

Health-charity fund-raising appeals always emphasize the critical need for funds to support disease research. But there is widespread public ignorance about the scope and significance of this research. Despite the impression given in fund-raising appeals that health charities are major participants in financing disease research, the health charities, at best, play only a minor role in research. The taxpayers, via the federal government's National Institutes of Health and other agencies, pay for more than 95 percent of all disease research. Furthermore, most of the "research" expenditures by health charities are not for research into causes and cures, but are seed grants given to researchers who use the funds to write research proposals to obtain government support for their work.

We argue that the Big Three hinder, rather than help, disease research by virtually monopolizing the direction of research through their close ties to the National Institutes of Health. Most cancer research, for example, is conducted at a relatively small number of institutions by a relatively small number of individuals who are members of a tightly knit group. Such a noncompetitive environment is not conducive to the kind of bold experimentation and challenging of the status quo that are the hallmarks of scientific breakthroughs. It's not as though the health charities discourage promising research out of evil motives, such as greed for the profits that would accrue to the firm holding a patent on a miracle drug that cured a disease. Rather, we show that research is impeded because the health charities and the researchers allied with them have the most honorable aims possible. But, once again, even the very best intentions do not guarantee good results.

Patient and Community Services

What distinguishes charities from other institutions in society is their ability to mobilize volunteers. In chapter 7, we present the many excellent programs administered by the ACS to show how much good can be accomplished when the energies of millions of volunteers are harnessed to help disease victims. Although a surprising number of health charities do not make use of volunteers, and many others use theirs exclusively for fund-raising, patient services provided by volunteer workers is unquestionably charity at its finest.

The Big Three also spend substantial sums on community services, such as disease screening to identify high-risk individuals so that preventive measures can be taken. On the surface, the benefits to the public of "disease avoidance" may seem obvious, but cost-benefit studies have shown that from both medical and economic perspectives the costs of prevention outweigh the benefits. Among other things, the side effects of medical treatments to reduce risk factors can cause other problems. Although disease screenings clearly benefit the medical establishment by increasing the demand for medical services, the public may not be better off. If volunteers rather than highly paid medical professionals were used more extensively in providing community services, the cost-benefit ratio might be more favorable.

The nation is in the midst of a health care crisis—millions of

Americans do not have adequate access to medical care. By using volunteers more effectively in providing more patient and community services and in cooperation with community-based free clinics, the health charities could do a great deal to alleviate the health care crisis.

Filling in the Gaps

Despite the efforts of existing health charities, much remains to be done. Although we may not be losing the battle against disease, major breakthroughs are few and far between, and the need for patient assistance is all but endless. There is a large gulf between the needs in the health and disease arena and what is being accomplished. As discussed in chapter 8, this gap has encouraged the formation of new health charities. Rather than welcoming the newcomers, however, the older, established health charities have been antagonistic toward them. After condemning the recently formed groups as frauds and unscrupulous look-alikes, the Big Three used their political clout to instigate congressional hearings, at which they denounced look-alike health charities.

Some of the criticisms of the newer health charities amount to a thinly veiled attempt to employ the power of the government to ban new groups simply because they may compete for funds. In reality, the so-called look-alikes not only provide healthy competition in fund-raising, but also aid in providing services and programs that existing health charities do not or cannot offer. We show how these new groups may actually increase the contributions to the established charities by comparing these with estimates of donations that would occur if no competition existed.

Finally, chapter 9 summarizes our findings and makes policy recommendations to improve the performance of health charities so that the public receives more and better services. America's health charities have an important role to play in alleviating the health care crisis and in helping those in need, and therefore must become more accountable to donors. There is no doubt that health charities do a great deal of good, but it is equally certain that much more can be accomplished with the resources that are already available. To quote a well-known politician, there is a need for change.

2

THE POLITICAL ECONOMY OF HEALTH CHARITIES

There is many a slip 'twixt the cup and the lip. —Palladas

In early 1992, the national president of United Way of America, William Aramony, resigned amid a controversy revolving around nepotism, cronyism, and extravagant expenditures of charitable donations on personal limousines, first-class air travel, condominiums for use by himself and other United Way executives, the creation of business spin-offs staffed by patronage employees, golf clubs, and other inappropriate uses.

Most commentators seem to believe that the United Way scandal was simply a matter of the personal negligence of a few individuals—perhaps just one person. Better or more effective leadership, therefore, would supposedly solve the problem. The new leadership at United Way of America may indeed put that organization's house in order, but this sorry episode highlights a more serious problem that is symptomatic of *all* charities. Because charities tend to be judged more by their self-professed good intentions than by their performance, they typically escape the close public scrutiny that private businesses (and even government entities) receive. Indeed, most of what the public knows about charities comes from the charities themselves; self-reported information, alas, is all too often self-serving.

Constrained neither by the pressures of the marketplace nor by the rigors of electoral politics, most charities—both large and small—suffer from bureaucratic inertia and diminished effectiveness. These problems are intensified as a charity ages and grows in size. Over time, the founders and their missionary zeal are replaced by professionals who consider the organization to be merely the source of their livelihoods. Fund-raising becomes the organization's primary function as economic security becomes paramount rather than the charitable services that motivated the entity's establishment. Self-selection encourages individuals who value the leeway and lack of restrictions offered by the non-profit organizational form to seek employment in charities. After all, no other entity in contemporary society permits a person to prosper financially while simultaneously asserting that his or her only goal is to "do good" through charitable acts. Our study of the incentive structures of the nonprofit sector in general and health charities in particular reveals that these structures permit, if not virtually guarantee, inefficiency and, if the executives are so inclined, malfeasance.

INCENTIVE SYSTEMS BY SECTOR

It is useful to compare the incentive systems in the for-profit, government, and nonprofit sectors, for there are major differences that have important consequences for organizational efficiency and effectiveness. The behavior of all managers and staffs in every organization is directly determined by the organization's incentive system—its structure of rewards and punishments—since everyone attempts to maximize his or her self-interest by seeking rewards and avoiding punishment.

The For-Profit Sector

The incentive system that determines the behavior of managers in private, for-profit businesses are very different from that in government or nonprofit enterprises, such as health charities. Managers of for-profits are more likely to get promoted if they strive for efficiency by cutting costs and reducing waste. A common practice in private industry is to base financial bonuses on the cost savings (and thus profit increases) achieved by managers. If costs can be reduced and profits increased, the manager's income—along with his or her prospects for promotion—rises. At the same time, executives who perform poorly can be (and often are) terminated—lax and careless managers can escape the consequences of their behavior for only a short time in the for-profit sector. Competition is a fact of life for private firms, and the ever-present threat of a loss of sales to more efficient, lower-cost competitors (assuming prices are increased to cover increased costs) forces managers to endeavor constantly to reduce costs and improve quality.

Many corporate giants have been humbled by lower-cost competitors in recent years. IBM Corporation, which for decades dominated the computer field worldwide, has taken a massive beating from small, highly efficient companies that sell personal computers by mail.

Known as Big Blue, IBM was regarded for years as the bluest of the "blue chip" stocks; today, IBM might more appropriately be called Big Black-and-Blue, after the drubbing investors gave the firm's stock.

The stock market also disciplines corporate managers of investor-owned business firms. Inefficient businesses whose managers do not closely monitor production and distribution in a continuous effort to lower costs and improve quality, or spend excessive amounts on executive salaries and perquisites at the expense of shareholders, will find their stock prices depressed. Disillusioned shareholders can easily vent their dissatisfaction with management's performance by selling their shares, which depresses the price of the firm's stock.

There is an entire industry of financial analysts who earn their living by studying corporate America to determine whether a company is undervalued—whether waste and inefficiency have caused its stock price to decline. When such a company is found, a corporate takeover specialist (often disparagingly called a "raider") bids for control of the company, usually by offering shareholders a higher price for their stock. Profits may be made by ousting the current managers and turning the company around by reducing waste and lowering costs. The mere threat of a takeover is a powerful mechanism to keep corporate managers on their toes.

Ultimately, for-profit firms must pass a market test by satisfying consumers with good-quality and competitively priced products or services. Business managers or entrepreneurs are widely believed to be in control of production in a market economy; as economist Ludwig von Mises once put it, "They are at the helm and steer the ship." Moreover,

> a superficial observer would believe that they are supreme. But they are not. They are bound to obey unconditionally the captain's orders. The captain is the consumer. . . . If a businessman does not strictly obey the orders of the public, . . . he suffers losses, he goes bankrupt, and is thus removed from his eminent position at the helm. [Others] who did better in satisfying the demand of the consumers replace him.[1]

The Government Sector

Governments throughout the world—from the central government of Russia to small U.S. towns—are turning to privatization (having private firms produce goods and services once produced by government employees) to deliver better-quality services at lower costs. Russia is now turning over many of its formerly nationalized industries to private ownership, an act that was unthinkable just a few years ago. And all across America, hundreds of municipalities are finding that privatizing everything from airports to street cleaning is a way to avoid unpopular tax increases and service reductions.[2]

Government bureaucracies are inherently less cost-effective and less accountable to consumers than for-profit, competitive businesses for a number of reasons. First, because there is no bottom line—no profit-and-loss statements—in the public sector, government managers are not rewarded for cost-cutting, nor are they penalized for cost increases. Since cost-cutting (in effect, saving the taxpayers' money) does not increase a bureaucrat's salary, which is set by civil-service regulations, there tends to be very little of it. While it is true that every president in recent memory has promised to "make government more efficient," every president has also failed to do so. The historical record thus offers little encouragement for the Clinton administration's current proposal to "reinvent government."

Second, incentives in the public sector are actually perverse. Government bureaucrats are not rewarded by cost-cutting or improving the quality of services, so other criteria are employed. As a rule, government managers are rewarded and promoted according to the size of their staffs, which creates an incentive for overstaffing. Bureaucrats are often "empire builders."

In other words, there are incentives for cost *maximization* in the public sector, which is why it is so notoriously inefficient and has been for as long as anyone can remember. As Mises observed almost a half-century ago,

> the terms *bureaucrat, bureaucratic,* and *bureaucracy* are clearly invectives. Nobody calls himself a bureaucrat or his own methods of management bureaucratic. These words are always applied with an opprobrious connotation. They always imply a disparaging criticism of persons, institutions, or procedures. . . . The abusive implication of the terms in question is not limited to America and other democratic countries. It is a universal phenomenon.[3]

Bureaucrats, as individuals, are no more lazy or dishonest than anyone else; the negative connotation of bureaucracy results from the incentive system in the public sector. All individuals respond to the incentive system that governs their behavior, and the incentives facing government bureaucrats do not reward or encourage efficiency.

There are, however, some constraints on bureaucratic inefficiency in government. At the local level, dissatisfied citizens can "vote with their feet" by moving to another jurisdiction. And at all levels of government, incumbents can be voted out of office in the next election. Electoral constraints have become increasingly weak, however, as the incumbents in Congress and elsewhere have rigged election outcomes by gerrymandering; expanded their taxpayer-paid staffs, which serve as full-time campaign organizations; abused the franking privilege; and employed other benefits of incumbency, such as access to the media, to make it all but impossible for a challenger to succeed. It is not unusual for nearly all congressional incumbents to be reelected.[4]

Political behavior is also influenced—for better or worse—by public opinion. Politicians who pander a little too much to special interests or who engage in grossly unethical behavior are often subjected to the scrutiny of the network news cameras, which report such behavior to the public. Newspaper columnists, radio and television talk-show hosts, and others in the media are also influential in shaping public opinion and, consequently, in monitoring and altering government behavior.

The media are also a forum for competing opinions regarding public policy. Despite complaints by conservatives of media bias, there is still a considerable amount of diversity of opinion over the nation's airwaves and in print. This diversity places an additional constraint on excessive government power.

The Nonprofit Sector

As with all nonprofit organizations, nonprofit health charities are largely isolated from both marketplace competition and electoral constraints. There are no shareholders in a nonprofit organization—indeed, that is what the legal definition of a nonprofit is. Consequently, there is no such thing as shareholder pressure, threats of legal action, or takeovers.

Nonprofit organizations do not rely on consumer patronage for their financial well-being—the recipients of charity are *not* generally the same people who donate the funds. Consequently, there is much latitude in the types and quality of service provided. Inefficient service providers are not weeded out by recalcitrant consumers, as is the case for all for-profit firms, nor are efficient service providers rewarded by those they directly serve.

Donors can and do apply pressure to ensure that their donations are well spent. But individual donor influence wanes as the size of an organization increases; most donors, especially those who make small contributions, simply rely on the organization's promises without examining its actual performance. All large health charities raise much of their revenue by getting a large number of small donations through mail solicitation or through door-to-door campaigns conducted by volunteers. Contributors who give $20 to a charity have little, if any, financial incentives to investigate the charity's activities, nor do they have the basic skills or the time required to unravel the charity's complex financial statements. Moreover, as we show in later chapters, much of the information about the operations of major health charities is difficult, if not impossible, to obtain; even when the information is available, it may be indecipherable or, worse, incorrect or misleading.

Like politicians, the managers of health charities and other nonprofits ostensibly serve the public good. On Election Day, every politician is judged by the voters on his or her performance in that regard. But unlike public officials, neither the members of the boards of directors nor the managers of nonprofits ever face an electoral judgment day.

Health charities and most other nonprofits are also in a unique position with regard to public opinion. For obvious reasons, most people are naturally suspicious about any self-serving claims made by businesses; after all, everyone knows that businesses are supposedly motivated by self-interest. And everyone knows that political campaign promises are nearly always broken. There have been enough political scandals in all branches of government in recent years that the public accords politicians, and especially members of Congress, low esteem.

But again, charities are different. Charities are viewed as motivated by neither profit nor political advancement. Supposedly, their only concern is "doing good." Therefore, criticisms of charities are often construed as criticisms of charitable activities themselves, and only a hard-hearted Scrooge or a dyed-in-the-wool Grinch with highly questionable motives would criticize charity. Charities have thus become sacred cows, even in the eyes of the media; nonprofits are therefore spared the public and media scrutiny that businesses and government routinely receive—at least until a scandal, such as the United Way fiasco, breaks. So health charities, and nonprofits in general, are not controlled by consumers, shareholders, voters, the media, or even public opinion, as is the case with for-profit businesses and government enterprises. And therein lies an enormous potential for mischief.

Many of the inefficiencies found in government enterprises, moreover, are found to an even greater degree in nonprofit organizations.

For example, one of the most notorious sources of government waste is the phenomenon of spending binges at the end of every fiscal year. In government, if an agency's budget is not spent during the fiscal year, it is difficult for its managers to make a case for a budget as large or larger in the following year. Consequently, even if the agency has come in under budget a month or so before the end of the fiscal year, its bureaucrats will typically go on a wasteful and needless spending binge to "prove" to the legislature or appropriations committee that it needs at least as much money, if not more, in the next fiscal year. This is yet another reason why government agencies tend to maximize rather than minimize costs.

Similar year-end spending binges occur in health charities for the same reason. If a health charity does not spend all of its budget in one year, an impassioned plea for increased donations from the public for the following year will be less convincing. Consequently, even research funds may be wasted in year-end spending sprees. One health-charity administrator candidly described what happened when leftover funds were discovered at the end of one fiscal year: "Our medical director would call up researchers frantically and beg them to accept grants, no matter how tenuous their projects."[5]

Researchers at the University of Pennsylvania medical school observed similar behavior:

> Some [health charities] have more money than they know what to do with. Such groups, having raised their money by advertising their need, naturally feel it must be spent or next year's campaign would be conducted at a disadvantage. So they raise the ante and attract talent and personnel to their field without regard to the opportunities for advancing it. Good investigators leave promising problems to work in fallow fields simply because money can be so easily picked up. . . . Another temptation in a research investigator's path is to publish results prematurely or make exaggerated claims to insure next year's grant by producing what is desired this year.[6]

The inefficiencies in and excessive bureaucratization of the major health charities have been known for decades, but very little is ever said or done about it. In 1945 the Rockefeller Foundation funded a study of health charities that produced "a devastating and carefully documented picture of useless activities, of failure to take up new problems and serve developing needs, of waste of contributors' money and failure to achieve health-protection goals that should long since have been reached and passed." The study concluded with a series of recommendations for improved efficiency, but "nothing was ever done to implement its recommendations and it was quietly forgotten."[7]

Fifteen years later, another Rockefeller Foundation study recommended the adoption of uniform accounting procedures. This time the recommendation was adopted—but it took the health charities about fifteen years to do it. As discussed in chapter 4, however, this so-called uniform accounting can be uniformly confusing and uninformative—as much is hidden as is revealed.

INTERLOCKING BOARDS OF DIRECTORS

At the heads of organizations in both the for-profit and the nonprofit sectors are boards of directors. In the for-profit sector, board members are elected by shareholders who have a financial stake in the corporation—if the firm is not well managed, the shareholders' investment in the company could become worthless. Board members have a fiduciary responsibility to protect the interests of shareholders and are liable for acts of malfeasance. Shareholders can, and do, file class-action suits seeking redress when they believe that their company has been mismanaged. If shareholders are unhappy with a corporation's performance, they can attempt to replace members of its board. Shareholder discontent and the stresses placed on corporate boards of directors were evident in early 1992, when the chief executive officers of several major *Fortune* 500 corporations—including such household names as General Motors, IBM, and American Express—were replaced.

In contrast, health charities and other nonprofits have no shareholders; no one—other than the executives and staff who earn their livelihoods from the organization—has a direct financial stake in a nonprofit's activities. The boards of directors are self-perpetuating and responsible to no one but themselves. Thus, there is no real incentive for board members to carefully monitor a charity's spending and operations, so the full-time executives and staff have wide latitude and considerable discretion in making decisions.

One particularly telling example of how board members are sometimes kept in the dark and relied on only for their prestige and fund-raising connections is an incident in the history of the National Foundation for Infantile Paralysis (NFIP). In 1972 it was revealed that the NFIP's "unpaid volunteer" president, Basil O'Connor, was actually paying himself a salary of $100,000 (more than $300,000 in current dollars), plus an expense account of over $70,000 for his "part-time volunteer" job. Remarkably, "only three of the NFIP's 28 trustees were aware that O'Connor was being paid."[8]

Health-charity board members usually serve without any compensation other than the prestige associated with involvement in community service. They also tend to be individuals with knowledge of or an interest in the health charity's disease. For example, medical professionals are heavily represented on the boards of directors of the Big Three (the American Cancer Society, the American Heart Association, and the American Lung Association) and other health charities. In 1988, seventeen of the thirty-six members of the American Heart Association's board were physicians, as were six of its ten officers. The medical establishment clearly plays a major role in the setting the agendas and controlling the policies of health charities.

Even though medical professionals may not represent a numerical majority on a charity's board of directors, they still exercise disproportionate control over the organization's activities. Every health charity must rely on the medical professionals in its field of interest to legitimate its programs and expenditures. The charity's managers cannot risk a dispute with the medical profession that might tarnish, perhaps irrevocably, the public image of the organization. Although the prestige given to the charity by the lay members of the board is important in providing public confidence, the endorsement given explicitly or implicitly by the medical professionals on the board is critical.

Other board members are frequently engaged in activities that are directly or indirectly related to those of the health charity. Although prohibitions against blatant conflicts of interest can reduce the chances of direct financial gain, board members or the organizations with which they are affiliated may still be able to derive financial benefits from an organization's activities (see chapter 6). The U.S. General Accounting Office found "overlapping interests" (a euphemism for conflicts of interest) at seventeen of the nineteen nonprofit hospitals it investigated. In six of the nineteen hospitals, 25 percent or more of the board members had conflicts of interest. One Washington, D.C., hospital, for instance, was governed by a forty-two-member board of trustees, of which

> 33 percent . . . had overlapping interests. The primary overlapping interest involved banks servicing the hospital, although board members were also identified with legal, investment, and three other types of firms.

Seven board members were associated with a bank which maintained a hospital savings account; checking account; and custody of hospital property, such as stocks and bonds. . . . Two members were associated with two other banks. . . . Three board members were associated with two firms providing legal services to the hospital. . . . One member was associated with a group of eight radiologists providing radiology services to the hospital. . . .[9]

The sociologists Amatai Etzioni and Pamela Doty argue convincingly that "omissions, ambiguities, and loopholes in the laws make it possible for the trustees and staff of not-for-profit corporations to engage in a variety of financial practices which bring them personal profits."[10]

Journalist Mary A. Mendelson studied another type of nonprofit in the health care industry, nursing homes, and concluded that

the term "nonprofit" does not mean what it would seem to mean: there are plenty of opportunities for profit in a nonprofit operation. All it means is that the [nursing] home by law does not produce profits for tax purposes: it does not return cash dividends to its owners. A church or a fraternal order or a union or a group of individuals can set up a nonprofit entity. . . . Once having achieved nonprofit status, the home enjoys some important advantages. It does not pay income taxes, in some states it does not pay the local property tax, and in various places it is exempt from water taxes. It also enjoys official favor. The federal government and foundations prefer nonprofit operations in giving grants for special projects.[11]

Because health charities have the same structures and incentives as nonprofit hospitals and nursing homes, the same potential for exploitation and conflicts of interest exists.

ORGANIZATIONAL SURVIVAL AND EXPANSION

Regardless of whether an organization is a for-profit business, a government enterprise, or a nonprofit entity, its most critical concern is always survival. As soon as an organization is created, interest groups form that derive economic benefits from its operations and therefore have a financial stake in its survival. The most readily identifiable interest group is comprised of the organization's executives and staffs, whose careers and incomes depend on the organization's success.

A closely related motivation is the desire for expansion. A large and growing organization offers greater opportunities for career advancement than a stagnant or declining one. In a for-profit business, expansion requires that the business continue to find—and satisfy— more and more customers with its products or services. If the customers become dissatisfied, or the product becomes obsolete, the business must find other products and customers or face extinction.

In theory, government and nonprofit enterprises share a primary goal: to go out of business. The government's welfare agencies, for example, ostensibly exist to eliminate poverty. If the nation's poverty problems were ever cured, however, there would no longer be any need for the agencies, the programs, or their employees. Consequently, regardless of how many trillions of dollars are spent on poverty, the poverty bureaucracy claims that the problem is only getting worse.

The so-called Poverty Pentagon has created an enormous propaganda machine to convince the public that poverty is worse than it actually is.[12] This is not to say that poverty isn't a serious problem in some parts of America; rather, the poverty bureaucracy has powerful incentives to exaggerate the extent of the problem, thereby increasing the likelihood that taxpayers will acquiesce when asked to pay more taxes to finance the army of bureaucrats, social workers, nonprofit organizations, university researchers, and "Beltway bandits" that regulates, administers, and analyzes the poor. Much of the money appropriated for poverty programs is skimmed off by this army and never reaches the needy.

Nonprofit organizations also have weak incentives to disband once their mission is accomplished. With regard to health charities, for example,

> two of the big five organizations were established to fight polio and tuberculosis, diseases for which cures and immunizations are now very much available. Rather than disbanding, the National Foundation changed its cause to fighting birth defects and the tuberculosis group added "respiratory disease" to its name. Together they account for $70 million of annual health-charity expenditures [in 1973].
>
> Why didn't they go out of business when they successfully conquered the diseases they set out to fight? The organizations say there was a public need and a public desire for them to enter new fields. But what about the executives who would have been out of work, the scientists who would have been forced to shop elsewhere for their research grants, the board members who would have had no charity to place beside their names in Who's Who?[13]

The American Lung Association (ALA) provides an excellent illustration of the survival and growth imperatives that require a health charity to generate sympathy for its cause and translate that sympathy into contributions. A decline in the perceived importance of the disease to which the health charity is devoted—whether because of reduced incidence or new methods of treatment—can seriously weaken the organization's fund-raising ability.

During its history, the ALA has changed its name four times: "Our Association has had four name changes during its 80-year history, which must cause some confusion in the public's mind, but a nonprofit agency such as ours cannot mount a million-dollar advertising campaign proclaiming a name change."[14] The most likely explanation for name changes is rooted in the quest for more donations: The old name no longer evoked the desired response from donors.

The last name change—to ALA—occurred in 1973, when the organization was known as the National Tuberculosis and Respiratory Disease Association (NTRDA). In 1972, its District of Columbia affiliate decided to administer tuberculin skin tests to fifteen hundred men who were at least twenty-five years old at their homes in the Upper Cardozo area of the city because "statistics show that the TB rate for the Cardozo area is almost twice that of the entire District." Cardozo residents were predominantly lower-income nonwhites, and "nonwhite males developed the disease about four and a half times as often as white men" and "three times the national rate." If the $10,000 program, funded by the NTRDA, proved successful, federal funds would be sought under the Model Cities program to extend the testing to other cities, reported Rufus Stephens, who was then director of tuberculosis and community health programs ,for the District of Columbia affiliate.[15]

The results of the tests were reported the next year and the incidence of the disease was found to be "lower than expected." In fact, *no cases of active tuberculosis were found.* For the residents of the Cardozo area, this was certainly good news. But it was a major problem for the D.C. branch of the NTRDA, which denounced the tests as "ineffective." Executive Director Robert G. Smith announced, "I'm essentially disappointed with the program. The rate should have been much higher. Obviously we're being misinformed [about] how much TB there is in the high-risk areas."[16]

The national association and its District of Columbia affiliate then faced a serious dilemma. If active tuberculosis could not be found even in high-risk areas, how could the association persuade the public to support a crusade against the disease? It decided not even to try; instead, it changed its name to the American Lung Association in 1973 so that *all* lung diseases, not just tuberculosis, came under its purview.

It should also be noted that the District of Columbia was chosen for the initial tuberculosis testing for strategic reasons. If a high rate of incidence had been identified in the nation's capital, the message would not have been lost on members of Congress who live and work there and might be personally exposed to the disease. The likelihood of federal funding would have been increased, and the publicity would have done wonders for fund-raising.

DISEASE MONGERING

It is not unusual for some health charities to exaggerate the extent and risk of certain diseases to assist their fund-raising efforts. Just as the government's poverty bureaucracy exaggerates poverty, the environmental bureaucracy exaggerates environmental problems, and the military-industrial complex exaggerates foreign military threats, health charities—and the medical profession—overstate the extent and severity of diseases and engage in "disease mongering," to borrow a phrase from the medical journalist Lynn Payer.[17]

Disease mongering—trying to convince essentially well people that they are sick—is big business, according to Payer. "For people to use a diagnostic product or service, they must be convinced that they MAY BE sick. And to market drugs to the widest possible audience, pharmaceutical companies must convince people—or their physicians—that they ARE sick." Payer concludes that "in my 20 years as a medical journalist, I have become more and more convinced that much of the so-called information we get about our health grossly oversimplifies and distorts reality." For example,

> I know that both blood pressure and cholesterol readings are rough
> approximations of the risk of dying of heart disease. But I also know
> that the readings themselves vary greatly according to the conditions
> under which they are taken and that even the same reading means
> vastly different things depending on your age, your sex, and various
> other risk factors. I also know there are studies showing that some
> people treated for mild hypertension are more likely to die than those
> who go completely untreated. I know that while four controlled stud-
> ies have shown that screening mammography performed in women

over the age of 50 does seem to cut the death rate from breast cancer, only one has shown any benefit in women under 50, something never acknowledged in the publicity urging women to get mammograms.[18]

Such disease mongering seems to be an essential part of the fund-raising strategies of nearly every health charity.

DONORS AND VOLUNTEERS

Organizational expansion requires additional revenues, which must be obtained through voluntary contributions. Americans donate more dollars to charity than all other countries combined, and they do so for a number of reasons, including altruism, guilt, social pressure, a desire for tax deductions, and because donations may be viewed as a form of social insurance. In the last case, an individual may support a charity because there is always some chance that in the future, he or she may benefit from or need the charity's services.

In a sense, volunteering is the equivalent of donating; volunteers simply offer a service—their time and effort—instead of (or in addition to) cash. Volunteers are presumably affected by the same basic motivations as donors to health charities—to ameliorate the suffering caused by disease, to educate others about it, and to find a cure. Many health-charity volunteers are people who have been personally affected by a particular disease, perhaps through the illness of a friend or relative.

No one knows exactly how many health-charity volunteers there are. Each health charity reports the number of its volunteers, and the numbers are indeed impressive. The American Cancer Society estimates that 2.5 million volunteers participate in its programs; the American Lung Association reports 150,000; and the American Heart Association claims 2.4 million volunteers.

Not all volunteers are equally committed to the charity's goals and programs; some may spend only a single afternoon a year collecting funds door-to-door, while others devote far more time and effort. For both public-relations and political reasons, however, it is important for a health charity to claim as large a number of volunteers as possible. A cause is more likely to be considered socially important and worthy of support if there are significant numbers of people willing to donate their energies to it.

In the political arena, politicians are much more sensitive to issues that appear to have a broad base of support, and large numbers of volunteers are an indication of widespread support. There are myriad interest groups in the nation's capital that compete for political influence by claiming millions of members, even though most of their "members" may simply be people who responded to a mass-mailed fund-raising appeal with a $5 donation but who have little or no knowledge about the actual operations of the organization.

The reasons why people donate to charity are vague enough; it is even more difficult to understand why individuals contribute to *particular* charities:

> The popular belief is that the magnitude of philanthropic effort in any particular direction bears a direct relationship to the urgency of the needs. The facts are that the emotion-stirring fund appeal and the efficiency of the soliciting organization determine the magnitude of the effort. For example, nearly four times as many people suffer from heart ailments as from cancer, but the American Cancer Society's annual take [in 1974] is $65 million whereas the American Heart Association's is $45 million. The Muscular Dystrophy Association of America raised more money (nearly $10 million) than the National Multiple Sclerosis Society ($7.5 million), although two and a half times as many people suffer from sclerosis as from dystrophy. The [March of Dimes] in its heyday was by far the most heavily supported agency in the medical care field, although—fortunately—polio afflicted only one out of every 30,000 Americans.[19]

Clearly, the importance of the disease in causing death or disability is not the prime determinant of a health charity's revenues; what is important is the pull of the fund-raising appeals on the donors' pocketbooks. If the charities raising funds for, say, AIDS are more effective at pulling the purse strings, then AIDS charities will receive more funding than those raising funds for other diseases, even though another disease might pose a far greater health threat to the public.

If donors are to respond positively, some emotional chord must be struck that will entice them to open their checkbooks and contribute. Guilt and fear are the emotions most frequently exploited. Consider a recent fund-raising appeal sent by the American Lung Association of Northern Virginia, which included the following brief letter:

> If you could help save someone who was dying—would you? We're asking you to do just that. To write a check and help save someone's life. The fact is, we've never needed your support more. Consider that chronic obstructive lung diseases—like emphysema—are now the fifth leading cause of death in this country. Please, won't you be gen-

erous? Your gift of $2 or more really could help save someone's life. Thank you.

Anne Logan Davis, M.D., who signed the letter, did not explain exactly how an individual donation of $2 could save a life; that was left up to the donor's imagination. The obvious purpose of framing the appeal in this way was to induce a feeling of guilt among those who might balk at contributing. After all, who would refuse to help save a life for a mere $2?

A good example of fear as a tactic is the long-standing fund-raising approach of the American Cancer Society. As one observer reported,

> The American Cancer Society of the 1960s used their education programs to build public panics to their diseases, leaving the lingering question of whether more reasonable means could have been used. . . . And among today's health charities, we encounter public-education programs designed to reteach us the warning signs we already know backwards. . . . The line between education and fund-raising promotion has become very thin indeed.[20]

Subtle deception, misleading statements, and even false advertising have also characterized some health-charity fund-raising, according to Carl Bakal. A "surprising, little-known fact" about the health charities, writes Bakal, is that their expenditures on research "represent only a small fraction of all the dollars spent on research in this country. . . . Most . . . now comes from the government, usually for programs to battle the same ailments as the health agencies." Nevertheless, "some health agencies tend to emphasize research in their fund-raising appeals because this come-on has been found to attract the most money, although many [health charities] actually devote larger portions of their budgets to other activities" (see chapter 5).[21]

Besides research, some health charities offer patient services. This too is often exaggerated in the heat of fund-raising campaigns. "All too frequently, the offer of help to medically indigent patients is nothing more than a referral to community agencies (which, in turn, are often unable to help). . . . Where care actually is provided, it may duplicate that already available from other resources in the community or be of questionable quality."[22]

Deceptive advertising by health charities is a very important issue (see chapter 8). It also occurs in the for-profit sector, but nonprofits have even more latitude than commercial entities to engage in false advertising. Since every business exists to make a profit, consumers are naturally skeptical of all commercial claims. Furthermore, false advertising is quickly pointed out by competitors, and any company that misleads consumers with its promotions will eventually bear the cost of the deception if only because every business must rely on repeat sales or positive endorsements from satisfied customers to prosper.

Competitive pressures do not eliminate false advertising by for-profit businesses, but they do limit it. In addition to market constraints, there are legal prohibitions against false advertising, which are enforced by the Federal Trade Commission and by state and local government agencies as well, including state attorneys general.

The nonprofit sector and especially health charities benefit from a reputation exactly opposite that of for-profit businesses: a "halo effect" surrounds all charitable entities. The mere claim by an organization that it is a charity allays the suspicions of most citizens. Since health charities are not part of competitive industry, the marketplace constraints on false advertising that exist in the for-profit sector are very weak. And by law, nonprofits are exempt from Federal Trade Commission scrutiny and from regulation by most state and local government agencies. They are regulated, however, by state attorneys general. But as shown in chapter 8, some state attorneys general are more like lap dogs than watchdogs; that is, they are charity advocates, a politically popular stance for those who aspire to higher political office—or simply wish to get reelected. Health and other charities are very active in the political arena. In short, the fund-raising appeals of most health charities are rarely challenged.

RATIONAL IGNORANCE

Most people spend much of their time tending to their personal affairs—working, taking care of children, paying the bills, getting the car fixed, filing their tax forms, and similar tasks. Most of us try to be as well informed as possible about these important, day-to-day decisions. When it comes to social or public-policy issues, however, "rational ignorance" prevails; that is, most people believe that it is not worth their time and effort to become well informed. Investigating complex issues is time-consuming and may require expertise that many do not already have; moreover, there is little prospect that our lives will be improved in any measurable way even if we do become informed.

In the context of politics, rational ignorance implies that legislators, prodded by special-interest groups, are often able to enact policies that go unopposed by the rationally uninformed general public. How many citizens are aware, for example, that Americans pay about double the world price of sugar because the federal government restricts low-cost sugar imports from foreign sources? Or that the average compact car costs as much as $2,500 more than it would without existing import quotas that benefit a small special interest—domestic auto manufacturers and their unions—at great expense to the consumers?

There is, however, a limit to the government's ability to cater to special-interest groups. Taxpayers have become so disenchanted with the federal government's inability to manage the nation's finances that voters in all fourteen states where it was on the ballot passed congressional term-limitation measures in the November 1992 election. The public's opinion of Congress—and the Washington establishment—is at an all-time low. Americans have developed a healthy skepticism about government and politicians.

Such skepticism, however, does not extend to charities. It's one thing to become cynical about politics, but charity is different. Most of us remain rationally ignorant about the programs and activities of health charities and judge them—if we judge them at all—by their own statements about their goals and performances. We have little or no knowledge of their activities other than the carefully crafted newspaper stories often planted by the charities themselves and accepted by a media wanting to do its part in the battle against disease. When asked to make a small donation to "fight lung disease and save lives," for example, who could say no? And almost everyone wants to do his or her part in the war against disease.

The point is that, to the extent that rational ignorance is a problem in the context of political decision making, it is every bit as much of a problem with regard to charitable activities. Not only are most citizens rationally ignorant of the activities of health charities, they are in awe of them. Some charities may indeed have earned such public respect because of their years of good works. But as will be seen in later chapters, the public's rational ignorance provides health charities with wide latitude to spend their revenues in many ways that seem ineffective or even counterproductive in the battle against disease and illness. To a large extent, some health charities seem to benefit primarily the medical establishment rather than disease victims, their families, or the public.

THE MEDICAL ESTABLISHMENT'S ROLE

*When I asked my husband for [a personal donation] for the American
Cancer Society to do research, he said, "No, I'm not going to give you
any money"—although he did. But he said, "The place to get the
money is the federal government." And I said, "I don't know anything
about the government." And he said, "There are unlimited funds. I'll
show you how to get them."*
—Mary Lasker, former Honorary Chairman of the American Cancer Society

The medical establishment has played a major role in the nation's
health charities. Indeed, the Big Three and similar health charities were
founded by physicians or other members of the medical establishment.
With regard to the American Cancer Society,

> a meeting of ten doctors and five laymen at the Harvard Club followed
> on May 22nd [1913], at which the Society was formally created. . . .
> The American Medical Association, the Congress of American Physi-
> cians and Surgeons, the American Gynecological Society, the Clinical
> Congress of Surgeons of North America, insurance companies . . .
> were all involved.[23]

Similarly, the American Heart Association was formed as "a professional, not-for-profit membership society of physicians and scientists. In 1948, it was reorganized as a voluntary health agency, admitting lay and professional members to its governing bodies. . . . About
60% of the Board of Directors are physicians or related health professionals."[24]

The desire on the part of health professionals to establish a society
devoted to research, education, and the curing of disease is certainly
laudable and deserving of public support. No one would deny that
there are many honest, hard-working health professionals who have
made enormous contributions to society through their efforts on behalf
of the health charities.

Realistically, however, it must also be acknowledged that the primary purpose of any professional association—whether it consists of
health professionals, college professors, attorneys, or truck drivers—is
to enhance the financial well-being of the members of the group. The
Big Three have been very successful in fulfilling this role on behalf of
the medical establishment.

If physicians were to advertise the need for more frequent checkups, some people would be suspicious that the ads were motivated

more by financial self-interest than by a concern for public health. But if the same advertisements are sponsored by a *charity*, which is only interested in "doing good," according to conventional wisdom, then the ads will have far more credibility; the physicians' mercenary intent is thus hidden behind the veil of charity. Because of this veil, the health charities confer legitimacy on policies that primarily benefit the medical establishment. Thus, a mutually rewarding "backscratching" arrangement exists: The medical profession provides legitimacy for the programs and activities of the health charity, while the health charity, surrounded by its aura of selflessness, advocates policies that primarily benefit members of the medical profession.

For example, the American Cancer Society (ACS) has long recommended routine mammography screenings for women between the ages of forty and fifty despite the fact that "most studies have shown that such screening does not reduce the death rate from breast cancer in women in this age group." Recent research indicates, moreover, that "adding mammography to breast examination may actually increase deaths from breast cancer in women between the ages of 40 and 50." One group of ACS medical advisers relayed these findings to the society, recommending an end to these screenings, and "found they were not invited back."[25]

"Cancerphobia must be inculcated into everyone over 31," Dr. James Coupal, President Coolidge's personal physician, said in 1928.[26] Coupal's objective seems to have been met. Thanks in large part to the public education campaigns of the ACS (see chapter 5), cancerphobia has greatly increased the demand for and incomes of physicians. Ralph W. Moss, formerly assistant director of public affairs at Memorial Sloan–Kettering Cancer Center in New York City, has asserted that the primary goal of the physician-founders of the American Cancer Society was "to urge the general public to consult their physician at the first suspicion of cancer."[27] The incessant pleas by the major health charities to "see your doctor" and "be tested" for this or that ailment may benefit some of the people some of the time, but not all of the people all of the time. The one group that always benefits, however, is the doctors themselves. For

> the way we pay doctors in the United States is based on the procedures they perform, and while surgeons make money based on the operations they do, the easiest way for the nonsurgeon to make much money is to perform diagnostic tests. Medical specialists who don't normally perform significant numbers of tests are among the lowest

paid. . . . The volume of testing in doctors' offices is increasing by 15 percent annually.[28]

An excellent example of "testing hysteria" is how the medical establishment and the health charities have created a sense of national anxiety over cholesterol. They have urged the testing of virtually all adults and even most children, drastic changes in diet, and treatment with cholesterol-reducing drugs. Such recommendations generate billions of dollars in income for the physicians administering the tests, the testing laboratories that analyze the blood, and the drug companies that sell the drugs. The health charities indirectly benefit from the publicity their cholesterol campaigns produce, since publicity brings increased contributions.

Medical researchers, however, have found virtually no evidence that the recommendations improve public health. According to the *British Medical Journal,* "Most researchers agree that a raised blood cholesterol concentration is a risk factor for coronary heart disease, yet most agree that lowering people's blood cholesterol (either by diet or by drugs) does not affect their overall mortality." Some studies have even shown *more* deaths in people treated for high cholesterol counts than in those not treated. These facts have not stopped the American Heart Association, in cooperation with the National Institutes of Health (NIH), from launching a National Cholesterol Education Program to "get all Americans to know their cholesterol level and presumably to try to lower it," even though the NIH's own scientific advisory council opposed the program. Dr. Eliot Corday, a past president of the American College of Cardiology, criticized the program in the *New York Times* by saying, "We don't know what we're doing. It's absolutely ridiculous."[29]

The NIH Connection

There has long been a close relationship between the major health charities, the medical profession, and the federal government. The federal government's National Institutes of Health is arguably the best biomedical research center in the world. The NIH consists of thirteen separate institutes, all but one of which are located in Bethesda, Maryland, in the suburbs of the nation's capital. Each deals with specific health issues: aging; allergies and infectious diseases; arthritis and musculoskeletal and skin diseases; cancer; child health and human development; deafness and communicative disorders; dental research; diabetes and digestive and kidney diseases; environmental health sciences; eye research; general medical science; heart, lung, and blood research; and neurological disorders and strokes.

Financed by the taxpayers, each of the institutes is funded *individually* by Congress, so that each must defend its budget proposal every year before Congress. Each institute, therefore, has strong incentives to rally its health-charity supporters to lobby Congress for funds that benefit medical professionals whose specialties are allied with that institute's work. As Ralph Moss has stated, for example, "The [American] Cancer Society and the National Cancer Institute work as partners."[30]

A system of interlocking directorates between the ACS and the National Cancer Institute (NCI), one of the NIH institutes, has apparently been long-standing. In 1960, Dr. John Heller, a former director of the NCI, declared that "the Director of the [National Cancer] Institute is a member of the board of directors of the [American] Cancer Society, and the scientific advisory committees of both organizations interlock."[31] In describing the ACS's lobbying role in the early days of the NCI, the historian Walter Ross wrote: "Spurred by the effective lobbying of the ACS, the NCI budget began growing rapidly. In 1950 it totaled nearly $19 million; in 1960 it had risen to $91 million; and by 1970 to $190 million."[32] Today, the NIH budget exceeds $7 billion annually, with about $2 billion going to the National Cancer Institute.

There is often fierce competition for funds as "the American Cancer Society, the American Heart Association, the American Lung Association, and dozens of similar organizations . . . lobby Congress—with considerable success—to gain more attention and more money for their areas of special concern."[33] The end result of this lobbying is that members of Congress, who have little knowledge of health issues and know even less about biomedical research, decide the relative benefits of allocating more funding to one institute over another. Research funding, therefore, is determined by the group that has the most lobbying and public-relations clout, not necessarily according to the most pressing public-health priorities.

But the health charities do not really compete with one another for taxpayers' money. Instead, in the political arena, they engage in that sure-fire, time-tested formula of pork-barrel politics: logrolling. The health charities operate under the dictum, "I'll lobby for funds for your NIH institute if you'll do the same for mine." Long ago, they found strength in numbers: By agreeing to political logrolling, they get higher funding for everyone at the expense of no one—except the taxpayers. As one observer portrayed this lobbying cartel, "The struggle for public-health dollars has become so intense that part of the disease lobby, trying to hold down the chaos, has organized itself into the Coalition for Health Funding, 60 national organizations that watch the [NIH] budget like hawks."[34]

There are close ties between the medical professions, the health charities, and the various institutes at the NIH. The medical profession, with the help of the health charities, has in essence captured the NIH and uses it to enhance the financial interests of its own members. The various health charities lobby for increased appropriations from Congress for the institutes of special concern to them. The NIH in turn awards grants and contracts to researchers who deal with these diseases and who work with the health charities to convince the public—and Congress—of the essential need for public donations to the health charities, as well as additional taxpayer support for research. Thus, the medical establishment benefits from both the health charities—which the establishment organized in the first place—and the NIH.

As discussed in detail in chapter 6, the close link between the health charities and the NIH has created a situation whereby the health charities play an important role in determining the direction of disease research. The NIH relies heavily on the health charities for their staffing of "advisory committees for counsel and critique with respect to both ongoing and proposed activities," particularly with regard to peer review of research grants and contracts.[35]

Implications for Medical Research

The professional and personal ties between the major health charities and the NIH gives the charities leverage in controlling disease research. The major health charities not only dominate the distribution of research grants, they also determine what gets published by producing many of the professional publications in their respective fields. Because most medical researchers, as in other academic disciplines, live under a "publish or perish" rule, their research and writings must conform to the standards largely set and maintained by the health charities if their work is to be published and supported by federal or health-charity grants.

The result of this centralization of research funding and publication is both conformity and powerful opposition to newer or riskier ideas—the kind of ideas that have historically been the source of breakthroughs in medical science (and in many other areas, for that matter).

The centralization of health-research funding has led to a bureaucratic mind-set that shuns risk and constantly seeks conformity. The perspective of the relatively small number of people who make the decisions on research grants is described as follows:

> The safest and most politic thing to do is to give priority to those applications coming from the more conventional and established researchers at well-known institutions. . . . Should anything go wrong, the grant giver can justify his or her decision by the prestige of the recipient institution and the supposedly high probability of success.
>
> To approve the grant application of a small research center (such as the Syracuse Cancer Research Institute or the Immuno-Augmentative Therapy Centre) is a difficult and dangerous undertaking for any bureaucrat or adviser. It is fraught with peril: if the project becomes an embarrassment, there inevitably will be inquiries to find out who approved the application in the first place.[36]

Another consideration is that many of the people who make the decisions regarding research funding—that is, the peer reviewers—are themselves distinguished researchers who, as is only human nature, do not want their own work contradicted. For example, Linus Pauling, the recipient of *two* Nobel Prizes, was repeatedly turned down by the National Cancer Institute. Dr. H. L. Newbold, who was familiar with Pauling's research proposals, explained the rejections: "They're jealous of him because he's too famous. Things are done through personalities. You think of scientists as being objective, but science is full of little men doing their own little things. This is true of people who grant research funds."[37]

Health charities also have powerful economic incentives to control the direction of disease research: If they are viewed by the public as the sole, selfless guardians of "the truth" about disease and public health, they will always be the major recipients of the public's contributions to health causes. The major health charities recognize this and have gone to great pains to label newer health charities as scams (see chapter 8) and out-of-the-mainstream researchers as quacks. "To the establishment, in general, such independent researchers are not innovators," explained Ralph Moss. "Nor are they really scientists. They are advocates of unproven methods or, more bluntly, 'quacks.'"[38]

The American Cancer Society even publishes a directory of "quacks" entitled *Unproven Methods of Cancer Management*. Moss has closely examined this directory and makes a convincing case that it is inaccurate and unfairly critical of many honest scientists. The book, according to Moss, "resembles the list of 'subversive' organizations once maintained by the House Un-American Activities Committee. Merely including a scientist's name on the list has the effect of damning that researcher's work and putting the tag of quackery on him and his efforts."[39]

Of course, there may well be some "quacks" on the ACS's list, but Moss shows that the majority of the names are highly credible people whose only transgression is that they are innovators who are not a part of the ACS/NCI "club." The ACS directory labels the scientists on its list as "ignorant, uneducated, misguided persons" and claims that only "a few" hold Ph.D. or M.D. degrees. But Moss discovered discrepancies between this characterization and the credentials of the directory's "quacks." According to the ACS's own information, 77 percent of the "snake-oil salesman" on its list are either physicians or hold Ph.D.s in such disciplines as chemistry, physiology, bacteriology, parasitology, and medical physics, having earned their degrees from Harvard, Yale, Northwestern, Oxford, the University of Illinois, and other respected institutions. "In most cases," Moss writes, these people "have spent their working lives treating and/or researching cancer."[40]

The ACS also attempts to belittle these "outsiders" by charging that their remedies are bizarre. The directory attempts to link contemporary scientists with the purveyors of nineteenth-century "cures," including clover blossom tea, cobwebs saturated with arsenic powder, tear extract, ox bile, llama placenta, and other exotic substances. None of these was ever marketed as a potential cure for cancer. But even if they were, the ACS attack is hypocritical given that many known treatments and cures for disease are equally strange. As Moss points out, the well-known drug Premarin, used by millions of women to relieve the symptoms of menopause, is made from pregnant mares' urine; penicillin is derived from mold; the commonly used anticancer agent Mustargen is a form of poisonous mustard gas; another anticancer agent comes from the periwinkle plant.[41] The drug Taxol, which comes from the bark of the yew tree, is now touted as a major advance in the battle against ovarian cancer. It would be just as easy to mock these present-day conventional medicines and therapies as it is the nineteenth-century cures.

The ACS's *Unproven Methods of Cancer Management* lists sixty-three "unproven methods," but, as Moss discovered,

in twenty-eight out of sixty-three cases (or 44.4 percent) no investigation at all was carried out by the American Cancer Society or any other agency before the method was condemned. In seven cases, or 11.1 percent, it appears that the results of the investigation were not negative at all, but actually positive. This does not mean, of course, that these seven methods are cures for cancer. Rather, the scanty data points in a positive, rather than a negative direction.[42]

Moss concludes that *"almost 72 percent of the methods on the unproven methods list have never been shown to be ineffective by any sort of rational scientific procedure."*[43] In summary, some of these "unproven methods" may indeed be fraudulent, but others may not be. They simply are untested and unproven.

The opposition by the health-charity establishment to newly proposed methods of treatment, according to Pat McGrady, a former ACS official, can be explained by the fact that

the establishment has turned the terror of this ugly disease to its own ends in seeking more and more contributions from a frightened public and appropriations from a concerned Congress. Still, undismayed by the futility of funds dumped into the bottomless barrel of its "proven" methods, it remains adamant in refusing to investigate "unproven" methods. . . . Forgetful of the fact that of the few really useful treatments, all, or almost all, were initiated under the kind of abuse now heaped upon "unproven" remedies, the establishment may be denying help for tomorrow's cancer patients as well as today's.[44]

As the foregoing discussion clearly shows, some critics are convinced that the close ties among the NIH institutes, the health charities, and the medical establishment have hindered the battle against disease. Implicit in the arguments of these critics is a conspiracy theory, which holds that the search for causes of and cures for various diseases is essentially a treasure hunt for patentable drugs. Because most of the unorthodox treatments—including hydrazine sulfate, Linus Pauling's vitamin C, and a whole raft of nutritional methods—cannot be patented, there is no money to be made from pursuing them. Hence, goes the theory, these methods are summarily condemned by the establishment as "quackery." And because there is also little money to be made from disease *prevention*—by reducing exposure to carcinogens, for example—patentable medical cures are emphasized and environmental causes are largely ignored.

This reasoning is not flattering to the medical establishment, the health charities, or the NIH, for the logic is based on greed. We reject

this view because it is too simplistic—the issues are far more complicated—and because we do not subscribe to the notion that the medical
establishment is callous or driven exclusively (or primarily) by mercenary motives; there is too much evidence that many health professionals are indeed concerned and caring. That having been said, however,
we agree fully with the contention that health-charity involvement in
disease research has been detrimental rather than beneficial. We treat
these critical issues in detail in chapter 6 and come to the same basic
conclusion as the other critics, but from a very different—and, we
believe, more reasoned and balanced—approach.

WHO'S REALLY IN CHARGE?

To the extent that health-charity mismanagement occurs, it is important to understand its causes and, even more important, who is ultimately responsible. As with all nonprofits (and even some corporations), health charities are essentially controlled not by their unpaid
volunteer officers, who are merely figureheads, but by their full-time
paid executives, with the assistance of a small number of activists on
their boards of directors.

Health-charity executives have a decided advantage over most
board members, who do not have the time, energy, or expertise to be
intimately involved in the details of the organization's operations. Most
board members are chosen for their ability to contribute to or organize
fund-raising drives for the charity, not for their expertise in managing
the charity. Since they are usually unpaid, they come to board meetings with the assumption that they are doing the charity a favor (which
they are) and are willing to "rubber-stamp," or approve with little
review, the executives' management decisions.

As we've discussed, most health charities were established by medical professionals who comprise an important block on the boards of
directors. To a large degree, health charities are operated primarily for
the benefit of health professionals. These professionals *are* active members of the boards of directors—much more so than others—for they
have financial interests at stake. The medical professionals on health-
charity boards are usually treated with deference by the lay members.
It is these professionals, along with management, who control America's health charities. These two groups have the most to gain financially from health charities, and they may do so at the expense of
donors, patients and their families, and the public.

3

HEALTH SCAMS AND HEART SCAMS

Since the mid-1980s . . . the Blue Cross–Blue Shield plan serving the Washington area . . . allowed executives to fly on the Concorde, courted clients at faraway spots such as Hawaii, threw parties at horse races in Virginia Hunt country, held retreats at exclusive vacation spas, hired relatives of some employees and transacted business with other family members.
—*Washington Post*, November 15, 1992

This kind of mismanagement and laxity appears to be prevalent in the nonprofit health area.
—Senator Sam Nunn (D-Ga.), December 1992

The wide latitude and discretion enjoyed by nonprofit managers due to the weakness of market controls and the absence of electoral constraints inevitably lead to a degree of mismanagement, if not outright scandal. Indeed, there is a long history of questionable behavior in the nonprofit sector. But because the public views the nonprofits as engaged exclusively in charity, such behavior is only rarely acknowledged and almost never publicized. Consequently, the abuse may persist for decades—until it gets so out of hand that it can no longer be swept under the rug.

More than seventy years ago, in 1921, the Rockefeller Foundation expressed concern that the myriad health charities that then existed were engaging in behavior that was "unscientific, wasteful, and misleading." These complaints went unheeded until 1945, when a three-year study of health charities funded by the Rockefeller Foundation was made public. The study, conducted by health experts Selskar M. Gunn and Philip S. Platt, presented "a devastating and carefully documented picture of useless activities, of failure to take up new problems and serve developing needs, of waste of contributors' money, and failure to achieve health-protection goals that should long since have been reached and passed."[1]

Nothing was ever done to implement the 1945 study's recommendations, and it was eventually forgotten. In 1961, the Rockefeller Foundation funded another inquiry whose authors recommended a national commission to oversee the activities of health charities. That recommendation was also ignored by the executives and members of health-charity boards of directors, who apparently were convinced that they were above well-meaning and constructive criticism.

For the better part of a century, the National Charities Information Bureau (NCIB), a charity watchdog organization, has publicly criticized the administration of various health charities. In 1957 the NCIB severely censured the March of Dimes (originally named the National Foundation for Infantile Paralysis) because it "consistently spent less on research than on fund raising which, the [NCIB] felt, was based on misleading or incomplete data." The March of Dimes' 1957 annual report, for example, depicted a dime divided into proportional "slices" to show how its money was spent; curiously missing was "a piece to represent the outlay that year of more than $6 million, or 14.4 percent, of the budget for fund raising."[2]

The NCIB also found many local chapters of the March of Dimes to be "less than candid" about their expenditures. The chapter in Fort Worth, Texas, for instance, claimed that its fund-raising expenses were below the 20 percent limit imposed by a local ordinance, but in reality the expenses exceeded 40 percent. Another local group in Florida had listed management salaries under "printing and supplies" in its annual reports, and its fund-raising expenses were as high as 80 percent of total collections.[3]

The American Lung Association (ALA), which can trace its origins to the Pennsylvania Society for the Prevention of Tuberculosis founded in 1892, raises millions via its annual Christmas Seal campaign, arguably the most ingenious charitable fund-raising technique ever. Notwithstanding its enormous success in fund-raising, its operations have been subjected to criticism almost from the very beginning. In 1919, when the ALA was known as the National Society for the Study and Prevention of Tuberculosis (NSSPT), it was boasting that its efforts had led to "a drop in the country's tuberculosis mortality rate of 33 percent," despite the fact that "as every epidemiologist knows, the tuberculosis death rate had been declining for years before the establishment of the [NSSPT]."[4] The NSSPT's efforts probably had an impact, but rising standards of living and improved diets were more likely responsible for the declining incidence of tuberculosis (TB). This interpretation is buttressed by medical journalist Frank Ryan's exhaustive history, *The Forgotten Plague: How the Battle Against Tuberculosis Was Won—and Lost,* which contains only one mention of the American Lung Association (or its predecessors)—in reference to lobbying for increased funding of TB causes during the 1980s.[5]

Many of the association's activities, moreover, were "characterized by inertia and complacency." As early as 1939, the ALA's own director of health education, Dr. H. W. Kleinshmidt, condemned its programs as little more than summer camps for children that had little or nothing to do with preventing or curing tuberculosis. However, "he did concede their usefulness in stimulating Christmas Seal sales."[6] (The last of these summer camps was held in 1968.)

In the late 1970s, the ALA was also criticized for its misleading advertising. In 1988, for instance, the ALA issued a press release entitled "Lung Disease Research Spurred by Christmas Seals," even though only about 2 cents out of every dollar in its total budget that year went to research. And in the 1940s and 1950s, health professionals took the ALA to task for ignoring the discovery of streptomycin and other important antituberculosis drugs because "they were afraid these drugs would put them out of business. If TB were licked, what would there be left for them to do?"[7]

FDR'S CHARITABLE LEGACY?

Mismanagement of the National Foundation for Infantile Paralysis (NFIP) was almost legendary in charity circles during the 1940s and 1950s. The NFIP (now the March of Dimes) was established in 1938 by President Franklin D. Roosevelt, himself a victim of polio. President Roosevelt appointed his former law partner and close friend, Basil O'Connor, as the organization's president. The board of trustees "was composed of Roosevelt's political and personal friends and of business people who were continually courting presidential favor."[8]

O'Connor was enormously successful at fund-raising, but his methods were strongly condemned. The NFIP's Fight Polio campaigns clearly implied that most of the money donated would go for research, but "actually, only about 6 percent of that amount . . . was spent for this purpose." Furthermore, trying to find out how the rest of the money was spent was "a frustrating undertaking. . . . Annual reports from this period are remarkably uninformative."[9] For many years, the NFIP did not even issue reports on the expenditures made by its local chapters; moreover, the annual reports that were published were based on its own treasurers' reports, not on those prepared by independent, external auditors.

Enough financial information was available, however, for O'Connor to earn the reputation of "one of the most spendthrift executives in American charity." For example, in 1951 O'Connor spent $500,000 in NFIP funds (more than $2 million in current dollars) to test a gamma-globulin component that was thought to offer protection against polio. The tests showed that, at best, gamma globulin provided very limited and temporary protection. Nevertheless, O'Connor spent another $5 million to buy up almost all the gamma globulin in the country. In 1954, when the Salk vaccine, a proven preventive against polio, was already in production, O'Connor spent another $9 million on gamma globulin.[10]

Although O'Connor received donations from throughout the country, the NFIP distributed a disproportionate share—$15 million—to the Georgia Warm Springs Foundation—FDR's small, 100-bed polio hospital. Incidentally, O'Connor was also president of this hospital. In 1956, O'Connor spent another $500,000 on a "study" to determine what the NFIP would do after polio was no longer a threat.

For his efforts, O'Connor was paid in excess of $100,000 annually (more than $500,000 in current dollars) and enjoyed a lavish expense account, which included an NFIP-provided suite at the prestigious Waldorf-Astoria Hotel in New York. As author Harvey Katz concluded, "the major initial consequence of the American public's massive investment in the polio fight was not a cure for polio. Rather, it was the erection of a gigantic bureaucracy where no organization had existed."[11]

This is not meant to be a comprehensive history of health-charity mismanagement. The point is that such mismanagement is *inherent* and pervasive and has been recognized, though not widely publicized, for decades. In every nonprofit entity, it is not a question of *whether* abuse of charitable contributions will occur, but rather *when* and *to what extent.*

HEALTH SCAMS

There is no better example of the type of mismanagement that is endemic to the nonprofit sector than the 1992 scandal at the United Way of America (UWA), which culminated in the resignation of the organization's national president, William Aramony. The UWA is not a health charity per se; it is best described as a fund-raising umbrella organization that coordinates national fund-raising drives conducted by local United Way affiliates. The income is then distributed to many different charities, including the health charities and particularly the Big Three (the American Cancer Society, the American Heart Association, and the American Lung Association). Indeed, the major health charities are intimately linked to the UWA. Lane W. Adams, a former chief executive officer of the American Cancer Society (ACS), has served on the boards of directors of such UWA spin-offs as United Way International, Mutual of America Life Insurance Company, Partnership Umbrella, Gifts in Kind, and Professional Travel Systems.[12]

Adams was one of Aramony's most outspoken supporters during the 1992 scandal, stating publicly that "he [Aramony] has done more to advance the cause of voluntarism than any professional I know."[13] The UWA certainly did thrive under Aramony's stewardship—as did the ACS and other funding recipients. But the question is not so much whether the UWA prospered, but rather, Would it have prospered even more had it been managed more effectively? The findings of a report to the UWA board of governors described the ways in which Aramony and his so-called cohorts, Adams among them, were "advancing the cause of voluntarism."

A Lavish Lifestyle

The report concluded that Aramony had apparently viewed UWA as his own personal cash machine. "What developed was a haphazard practice of expenditures without adequate documentation, the proliferation of spin-offs not accountable to UWA, the payment of unjustified consulting fees, and the hiring or supporting of a number of persons who were either related to or personally associated with Mr. Aramony." These practices "too often brought little demonstrable benefit—and some outright harm—to UWA."[14] Among the inappropriate uses of charitable donations to the UWA are as follows:

- From 1988 through 1991, the organization spent more than $92,000 for limousine services for Aramony.[15] During 1991, the UWA spent $20,000 for limousine services because, according to Aramony, "I can't afford to be waiting on cabs."[16] Aramony once described himself as a social worker to Ted Koppel on ABC's "Nightline." There must be very few social workers whose time is so valuable that they must use limousines. Even Mother Theresa—the very epitome of a selfless social worker—does not travel by limousine; by Aramony's standards, her contribution to society must have been worth much less than his.

In 1990, the UWA paid $54,365 to one limousine company to transport Aramony and some of his associates around the city of New York.[17] Aramony also ran up thousands of dollars in limousine bills during trips to Los Angeles, San Diego, Chicago, San Francisco, Detroit, Atlanta, and London.

- From 1987 through 1990, the UWA spent at least $40,762 for airfare on the Concorde supersonic jet for Aramony and his traveling companions. In 1989, he took a 20-year-old female friend along on a trip to Egypt, with the UWA paying all of her expenses and personal costs.[18] Aramony did so much traveling that in some years the budget *overruns* for his travel expenses alone exceeded $100,000.

- Aramony owns a condominium in southern Florida, where his daughter lives.[19] Consequently, he charged thousands of dollars for trips to southern Florida—especially at Thanksgiving and Christmas—to the UWA.

- Between early 1988 and the end of 1990, Aramony made at least thirty-two trips,[20] at UWA's expense, to or through Gainesville, Florida, although no UWA business was ever conducted there. The female friend who had earlier accompanied Aramony to Egypt, however, lived there.

- Aramony and some of his UWA associates also appear to be avid gamblers. "In early 1988, Aramony booked airline trips to or through Las Vegas . . . costing $15,236.56. In 1989, Aramony made 13 such trips at a cost of $12,455."[21]

- Tens of thousands of UWA dollars were also spent on trips to Venice, Nassau (for a one-hour business meeting), Puerto Rico, Paris, Moscow, and an annual junket to the Super Bowl.[22]

- From 1988 through 1991, the UWA spent more than $19,700 for meals, entertainment, gifts, clothes, flowers, mail-order purchases, and golf equipment for Aramony.[23]

- Aramony's Alexandria, Virginia, UWA office was furnished with a kidney-shaped rosewood desk, motorized blinds on windows that gave him a view of the Potomac River, and a bank of television monitors that allowed him to watch his secretaries at work.[24]

- Aramony used UWA funds to conduct a study that was used to justify his $390,000 annual salary and some $80,000 in fringe benefits (not including the perks mentioned above).[25]

In the wake of the UWA scandal, *Regardie's* magazine concluded that Aramony had "crafted United Way of America into a personal empire that allow[ed] him to lead a lavish lifestyle while it provid[ed] jobs for his friends and family."[26] No one could deny that his lifestyle was indeed lavish—all paid for by tax-deductible, charitable contributions. As the report to the UWA's board of governors concluded, Aramony "appears to have developed a taste—if not a habit—for a lavish lifestyle and all its trappings. The world of Mr. Aramony became one of limousines, first-class travel, and expensive restaurants." All of this was made possible because, as the report to UWA's board of governors explained, under Aramony's leadership there simply were no policies in place outlining the appropriate documentation and expenditure of travel funds.[27]

Nepotism

Aramony also practiced nepotism and cronyism on a grand scale. His son, Robert D. Aramony, was appointed president and chief executive officer of four profit-making spin-offs of the UWA. When questioned about nepotism, Aramony claimed that he "had nothing to do with his hiring."[28]

Aramony also hired, as UWA's chief financial officer, Thomas J. Merlo, an old friend from Boca Raton, Florida, who "played poker and gin rummy and visited the racetrack" frequently with Aramony. Of all the talented and experienced financial advisers in the country who were eminently qualified to be the chief financial officer of this $3 billion organization, it is odd that Thomas Merlo was chosen: When he was hired, "his business enterprises in Florida were in trouble" and he had been "a defendant in several lawsuits over unpaid loans and fiduciary duties relating to his business ventures." Nevertheless, Aramony apparently believed he needed to pay Merlo a $211,000 salary— $40,000 more than the previous chief financial officer—to "lure" him away from his failing Florida businesses. Merlo was also paid housing and commuting expenses for his first eighteen months so that he could "continue to live in Florida." Meanwhile, the UWA paid for a $1,050-a-month condominium in Alexandria, Virginia, and for Merlo's *weekly* flights back to Florida.[29]

And Aramony always displayed a certain "kindness" toward young female employees. According to *Regardie's,* "several of his young female assistants had been promoted to mid- and top-level management posts so quickly that employees complained it was damaging to morale. At one point, Aramony hired his hairdresser's receptionist to run the office's subsidized food-service operation."[30] One of UWA's spin-offs "hired a woman whom Aramony had met at an airport; she had no experience for the job she was given."[31]

Squandering Endowment Funds

In 1987, the UWA threw a party to celebrate its one-hundredth birthday. Mutual of America Life Insurance Company, a UWA spin-off that manages pension funds for local UWAs, created a $1 million endowment; its interest income was to finance the William Aramony Initiatives in Voluntarism program, which would "foster entrepreneurial spirit" in expanding the "voluntary sector." Assuming a 10 percent rate of return at the time, the endowment would have provided $100,000 annually in interest income. It appears, however, that Aramony quickly spent far more than that on things that were not exactly designed to promote voluntarism. In the first year alone, the endowment spent $125,526 for a condominium in Coral Gables, Florida, described in the development's promotional literature as "the most desirable address in Coral Gables" and featuring a rooftop swimming pool and an expensive French restaurant in its lobby.[32]

Aramony did establish the Initiatives in Voluntarism program by appointing his son, Robert Aramony, as its president. In 1990, that organization received about $200,000 from the UWA, spent about $14,000 on operating costs, and made only $3,000 in grants, according to its public tax returns. In 1988, another UWA spin-off, Partnership Umbrella, purchased a $430,000 condominium in New York for Aramony's use.[33]

Incredibly, United Way of America's books were audited by the Arthur Andersen & Company accounting firm (the same firm, incidentally, also audits the American Cancer Society's accounts), which apparently found nothing wrong with Aramony's expenditures of charitable funds. The report to the UWA's board of governors concluded that

> the numerous abuses of the UWA financial system involving avoidance of financial control procedures, use of restricted funds for other than the stipulated restricted purposes, payment of questionable fees, financial transactions with the spin-offs, and related matters were not brought to light by the annual audits.[34]

Business Spin-Offs

Another source of criticism aimed at the United Way of America has been the activities of its numerous for-profit spin-offs (see table 3.1). The spin-offs were supposedly established to reduce the operating costs of the nationwide network of local UWA affiliates. One spin-off, for example, centralized the purchasing of office materials used by UWA affiliates, a move that allowed discounted bulk orders.

But many of the spin-offs were grossly mismanaged. *Regardie's* reported that the spin-offs amounted to a "merry-go-round" where "Aramony and several of his cohorts constantly show up on the boards or the executive lists of United Way of America and its affiliates. . . .

TABLE 3.1
United Way of America Spin-Offs

1. *United Way International, Inc.* A nonprofit organization created to promote United Way–type charities in foreign countries.

2. *Sales Service/America, Inc.* A for-profit corporation that sells United Way promotional and other products displaying the United Way logo to local United Way affiliates. Handles all sales of UWA films and publications.

3. *The Partnership Umbrella, Inc.* A for-profit corporation established to develop and manage national discount volume-purchasing programs for such items as telephone services and equipment, insurance, and travel.

4. *Charities Funds Transfer, Inc.* A nonprofit organization that disburses to local UWA affiliates the funds that have been received by the national UWA from corporate contributions and government grant programs.

5. *Voluntary Initiatives America, Inc.* Officially named the *William Aramony Incentives in Voluntarism Program,* this entity's goal was to promote "voluntarism in the public sector."

6. *Mobilization for America's Children.* A nonprofit organization developed by William Aramony to build "local and national coalitions to facilitate system, educational, and social service delivery change for children."

7. *Professional Travel Systems, Inc.* A for-profit spinoff established to provide the nonprofit sector with "travel planning services" and to "establish discounted rate programs with hotels and car rental firms."

8. *PTS International, Inc.* A for-profit entity incorporated as an international travel agency.

9. *Gifts in Kind America.* A nonprofit entity organized to "coordinate the disbursement of charitable donations by businesses" of tangible personal property such as computer equipment, clothing, and furniture.

The executives draw salaries, board stipends, and consulting fees from a variety of sources and for vague purposes. Ultimately, the money isn't traceable."[35]

One particularly active cohort was Lane W. Adams, formerly chief executive officer of the American Cancer Society, who had been on the boards of Mutual of America Life Insurance Company, United Way International, Partnership Umbrella, Gifts in Kind, and Professional Travel Systems. UWA employees apparently knew very little about the operation of these organizations and were generally surprised to learn that "one spin-off spent more than $500,000 on two out-of-state condominiums. Another hired a woman whom Aramony had met in passing at an airport. . . . [And] Aramony's son . . . has worked for . . . three."[36] By staffing the boards of directors of these spin-offs with such cronies as Adams, Aramony was able to place them beyond the purview of the UWA board of directors and to spend large amounts of money generated by or laundered through the spin-offs on himself and his friends.

Professional Travel Systems (PTS) was purportedly established to provide discounts on travel expenses to UWA affiliates. PTS opened offices in Alexandria, Virginia (the location of UWA's headquarters), Washington, D.C., New York, and Chicago. PTS quickly developed financial problems and lost $47,000 in its first five months of operations; by then it had spent $18,770 just on travel by its own managers to meetings! UWA officials were never able to locate PTS's records, so it has no idea where Aramony, Adams, and others may have traveled to. Only a few travel vouchers—for trips to Las Vegas—were ever discovered.[37]

PTS also paid $550 to cover the moving expenses of the 19-year-old woman Aramony "recruited" from Ohio during "a chance encounter at an airport." Even though PTS was incurring large losses, Aramony expanded the business by opening new offices in Miami and elsewhere. PTS eventually drowned in its own red ink, and its operations were taken over by another UWA spin-off, Partnership Umbrella.[38]

Partnership Umbrella was ostensibly established to make discounted bulk purchases of goods and services for local UWA affiliates. As with the other spin-offs, the UWA board of directors had little knowledge of Partnership Umbrella's activities; as usual, Aramony appointed his "cohorts" to serve on the Partnership Umbrella board. The UWA provided nearly $1 million in start-up funds for Partnership Umbrella; additional funds were obtained through a special arrangement with AT&T. AT&T offered the UWA and its affiliates a discount on phone services; the amount of the discount was determined by the volume of business the UWA affiliates did with AT&T. The larger the volume, the bigger the discount. Since the volume of telephone sales could not be predicted accurately, the discounts came in the form of rebates given months, or sometimes years, after the arrangement came into being. The rebates received from AT&T would be split 50-50 between the UWA and Partnership Umbrella.

The arrangement among AT&T, UWA, and Partnership Umbrella appears to be advantageous to all parties. Nevertheless, the 1992 report to UWA's board of governors leads to the conclusion that these funds were used improperly. Rather than assisting local UWA affiliates in cost-cutting, "$932,000 of AT&T funds appears to have been used . . . to purchase an office building in Virginia and condominiums in New York and Miami," primarily for the use of Aramony and his "cohorts."[39]

It was also discovered, according to the report, that Partnership Umbrella had been receiving "management fees" from the UWA, but the report's authors could not determine exactly what kind of management advice was provided in return for these fees. The 1991 financial statements of Partnership Umbrella, audited by Arthur Andersen & Co., showed "significant amounts expended for salaries, consultants, benefits, and travel."[40] The same audited statements, however, never disclosed such items as Partnership Umbrella's purchase of the condominiums. When questioned about this omission by the *Washington Post,* a UWA spokesman conceded that "it would be our intention to put that on there."[41] His response highlights an important issue explored in detail in later chapters: the questionable reliability of even the *audited* financial statements of health charities.

It is worth repeating that although the United Way of America is not a health charity per se, it *is* a nonprofit organization with the same incentive structure that applies to all nonprofits. It is also intimately involved in funding health charities and in fund-raising on behalf of them, particularly the Big Three.

Lack of Oversight

Where Was the Board? The abuses listed above didn't just suddenly materialize in 1992—they had been going on for years and years. This brings up the crucial question: Where was the UWA board of directors? In theory, it's the responsibility of the UWA's vaunted "blue-ribbon" board to keep an eye on the UWA's activities. How did the board let matters get so far out of hand?

The answers to these questions are related to the dynamics of all nonprofit boards of directors. Typically, a board member simply does not have the time, incentive, or inclination to become an activist or even to get very deeply involved in the organization's internal operations. These individuals may be of "blue-ribbon" quality when it comes to running their own organizations, but their expertise and reputation for keeping a tight rein on their own firms does not necessarily apply to their work on behalf of the UWA. Clearly, Aramony and his cronies were able to manipulate the UWA's board into acquiescence about their spending programs by withholding important information from them and by telling them only what they wanted to hear.

Where Were the Auditors? The auditing firm of Arthur Andersen & Company was also unable to detect the problems at the UWA. This is not at all surprising since auditors do not make substantive judgments about whether limousines, condos, and first-class trips to Las Vegas and elsewhere are appropriate expenditures for a charity. The auditors' main concern is whether the expenses are listed in the right categories; that is, that travel costs are listed in the travel category, and managerial salaries are not listed under, say, the supplies category. The auditors are also interested, of course, in whether the numbers add up correctly— they are to ensure that there are no discrepancies. For this reason alone, an audited financial statement of the UWA—or any other charity —is of very limited use. It does not tell us whether a charity is using its funds appropriately; that is, in a manner consistent with the intent of the donors. Few would donate to any nonprofit organization if they knew in advance that the money would be spent on an executive's Concorde flight to Europe.

Although charity executives often claim that their audited financial statements are, in effect, a "seal of approval" on their expenditures because they are provided by an unbiased, independent, highly respected accounting firm, such claims are empty. From the auditors' perspective, the expenses incurred on a gambling junket to Las Vegas are just as legitimate and appropriate as those incurred in providing charitable assistance to the poor. Auditors do not make judgments about whether a trip was necessary or whether, if the trip was justified, the traveler should have flown coach rather than first class. If this were not the case, Arthur Andersen & Company would be culpable for the years of flagrant abuse at the UWA. Part of the problem is that the auditors have no responsibility to ask whether particular expenditures are appropriate. Contributors cannot sue the auditors (which they can do and have done in the for-profit world), for contributors do not have any standing in court. They gave voluntarily, so they cannot claim to have been harmed by mismanagement.

The Investigation Continues

One year after the 1992 scandal at UWA, Federal Bureau of Investigation and Internal Revenue Service agents were conducting a criminal investigation of Aramony and his former aides. The New York state attorney general was also conducting a separate civil investigation of the UWA board of directors' performance. According to the assistant attorney general, Pamela A. Mann, the state was investigating whether or not the UWA board "did everything they should have done to make sure that United Way's money was used for the purposes of United Way and not for the benefit of any particular individual."[42]

Meanwhile, a new scandal appeared to be brewing at numerous local UWA affiliates. Apparently, a common practice of these affiliates is to organize fund-raising drives for charities that are not associated with the UWA; they also often organize, for a fee, fund-raising drives for city and state governments. Questions have been raised about the propriety of counting these non-UWA funds as part of United Way's fund-raising receipts, which would overestimate the organization's success in raising funds for its own campaigns.[43]

BLUE CROSS–BLUE SHIELD OF WASHINGTON, D.C.

A 1992 congressional investigation of the nonprofit Blue Cross–Blue Shield health-insurance organization serving the Washington, D.C., area (BC–BS/DC) revealed a pattern of managerial misbehavior that recalls the UWA episode, although on a smaller scale. The U.S. Senate's Permanent Subcommittee on Investigations found "poorly conceived for-profit subsidiaries, weak financial controls, infrequent audits, bloated travel budgets and excessively high salaries" that make BC–BS/DC "the most financially unhealthy of the 72 health plans in the nationwide Blue Cross and Blue Shield system." The nonprofit local organization lost nearly $40 million in 1992, but its executives lived luxuriously while its customers picked up the tab. From 1988 to 1991, a Washington-area family's average insurance premium rose from $194.06 to $410.90 per month.[44]

Among the examples of mismanagement uncovered by the Senate hearings were:[45]

- Forty-five for-profit subsidiaries were so poorly managed that they lost over $100 million over eight years, including $50 million in 1992 alone.
- More than half of the local organization's investments were in risky securities; the average Blue Cross–Blue Shield company invests only 15 percent in such securities.
- The board of directors was kept in the dark or "deliberately misled" about many issues.
- Like the United Way of America, Blue Cross–Blue Shield's Washington-area managers apparently developed a taste for luxurious lifestyles, frequent travel around the world, and fine dining:
  - Joe Gamble, the chief executive officer, spent 202 work days out of the office traveling in 1990, running up expenses of $447,007. Like other company officials, he routinely flew on the Concorde—twenty-two times to Europe alone at $7,400 per flight, compared to an average coach fare of under $1,000 per flight.
  - Accompanied by his wife, Gamble spent $28,839 on a twenty-one-day trip to Hong Kong, flying first class all the way.
- When Gamble retired in November 1992, BC–BS/DC spent $28,000 on a three-dimensional collage presented to him as a tribute; the collage, appropriately enough, included a picture of the Concorde.
- While the company was losing millions of dollars and its insurance premiums were more than doubling between 1988 and 1991, top executives received pay raises of 85 percent; by contrast, the average employee's raise was 13.2 percent during the same period.
- One top executive traveled to Bermuda, Portugal, and Switzerland to inspect the restaurants, hotels, and beaches of some of the world's most exclusive resorts just to make sure they were "appropriate" for future business meetings.
- More than $1,000 was spent on vintage wine during a single evening at a Tyson's Corner, Virginia, restaurant.
- More than $100,000 in food and beverage bills were rung up at the City Club of Washington; BC–BS/DC owned ten corporate memberships there, as well as two memberships at the Congressional Country Club in Bethesda, Maryland.
- One executive spent $891 for a single night at the Grand Barbados Beach Resort.
- BC–BS/DC rented a skybox at Orioles Park in Baltimore so that

top executives could watch America's national pastime in air-conditioned comfort.

- The company sponsored a tent at the International Gold Cup equestrian hunt in Virginia, which cost $6,000 for one day (the link between fox hunting on horseback and health insurance is anybody's guess).
- The company sent over one hundred employees on vacations to Pebble Beach, California, as rewards for selling insurance. The cost exceeded $200,000.
- BC–BS/DC provided six top executives with luxury cars, including Buick Park Avenues equipped with car phones.
- Top executives were also given up to $14,000 for such miscellaneous expenses as golf clubs, health- and country-club dues, and other perks.
- Several executives took their spouses to Hawaii at BC–BS/DC expense.[46]

Like United Way of America, BC–BS/DC became less and less efficient because of the almost total absence of the marketplace discipline that reduces (though it doesn't totally eliminate) such gross inefficiencies in for-profit firms. For-profit firms operating in a competitive marketplace would eventually go out of business or be taken over by a corporate "raider" if they exhibit the kind of behavior routinely displayed by BC–BS/DC executives.

HEART SCAM?

Charity scandals have not been limited to the Northern Virginia/Washington, D.C., area in recent years. In early 1992, the Chicago Heart Association (CHA), one of that city's oldest and most prominent charities, underwent a management shake-up following "an inquiry into alleged staff misconduct and fiscal abuse."[47]

Like the UWA board of directors, the CHA's board employed an outside auditing firm to conduct an investigation of rumored "irregularities." Among its findings were illegal campaign contributions to former state senator John D'Arco, who was convicted in December 1991 of taking bribes to influence legislation.[48] Tax-exempt, nonprofit charitable organizations are prohibited by law from making campaign contributions.

The investigators also uncovered considerable nepotism, such as the hiring of both a nephew and a son of the association's former executive director, Raymond M. Restivo, and the son of the former chief financial officer, Jay Zimmerman, who was fired in September 1991 from his $107,250-a-year job. As did the UWA's Aramony, these CHA executives claimed to have had nothing to do with the hiring of their relatives. Improper expenditures were also uncovered, after which the association's staff returned thousands of dollars to the organization.

Arthur Andersen & Company was commissioned in 1992 to investigate the CHA and, in view of the firm's failure to uncover the abuses at UWA, the result was not surprising. "There was nothing they found that was illegal or immoral. They found no gross malfeasance," said the association's new president, Patrick J. Scanlon.[49]

NONPROFIT HOSPITALS

According to the American Hospital Association, 51.5 percent of all hospitals in the United States are nonprofit; 33.9 percent are operated by state or local governments; and 14.6 percent are proprietary, meaning they are for-profit commercial operations.[50] The hospital industry was vastly different at the turn of the century, when 56 percent of the hospitals were proprietary. This change was no accident: Government policy has, for the past century, favored the creation and growth of government and nonprofit hospitals at the expense of proprietary ones. Nonprofit hospitals are exempt from all taxation and from many regulations that apply only to proprietary hospitals; they receive direct government subsidies for both capital and operating expenses; and they can solicit more charitable donations and volunteer labor than for-profit hospitals.[51] All of these factors have given nonprofit hospitals competitive advantages over their proprietary rivals.

One of the biggest advantages was given by the Hill-Burton Act of 1947, which earmarked federal-government funds for the construction of government and nonprofit hospitals. From 1947 through 1971, almost $4 billion in federal funds supported over ten thousand hospital construction projects.[52] (No appropriations have been made under the Hill-Burton program since 1974.) The Hill-Burton program provided a major stimulus for the expansion of nonprofit hospitals.

The ostensible reason for the tax and regulatory exemptions of nonprofit hospitals is that, unlike proprietary hospitals, they are charitable institutions that provide medical care to poor people who would be turned away from for-profit hospitals. But in many cases, nonprofit hospitals are no more charitable than their for-profit counterparts. Indeed, they are sometimes even *less* charitable.

In a Utah court case, *Intermountain Health Care v. Utah County*, evidence showed that the nonprofit Intermountain Hospital chain, the largest nonutility employer in the state, had a profit margin of 10.9 percent in 1985. Yet "Intermountain was losing an amount equivalent to only 3.3 percent of revenues on patients who couldn't pay, while for-profit hospitals in the state were losing 4 to 5 percent." The Utah Supreme Court "found a nonprofit hospital system to be no different than profit-making systems, and refused to give it state property tax exemption."[53]

The *Intermountain* case raises serious doubts about the degree to which nonprofit hospitals are willing to serve the poor. Evidence from cases brought under the terms of the Hill-Burton Act also raises questions about the charitable activities of nonprofit hospitals. In order to receive funds under the Hill-Burton program, hospitals had to agree to be available to "all persons residing in the territorial area" of the facility and to make available "a reasonable volume of hospital services to persons unable to pay."[54] But the act never seems to have achieved its intended effect.

> Despite good intentions, ... the Hill-Burton program has been a giant giveaway to private [nonprofit] hospitals, which have received 60 percent of the grants. For the first twenty-five years after the Act's passage, the government did nothing to insure that recipient hospitals were meeting their obligations to provide community service and free health care. Most Hill-Burton recipient hospitals turned away patients who could not pay, who did not have a private physician, or who were on Medicaid. Critically ill patients were even refused admission to emergency rooms.[55]

In 1970, the first of numerous lawsuits were filed claiming that indigents had been denied services at Hill-Burton–subsidized hospitals. The lawsuits forced the federal government to issue a new set of regulations enforcing the law, but nonprofit hospitals have apparently dragged their feet rather than comply. "An April 1982 Government Accounting Office investigation disclosed that, among hundreds of other deficiencies, over the preceding two years only 17 of 690 complaints pending against hospitals had been resolved by the Department of Health and Human Services, the agency responsible for insuring compliance."[56]

In addition to not doing as much as could be done to assist the poor with indigent care—the principal justification for the tax-exempt status of nonprofit hospitals—there is evidence that, for many of the reasons discussed in chapter 2, nonprofit hospitals tend to be managed much less efficiently than their for-profit counterparts. Harvard University professors Regina E. Herzlinger and William S. Krasker analyzed the performance of fourteen major hospital chains—six for-profit and eight nonprofit—in 1977 and 1981. Their sample consisted of 725 hospitals representing 90 percent of the hospital beds in the for-profit sector and 68 percent of the beds in the nonprofit sector in the United States. They made adjustments so that accounting data for both types of hospital were comparable and corrected for factors that could influence financial performance, including location, scope of services, the presence of teaching and research activities, care to indigent patients, quality of care, size, and prices charged for services. Based on this very careful, comprehensive analysis that they knew would be controversial—no matter what the results showed—they reported the following four major findings in the *Harvard Business Review:*

1. Although nonprofit hospitals receive more social subsidies than for-profits, they do not achieve better social results. They are not more accessible to the uninsured and medically indigent, nor do they price less aggressively. They are also more oriented toward short-term results, replacing plant and equipment much more slowly than for-profits.
2. Nonprofits, however, do more to maximize the welfare of the affiliated physicians, who are their main customers. These hospitals make large numbers of staff and beds available to these physicians, and they finance these benefits through social subsidies, tax exemptions, and delays in replacing plant and equipment. Today's physicians are subsidized by current taxpayers and future patients.
3. For-profit hospitals, in contrast, produce better results for society and require virtually no societal investment to keep them afloat. They are more efficient than nonprofits, reinvest their earnings in newer plant and equipment, and offer just as broad a range of services to a large number of patients, including the medically indigent.
4. Our data suggest that, at the very least, nonprofit hospitals do not inevitably improve social welfare in their communities. Indeed, the hospital's professional staff—and not the patients or society—may be capturing many of the benefits inherent in the nonprofit form.

This imbalance is unlikely to happen in a for-profit organization subject to stock market discipline.[57]

Herzlinger and Krasker conclude that nonprofit hospitals have not "fulfilled their social promise" and that the quality of services is higher at for-profits than at nonprofits, with the services offered at comparable prices.[58]

Who Profits from Nonprofit Hospitals?

Of course, the term *nonprofit* does not mean that "profits"—revenues in excess of expenditures—are not earned by nonprofit hospitals. It only means that such surpluses are not distributed to shareholders—after all, there are no shareholders. Nonprofit managers and administrators may not directly benefit from the "profits" made by their organizations, but they can and do benefit indirectly.

Herzlinger and Krasker further concluded that "nonprofit hospital chains acted for the self-interest of the professionals within them, not just for the welfare of society. They increased professional staffs' comfort level through tax exemptions and the deferral of capital replacement without providing better, cheaper, or more accessible health care in return."[59] Since they pay no taxes, receive government subsidies, and frequently do not even serve more indigent patients than do for-profit hospitals, it is not surprising that many nonprofit hospitals are flush with "profits." These surpluses are not necessarily taken home by hospital administrators, but are used to create a comfortable working environment for staff physicians by making an excessive number of beds available, by offering a wide range of services, and by acquiring a large support staff. Such expenditures, of course, are paid for by the hospitals' customers and contribute to rapidly escalating health care costs.

Etzioni and Doty have identified four avenues through which nonprofit hospital staffs and administrators can personally profit: (1) income tied to entrepreneurial activity; (2) self-dealing; (3) real-estate transactions; and (4) unreasonable and uncustomary fees, salaries, and fringe benefits.[60]

In the first category, a common practice among some medical specialists, such as pathologists, radiologists, and anesthesiologists, is to receive all or part of their remuneration based on a percentage of their department's gross or net income. Pathologists have even gone so far as to institute a professional code or rule requiring each new pathologist to take an oath that "I shall not accept a position with a fixed stipend in any hospital."[61] It is not uncommon for some stipendless pathologists to earn over $500,000 a year.

Self-dealing occurs when both parties of a transaction appear on both sides; that is, as both buyer and seller. A General Accounting Office study found cases of self-dealing among trustees or key employees at seventeen of the nineteen nonprofit hospitals it investigated.[62] In six of the nineteen hospitals, 25 percent or more of the board members had "overlapping interests"—meaning conflicts of interest. For example:

- A Washington, D.C., hospital was governed by a forty-two-member board of trustees. Twelve board members had overlapping interests, such as associations with banks, law firms, and other businesses servicing the hospital.
- Seven board members were associated with a bank that maintained a hospital savings account and checking account, and had custody of the hospital's investment portfolio. Three board members were associated with law firms doing business with the bank, and one member was associated with a group of eight radiologists providing radiology services to the bank.
- In 1970, Jose A. Blanco was controller and assistant administrator of Washington Hospital Center, the largest private nonprofit hospital in the District of Columbia. Blanco, who managed the hospital's data processing operations at an annual salary of $39,000, decided that the existing system needed improvement, so he formed a private company—Space Age Computer Systems, Inc. He was certain of one customer—Washington Hospital Center. As reported in the *Washington Post*,

  Blanco's boss, Richard M. Loughery, administrator of the hospital, accepted stock free of charge in the new company, and became one of its directors. Blanco concedes that five other administrative officials of the hospital, including the assistant controller and the internal auditor, bought stock in Space Age at $1 a share. To further help the new company along, it was given $50,000 by the hospital. The payment was described as a "deposit."[63]

These examples of self-dealing at nonprofit hospitals have become so commonplace that Herbert S. Denenbery, a Pennsylvania insurance commissioner who has investigated hospital finances, has concluded that nonprofit hospitals are "public institutions and they ought to be

above suspicion, but you'd never know it from the way they operate."
Marilyn G. Rose, director of the Washington, D.C., office of the
National Health and Environmental Law Program, was even more
forceful in her conclusion that "there's no such thing as a nonprofit
hospital. The money goes to the staff, trustees, and administrators
through high salaries and various arrangements."[64]

INPUT AND OUTPUT IN MEDICAL CARE

*In a bureaucratic system, . . . increases in expenditure will be matched
by fall[s] in production. . . . Such systems will act rather like "black
holes" in the economic universe, simultaneously sucking in resources,
and shrinking in terms of "emitted" production.*

—Dr. Max Gammon

*A casual glance at figures on input and output in U.S. hospitals indi-
cates that Gammon's law has been in full operation for U.S. hospitals
since the end of World War II.*

—Milton Friedman, *Input and Output in Medical Care*, 1992

Nobel laureate economist Milton Friedman recently "discovered" the
research of Dr. Max Gammon, a British physician who also researches
the medical-care industry. Dr. Gammon's research, says Friedman, has
important implications for the U.S. health care system and for understanding the role of health charities in that system.[65] Friedman and
Gammon have both noted that in bureaucratic systems, such as America's health care system, there is a tendency for increased inputs (meaning expenditures) to be matched by *reduced* levels of output, however
measured.

As discussed in chapter 2, many incentives found in government
bureaucracies are also prevalent in nonprofit organizations, including
health charities. In fact, an argument can be made that the inefficiencies will be even greater in the nonprofit sector because of the absence
of market or political discipline and because of the "halo effect"—by
definition, all charities must be "doing good"—that dissuades the public from closely examining the operations of most charities. Thus, it
should not be too surprising that as the amounts spent on health care
rapidly increased, progress in improving public health has proceeded
only slowly, if at all. There have, of course, been major advances in
health care over the past century, but, as Friedman correctly observes,
"the question remains whether these gains were promoted or retarded

TABLE 3.1
Summary Data on Hospital and Medical Expenses, Selected Years,
1923–89

	1923	1940	1965	1989
Output				
Beds per 1,000 population	6.8	9.3	8.8	4.9
Percentage of beds occupied	73.0	84.0	82.0	69.6
Cost per patient-day (in 1982 $)	NA	$22	$71	$545
Input				
Personnel per occupied bed	NA	NA	1.4	4.6
Hospital expenses as percentage of total medical expenses	NA	24.3	32.1	35.6
Annual medical cost per person (in 1982 $)	$136	$216	$593	$1920

Source: Milton Friedman, *Input and Output in Medical Care,* Hoover Institution Public Policy
Essay (Stanford, Calif.: Hoover Institution Press, 1992), p. 2.

by the extraordinary rise in the fraction of national income spent on
medical care."[66]

Friedman's examination of inputs and outputs in U.S. hospitals
from 1923 to 1989 suggests that Gammon's law has apparently "been
in full operation . . . since the end of World War II"—precisely the
period when the Hill-Burton Act and other government programs
transformed the hospital industry from one in which proprietary firms
dominated to one in which nonprofit and government hospitals now
comprise more than 85 percent of the industry's capacity.

As seen in table 3.1, before 1940 both input and output rose in
U.S. hospitals. The cost of hospital care per patient, adjusted for inflation, rose at about 5 percent per year from 1929 to 1940; the number
of occupied beds rose by 2.4 percent; and costs rose only modestly.

The situation after the war was dramatically different. Between
1946 and 1989 the number of beds per one thousand population fell
by more than half; the occupancy rate dropped by an eighth. Inputs,
on the other hand, skyrocketed as hospital personnel per occupied bed
multiplied nearly sevenfold, and cost per patient-day, adjusted for
inflation, rose an amazing twenty-sixfold, from $21 in 1946 to $545 in
1989 in constant 1982 dollars.[67]

Part of the reason for the decline in output, according to Friedman, can be explained by improvements in medical science: A healthy population needs less hospitalization. But that does not explain the meteoric rise in inputs and their associated costs. Moreover, "improvements in health and in the quality of hospital care do not appear to have proceeded more rapidly after 1965 [the year Medicare and Medicaid were established] than before."[68] In fact, there is some evidence that

the reverse is true. Whereas reported expenditures on research (per capita and in constant dollars) rose at the rate of 15 percent a year from 1948 to 1964, they rose at less than 2 percent a year from 1965 to 1989. Yet the number of occupied beds per thousand population fell by 1 percent a year from 1946 to 1964 and by 2.5 percent a year from 1965 to 1989. Cost per patient day rose by 6 percent in the first period, 9 percent in the second.[69]

Gammon's law was at work, not medical miracles.

Along with government subsidies to nonprofit and government hospitals came a massive bureaucratization. "Personnel per occupied bed, which had already doubled from 1946 to 1965, more than tripled from that level after 1965," while "cost per patient day, which had already more than tripled from 1946 to 1965, multiplied a further eightfold after 1965."[70]

Government policy, therefore, caused a dramatic increase in hospital and other medical costs, especially administrative costs. Having caused these costs to skyrocket, the government then instituted myriad regulations purportedly designed to control these costs. But these additional regulations only added to administrative expenses. This phenomenon typically occurs whenever *any* organization accepts government subsidies: Costs increase; regulations and controls inevitably follow; the additional regulations result in costs being driven even higher, which then leads to even more regulation; and so on.

Gammon's law of bureaucratic systems provides an important explanation of why health care costs in general, and the costs of operating nonprofit hospitals in particular, have risen so dramatically since the mid-1960s. The essential problem, as Friedman recognizes, is that because of massive government interventions, "the U.S. medical system has become in large part a socialist enterprise" as "medicine in all its aspects has become subject to an ever more complex bureaucratic structure."[71]

The nonprofit health charities have become an important element of that "complex bureaucratic structure."

4

THE BUSINESS OF HEALTH
CHARITIES

Things are seldom what they seem;
Skim milk masquerades as cream. . . .
Black sheep dwell in every fold;
All that glitters is not gold.
—W. S. Gilbert, *H.M.S. Pinafore*

What do health charities really do? There are many answers to this
question, but none is acceptable or useful. At one extreme, the answer
is deceptively simple: Health charities, like others, "do good" for society. After all, the unabridged *Random House Dictionary of the English
Language* defines charity as "charitable actions, as almsgiving or per-
forming other benevolent actions of any sort for the needy with no
expectation of material reward." Thus, conventional wisdom holds that
charities serve the most vulnerable in society—people who are in need
because they are poor, homeless, unemployed, hungry, sick, or dis-
abled. But, as chapter 2 revealed, nonprofit organizations have incentive systems that may permit their executives and staffs to obtain significant material rewards, always at the expense of programs; in some
cases, such as the unsavory episode at United Way of America detailed
in chapter 3, charitable donations have been flagrantly misused. Obviously, the dictionary definition of charity is overly simplistic and not
very helpful in understanding what charities in general, and health
charities in particular, really do.

One source of information on the programs and activities of charities is each organization's annual report, but this self-serving information must be viewed with considerable skepticism. Because a primary
function of these reports is to impress both potential contributors and
the government agencies that oversee charities, they tend to be long on
self-promotion and praise and short on self-criticism. The most important asset of every charity seeking donations from the public is its rep-

utation for efficiency and program effectiveness; thus, one could hardly expect a charity to raise questions or criticisms about its programs and priorities in its annual report. Whether true or not, all charities claim that their programs are urgently needed, effectively executed, and highly beneficial to society. In fund-raising appeals, such claims are inevitably accompanied by the plea that much more needs to be done and, indeed, would be done if only additional funds were available.

A conscientious contributor who tries to dig beneath the surface to determine whether a charity's fund-raising rhetoric accurately reflects its spending priorities immediately encounters numerous and complex problems. Among the questions the contributor may ask are the following:

1. Does the charity use its funds efficiently by producing services and programs at the lowest cost?
2. Does the charity use its funds for the purposes described in its fund-raising appeals?
3. Do those in need benefit from the charity's programs?
4. From the perspective of society and contributors, could better results be achieved by redirecting resources to other activities; in other words, are the charity's programs appropriate?

Although these questions appear straightforward and are essential to understanding a charity's activities and programs, finding accurate answers is fraught with difficulties.

FINANCIAL DATA: FACT OR FANTASY?

Tracking a charity's expenditures would appear to be a straightforward task, since all legitimate charities issue audited financial statements each year. For health charities, these financial statements report spending for program services in five categories: public education, research, patient services, professional education, and community service. In addition to these expenditures, fund-raising costs as well as management and general expenses are also reported. This breakdown follows the *Standards of Accounting and Financial Reporting for Voluntary Health and Welfare Organizations,* which is published by the National Health Council (NHC), the United Way of America, and the National Assembly. The NHC is "a private nonprofit association of national organizations which was founded in 1920 as a clearinghouse and cooperative effort for voluntary health agencies" (health charities are also known as "voluntary health agencies"). Each year, the NHC "requires member agencies to provide audited figures for national and affiliate offices combined whenever possible" and, based on these data, issues a publicly available *Report on Voluntary Health Agency Revenue and Expenses* that summarizes and compares the spending patterns of member organizations.[1]

According to the NHC, the five program services conducted by its members are defined as follows:[2]

Public education: Programs that inform the general public about how to promptly recognize the symptoms of ill health, disease, and/or physical disorders. Also included is the dissemination of facts and information designed to encourage periodic physical examinations, reduce indifference toward health problems, and eliminate unwarranted fears or misconceptions.

Research: Awards or grants-in-aid to support scientific studies or investigations (plus all associated costs or expenses) to find causes of, cures for, and prevention of specific diseases or health problems.

Patient services: Activities performed or programs conducted for the purpose of providing physical, emotional, and other assistance to individuals afflicted with a disease or health impairment, or to their families. Also included is the furnishing of medical care, hospitalization, equipment, drugs, and other tangible items to those in need.

Professional education: Activities or programs designed to improve the knowledge, skills, and critical judgment of physicians, dentists, nurses, and others directly or indirectly engaged in health work by keeping them abreast of new medical advancements, diagnostic techniques, and similar information. Also included is the provision of educational opportunities for those who have displayed the interest, aptitude, and intelligence to enter the medical field or to undertake scientific investigations, as well as the expansion or improvement of health-education courses in universities and the stimulation of health and/or scientific careers.

Community services: Activities such as the detection of disease or health problems, planning and improving health practices, supporting clinics or other public-health facilities, and conducting rehabilitative or similar programs.

With regard to fund-raising and management and general expenses, the NHC notes that management and general expenses provide for accounting, financial reporting, and other services to meet regulatory requirements and sustain agency operations. Fund-raising expenses are the costs incurred in appeals to the public.[3]

The aggregate data for all thirty-nine health charities in the NHC's fiscal year 1990 report is impressive: Out of total expenditures of $3 billion, program services accounted for $2.52 billion, or 84 cents of each dollar spent, while 9 cents went for fund-raising and only 7 cents was spent on management and general expenses. Thus, it appears that contributors are getting a bargain—for each dollar spent on fund-raising and on management and general activities, $5.25 worth of program services were produced for the benefit of the community—and health charities are apparently highly efficient, since all but 16 percent of their expenditures are spent on programs.[4]

Among the thirty-nine health charities, 42 percent of program-services expenditures went to community services, 4 percent to professional education, 13 percent to research, 17 percent to patient services, and 24 percent to public education.[5] Although all health charities have fund-raising expenses and management and general expenses, not all health charities are engaged in all five program-services activities. For example, the Damon Runyon–Walter Winchell Cancer Research Fund, as its name suggests, limits its program exclusively to funding cancer research; the Juvenile Diabetes Foundation does not engage in patient services, professional education, or community services, but concentrates instead on public education and research; and the American Heart Association does not provide assistance to individual patients.

The NHC's statistics might seem highly reassuring to a potential donor considering a contribution to the health causes addressed by NHC members. But much can be obscured when information is aggregated; by lumping together thirty-nine charities, differences in spending patterns among individual entities cannot be detected. Clearly, a potential contributor would be concerned about how much of each dollar donated to a particular health charity was spent on program services relative to the amount spent on fund-raising and on management and general expenses. The obvious conclusion is that the charity that spends the lowest proportion of its revenue on fund-raising and on management and general expenses, and thus the largest proportion on program services, is the most efficient and effective.

Things are seldom what they seem, however, and such a conclusion may be totally erroneous. It is difficult, if not impossible, to determine from audited financial statements what a charity does with its money that actually benefits those whom the charity purportedly serves. Put another way, the NHC data—though flattering to its members—tells very little about efficiency and nothing about effectiveness.

The reason that financial information offers few insights into charitable activities is simple: By accounting convention, *the costs of providing program services are counted as part of the services themselves.* The problems created by this accounting practice are easily illustrated by a clear-cut example. Suppose that two health charities, A and B, spend all of their income each year on aid to disease victims. Both charity A and charity B collect $100,000 in a given year and both report spending $100,000 on patient services. Both appear to be highly efficient and equally deserving of support, but these "facts" can be deceiving. Charity A has one staff member paid $20,000 per year to distribute $80,000 in cash assistance to patients, while charity B hires four staff members at $20,000 each to distribute $20,000 to patients. Charity A is apparently far more efficient and deserving of support than is charity B, since four times as much cash assistance reaches those in need. Yet the amount reported spent on patient services in the audited financial statements is the same for both charities: $100,000! Thus, it is not possible to determine whether expenditures on staff are as low as possible or whether the payroll is padded with paramours, cronies, or nepotistic nieces and nephews.

To carry the exercise a bit further, it is important to understand that even though charity A is relatively more efficient in distributing cash to patients than charity B, no claim can be made that charity A is efficient in any absolute sense. After all, a full-time staff member might not be needed to distribute cash to disease victims. Perhaps a part-time worker paid $10,000 per year (or even less) could provide this service or, better yet, if one or more unpaid volunteers could accomplish this task, the entire $100,000 could help needy disease victims. Using financial data to assess efficiency, even in a relative sense, leaves much to be desired.

Three Broad Categories

Additional insights into health-charity expenditures can be obtained by looking at more detailed financial information; that is, the cost components associated with each of the seven major spending categories. Unfortunately, the NHC does not provide such details; one must delve into the financial statements of each individual charity. For each of the

TABLE 4.1
Expense Items by Category

Executive and Staff Compensation	General Overhead	Direct Services
Salaries	Professional fees	Printing, publications, and films
Fringe benefits	Supplies	Meetings and conferences, including related travel
Payroll taxes	Telephone	Specific assistance to individuals
	Postage and shipping	Awards and grants
	Occupancy	
	Interest	
	Information processing and other services	
	Other travel	
	Insurance	
	Depreciation	
	Other expenses	

Authors' categorization of health-charity expenses.

five program services as well as for the fund-raising and management and general activities, expenditures are broken down into as many as eighteen different items. For our purposes, these expense items can be placed in three broad groupings, as shown in table 4.1: executive and staff compensation, general overhead, and direct services. This classification system provides insights into health charities' activities and helps put their priorities in perspective. For a highly efficient volunteer group, one would expect expenditures for compensation and general overhead to be small relative to the amount spent for direct services, which, in broad terms, are the programs that benefit the general public and disease victims.

Executive and Staff Compensation. Health charities often describe themselves as "volunteer" organizations. For example, when the American Cancer Socity (ACS) financed *Crusade: The Official History of the American Cancer Society* by Walter Ross (formerly the ACS's director of special publications), the book was dedicated

> to the 2,500,000 volunteers of the American Cancer Society—more than two of every one hundred U.S. volunteers—in honor of the organization's seventy-fifth anniversary.

The purpose of this book is to illustrate how the American Cancer Society became the world's largest volunteer health organization.

It tells why volunteers started the Society and how they made it grow.
It is designed to provide a view of how volunteers go about setting
the organization's goals and achieving them.[6]

The role of ACS volunteers is also routinely touted in its annual
reports, and other health charities also praise their volunteer cadres.
The 1991 annual report of the American Heart Association (AHA)
states, "Today the AHA is one of the world's premier health organizations with about 3.5 million volunteers."[7] The reason that the role of
volunteers is stressed is straightforward: In theory, volunteer organizations spend little of their funds on executive and staff compensation,
so that most of the expenditures are for program services. The ACS's
1991 annual report makes this point by stating, "We also highly prize
the effective partnership of American Cancer Society volunteers and
staff. . . . Again, one of our keys to success has been the low ratio of
staff to volunteers. The present ratio of one staff person for 458 volunteers translates into high productivity in program delivery at low program cost."[8]

Despite the self-proclaimed volunteer status of health charities,
executive and staff compensation account for a significant percentage
of their expenditures. For fiscal year 1991, 38.9 cents of each dollar
spent by the ACS went to compensation; for the AHA, compensation
took 34.3 cents of each dollar spent; and the American Lung Association (ALA) spent 42.5 cents of each dollar on compensation.[9] Despite
the major role attributed to unpaid volunteers by the nation's health
charities, salaries, fringe benefits, and payroll taxes account for a significant proportion of each dollar spent—for some organizations, as
much as half.

Although no one would expect a large health charity to function
without some paid employees to provide specialized expertise and continuity and to mobilize and direct the energies of volunteers, the notion
that a very low percentage of expenses goes for executive and staff
compensation is contradicted by the financial facts.

Most volunteers contribute their time and effort at the state,
regional, and local levels of health charities, not at national headquarters. The national office is concerned not so much with volunteer services to individuals as with such matters as allocating funds for
research and providing information and guidance to affiliates on fund-
raising and other programs. The loyalty of volunteers is primarily to
the communities where they live, not to the distant headquarters.
Thus, it is more appropriate to look at compensation for executives

and staffs of state affiliates rather than the consolidated national-and state-office financial reports, which combine the expenses of the national office with those of the state, regional, and local units.

The ACS alone has fifty-seven divisions—fifty state units, plus four regional affiliates in New York and affiliates in Puerto Rico, Philadelphia, and the District of Columbia—and nearly 3,500 community-based units.[10] Only the fifty-seven divisions issue audited financial statements each year. One might expect that at the state level—where volunteers are concentrated and their efforts most in evidence—the percentage of expenses going to compensation would be much smaller than that reported in the consolidated financial statements. But the reverse is true: At the state affiliates, executive and staff compensation accounts for a much higher percentage of expenditures than for the organization as a whole.

Rather than attempt to obtain financial reports from all fifty-seven ACS divisions, we reviewed audited financial reports for a sample of ten geographically dispersed state divisions. The percentage of expenditures accounted for by compensation ranged from a low of 45 percent at the Texas affiliate to a high of 60 percent in Missouri; percentages for the other eight state divisions reviewed were: Arizona, 53.9; California, 58.9; Colorado, 52.3; Florida, 48.7; Ohio, 56.4; and Wisconsin, 52.5.[11] In short, the single most important spending category for state divisions is executive and staff compensation (salaries, fringe benefits, and payroll taxes), a rather surprising result for an organization that describes itself as "volunteer."

The traditional view is that charity should be self-sacrificing and noble, a picture that is often painted in fund-raising appeals.[12] Indeed, in keeping with this vision, the glossy annual reports issued by most ACS state divisions contain no information on salaries, and the audited financial statements must be specifically requested and consulted to obtain such data. Self-sacrifice implies selflessness; that is, the public does not expect charity executives to enrich themselves while serving the needy. Though never publicized by the charities themselves, the salaries of the highest-paid executives must be reported on IRS Form 990, the tax form for charitable organizations, which are subject to public inspection. Compliance with this provision of the law is often grudging at best. Charity executives apparently believe that contributors might not appreciate the generous salaries paid to the executives who "do good."[13] And salary information readily reveals that charity executives can do very well financially by purportedly "doing good."

Six-figure salaries are commonplace at ACS national headquarters and for top executives at the state divisions. After studying the ACS's 1990 income-tax returns, Kurt Loft of the *Tampa Tribune* reported that "the American Cancer Society pays its top officers more than most nonprofit groups. . . . Salaries for the top five officers [at national headquarters] exceed $800,000." In 1990, Executive Vice-President and Chief Executive Officer William Tipping was paid $208,000; John Laszlo, senior vice-president of research, $168,000; Gerald Murphy, group vice-president, medical, $164,000; Lowell Luepto, group vice-president, operations, $149,000; and Daniel Nixon, vice-president, professional education, $124,000.[14] In addition to such salaries, top executives at health charities can also enjoy generous fringe benefits, such as personal vehicles; health, life, and disability insurance; club memberships; travel and expense accounts; and, in some cases, "golden parachutes," that is, their employment contracts award them generous benefits when they leave the organization.

Salary levels of the top executives at ACS headquarters are not out of line with those at other health charities. In 1992, the American Heart Association paid its executive vice-president $246,000, plus $38,846 in benefits, while the American Lung Association's managing director earned $195,000, plus $9,271 in benefits.[15]

Executives at ACS state divisions also fare well. In 1991, the executive director of ACS-Ohio earned $120,000;[16] the executive director of the Hamilton County subunit earned $58,600 in 1992.[17] ACS federal tax returns for 1990 reveal that the executive vice-president of the Texas division was paid $145,000; his Florida and New York City division counterparts made $115,000 and $122,127, respectively.[18]

Salaries at the ACS-California division are particularly interesting: At the end of fiscal year 1989, the chief executive and the vice-president of "cancer control" were two of the highest paid ACS officials outside the national office, earning, respectively, $135,000 and $116,500 per year. In addition, both of these executives received retirement and insurance (health, dental, disability, and life) benefits costing more than $13,000. The five officers with the highest salaries together earned of $400,250, and 151 employees each earned more than $30,000 per year. In contrast, at the end of fiscal year 1990, the five top officers together earned $509,190—an increase of 27.2 percent in only one year—and 197 employees earned more than $30,000 per year.[19] Throughout ACS, 682 employees were paid more than $30,000 per year in 1990, only 176 of whom worked at the national office.[20]

The ACS justifies the generous salaries of executives by arguing that they are comparable to compensation paid to managers in the private sector: "Cancer society officials . . . say their salaries aren't out of line. They say their chief executives would earn similar salaries at a private company of similar size."[21]

Although there may be an element of truth in this assertion, it is troublesome that ACS officials apparently think of their organization as a business. Such a psychological bent or mind-set is not conducive to the conduct of charitable activity. Businesses seek a monetary return for their goods and services; charities claim to serve those who cannot afford to pay. Indeed, the fundamental reason that nonprofit organizations enjoy such a long list of government-granted special privileges and exemptions is that their objectives and operations are not—or at least should not be—primarily motivated by concern over revenue and profit. As shown in later chapters, however, the "business" mind-set can explain a great deal of the activities of health charities.

General Overhead. All organizations have overhead expenses and, as every student of basic accounting is aware, the allocation of overhead expenses is largely arbitrary. To illustrate the problems associated with allocating overhead expenses among programs, consider the receptionist who answers the telephone. Telephone calls may be related to any of the seven activities for which costs are reported: the five program services, plus fund-raising expenses and management and general expenses. Theoretically, the receptionist's salary should be allocated to each of the seven activities in direct proportion to the number of calls received for that activity. Specifically, if half of the telephone calls are concerned with fund-raising, half of the receptionist's salary should be counted as a fund-raising expense. Similarly, half of the telephone bill should also be charged to fund-raising, as should half of the cost of message pads. But expenses aren't allocated this way because the record keeping required to do so is costly and time-consuming; equally important, matters are never so simple. For example, long-distance calls are much more costly than local calls, so if most of the calls about fund-raising are local, less than half the phone bill should be charged to fund-raising. To complicate matters further, if the executive in charge of fund-raising was always available so that it was never necessary for callers to leave a message, then none of the cost of message pads should appear in the fund-raising account.

This nitpicking exercise shows that the allocation of overhead expenses to programs, if carried to extremes, quickly becomes very complicated, time-consuming, and costly—which is why it is not carried to extremes. Rather, managers have considerable discretion in allocating overhead costs among programs. And because managers want the public to think that virtually all the funds donated to their organizations go to program services rather than to fund-raising expenses and management and general expenses, there is a strong (and understandable) incentive to overallocate overhead expenses to program services. This interpretation is confirmed by Arthur F. Stocks, a thirty-year veteran of ACS's Iowa division who served as executive director there from 1960 until he retired in 1985: "It is terribly easy for a staff person working with volunteers in a field area to be tempted to place 'fund-raising activity' (which the public identifies as 'bad') under some activity such as 'Public Education' (which the public identifies as a 'good' use of donated funds)."[22] If, when all is said and done, the allocation of overhead costs is basically arbitrary, why not be arbitrary in a way that makes the organization look good to potential donors and government regulators?

There is nothing inherently illegal about "padding" the overhead for program services and reducing the overhead for management and fund-raising. But what assurance does a donor have that the numbers have not been substantially distorted so that a lot of the fund-raising costs show up in the financial statements as, say, public education expenses? Health-charity financial officers would claim that the books can't be cooked because auditors check them each year. But there are several reasons why little faith should be placed in the power of auditors. First, although the books are indeed audited annually, they can still be seasoned with more than a grain of salt. In the audited financial statements for the ACS as of August 31, 1991, for instance, Arthur Andersen & Company authoritatively stated that "expenses are allocated into functional categories depending upon the ultimate purpose of the expenditure."[23] On close examination, however, this statement tells us absolutely nothing.

The auditors for the American Lung Association, Loeb and Troper, explain in the ALA's 1991 financial statements that the national headquarters and ALA affiliates incurred "joint costs of $24,770,193 for information materials and activities that included fund-raising appeals. Of these costs, $12,480,390 were allocated to fund-raising, $1,451,912 to environmental health, $3,555,654 to smoking education, $4,069,780 to lung disease, $2,838,028 to community services, and $374,429 to management and general."[24] Thus, fund-raising costs are distributed as overhead to programs and to management and general. The ALA's financial statement shows how much was allocated to what program categories, but how the amounts were determined remains a mystery. Moreover, no information is offered about how other ALA overhead expenses are allocated across programs, and the same is true for the ACS and the AHA.

The absurdity of this state of affairs has been highlighted and dramatized by Clarine Nardi Riddle, the attorney general for Connecticut, who satirizes the inclination of charities to write off fund-raising costs as public education expenditures.

> She describes a hypothetical organization dedicated to wiping out the common cold. The charity's direct-mail package includes statistics on the incidence of sniffles and offers tips on avoiding them: Wear a hat, eat soup, stay away from people who are sneezing. Three years of imaginary mailings bring in $10 million in play money. The fundraiser bills the charity a plausible $9.75 million. And in its financial statements, the charity calls 50 percent of the fund-raiser's bill a program expense because the package has educated the public. "What exactly is the benefit to society," asks Ms. Nardi Riddle, "that makes this charity worthy of donor support and tax exemption?"[25]

Second, the relationship between nonprofit organizations and their auditors is a cozy one—not at all like the "arm's length" relationship between private firms and their auditors. "In the business world, you have the Securities and Exchange Commission and investors who would sue if they got information that would lead them to make a poor investment decision. In the nonprofit world, there's not that much pressure on having good information that accurately portrays what is going on."[26] Because donors do not have a large or long-term financial stake in charities, there is little likelihood that the auditors might be sued if some of the numbers were moved around a bit.

Another reason for the cozy relationship between charities and their auditors is the substantial auditing fees that major charities pay. The ACS's federal tax returns (IRS Form 990, Part II, line 31, column A) reveal that accounting fees totaled $2.8 million during the fiscal year ending August 31, 1990. When large fees are at stake, what auditor of any health charity will raise the roof about shuffling a few numbers around here and there, especially if there is no absolute prohibition against it? After all, it is not the job of the auditors to determine whether the funds were appropriately spent on charitable purposes; if that were the case, the United Way of America scandal should have been uncovered years earlier. Longtime ACS executive Arthur Stocks explicitly discusses the friendly ties between ACS and its auditors:

I believe that in order to maintain the ACS as a lucrative account, the Arthur Andersen & Co. auditing firm has compromised its accounting standards.

Now, a "new agreement" [between ACS and Arthur Andersen & Company] . . . allows division financial staffs to assume greater responsibility for the preparation of workpapers and timely reporting for consolidation purposes. . . . In other words, divisions are virtually allowed to develop their own audits! Also, some of the smaller Divisions are not audited annually because of their size, but "instead, are scheduled for financial review by Arthur Andersen."

That is really retrogressive! Thirty years ago, EVERY DIVISION, large and small, was required by the Society to have an annual audit. Why the backsliding at a time when, more and more, charity organizations are being questioned about their financial activities?[27]

A third reason to be skeptical is that there is little likelihood that the Internal Revenue Service (IRS) will question the accounting practices of the major charities, which have considerable political clout. This is true even though the IRS is well aware that the financial statements of charities are questionable. Indeed, Marcus Owens, director of the IRS Exempt Organizations Technical Division, has stated that "the level of tax compliance among a number of tax-exempt groups is at a 'Third World level.'"[28] The accounting rules governing charities permit them to classify many fund-raising expenses as "public education" because "pleas for cash are wrapped in verbiage that might raise public awareness of a problem." According to Kenneth Albrecht, president of the National Charities Information Bureau, the charity watchdog and rating group, "There's vast misrepresentation of expenditures going on right now, and it's growing. . . . People are being duped. They are being lied to."[29]

The misrepresentation to which Albrecht refers is the practice of shifting fund-raising expenses and management and general expenses to "public education" and other program services. These costs can be substantial for a large charity, particularly if a determined effort is made to disguise fund-raising as public education—as is the case with ACS. In his official history of the ACS, Walter Ross makes the incredible claim that the fund-raising Crusade conducted each April is more like a public education program than a fund-raising drive, for

[the Crusade] is unique among fund-raising drives because its campaign handbill, known as the mass distribution leaflet, does not mention or request money. It is always an educational piece, accenting some aspect of cancer prevention or safeguard. Some 35 million were printed this year [1987] on about five railroad-carloads of paper, making it one of the largest editions of any nongovernment document in the United States.[30]

Several paragraphs later, however, Ross admits that the "main activity" of the Crusade is "door-to-door solicitation."[31] Arthur Stocks questioned the ACS's fund-raising practices: "I have in recent years become highly critical of the Society. I feel [that] there is tremendous waste of funds in the management levels of the organization, that fund-raising protocols are highly risky, inefficient and thus, highly costly, both in terms of money and . . . in the vast number of volunteer hours required."[32]

The temptation for charity executives to report most, if not all, of the organization's fund-raising costs as public education or other program services must be great, especially since there is little likelihood that the auditors or the IRS will make an issue of it. The most important asset of every charity, however, is its credibility and reputation. Everyone knows that hundreds of millions of dollars cannot be raised year after year without considerable expense. If the ACS or another charity reported unbelievably low fund-raising costs, its public image could be damaged if the facts were brought to light. And if fund-raising costs were seriously understated, competing charities that seek funds from the same donors for similar purposes would have a powerful incentive to expose the misrepresentation.

In sum, this discussion of overhead accounting practices demonstrates that (1) the allocation of overhead is arbitrary; (2) there are powerful incentives for overhead costs to be allocated to program services rather than to the management and fund-raising categories; (3) there is little to prevent such creative accounting from occurring; and (4) there is ample evidence that many charities write off much of their fund-raising costs as public education or other program-service expenses to inflate the reported spending for program services and to reduce reported fund-raising costs. The audited financial statements, in other words, add to the confusion about what charities do and how they spend their funds rather than provide insights and understanding.

Direct Services. Contributors should be most concerned about how much of their donation actually reaches those in need or is used for programs that donors view as worthwhile, such as research. Among the eighteen expense categories that appear in the audited financial statements of most health charities, four seem to correspond most closely to that requirement: printing, publications, and film; meetings and conferences, including related travel; awards and grants, primarily for research; and specific assistance to individuals. These four categories are easily distinguished from salaries and general overhead.

For the ACS as a whole in fiscal year 1991, these four expense categories together amounted to $146.7 million, or 40.5 percent, of the total expenses of the ACS. The vast majority—$100.7 million—of this $146.7 million was spent on research activity, which is, with minor exceptions, the exclusive responsibility of the national headquarters. About seven state divisions also fund research grants from time to time, but these grants are small and often sporadic. Thus, a very different picture is obtained when one looks at the direct-services component of spending by the ACS divisions. Among the ten ACS state divisions we reviewed, the percentage of expenditures accounted for by direct services ranges from a high of 22.5 in Texas to a low of 8.6 in Missouri; the percentage figures for the other eight states are: Arizona, 9.5; California, 11.0; Colorado, 17.7; Connecticut, 18.2; Florida, 18.0; Minnesota, 17.9; Ohio, 22.1; and Wisconsin, 11.2.

One might be tempted to believe that states with higher percentages of their expenditures spent on direct services are doing more "good" than those with lower percentages, but such a conclusion would be unjustified. Once again, the problem is that the costs of direct services are counted as part of the service itself. Consider the "meetings and conferences, including related travel" component of direct services. Expenditures for this purpose can be very large because the meetings are held at expensive, first-class hotels. For example, ACS-California held its 1992 annual meeting at a Hilton Hotel between May 14 and May 16. In this short period, ACS-California officials signed twenty-three banquet, restaurant, and bar tabs totaling $13,480.56![33] On May 14, a buffet was held for sixty-five people at $25 each. By the time a 17 percent service charge and the 8.25 percent sales tax were added, the tab, signed by Semiramis Shabbas, totaled $2,058.10, and would be tacked on to ACS-California's "master bill." On May 15, twenty members of ACS-California's marketing communications group met in the Hilton's Roosevelt A room and enjoyed coffee, muffins, and juice in the morning; dined on the $17.95-per-person California Bistro luncheon selection; and, at three in the afternoon, enjoyed soft drinks, mineral water, and two dozen cookies—at $15 per dozen. When Mr. Ron Hagen signed the chit, it totalled $1,173.72.

It seems ironic that, in fund-raising campaigns throughout the nation, the ACS stresses the critical and urgent need for donations to support program services, and yet the organization can spend thousands of dollars on food, meeting rooms, and bar and restaurant charges at a two-and-a-half-day meeting. A donor might justifiably ask: Was it necessary to go to a Hilton Hotel? Might not some less-elegant and lower-cost setting have served equally well? Are donors—not to mention the needy, purportedly the prime beneficiaries of charity— getting the most from their contributions, which are used to finance these meetings? Surely, the annual meeting of ACS-California could have been far less costly and equally effective.

In a similar vein, direct-services expenditures can be increased by paying first-class rather than coach fares to conferences and meetings. In neither case is the donor well served. Meetings and conferences should have the same content and effect, whether held at a lower-budget venue or at a Hilton; coach passengers get to the same destination at the same time as those in first class. Although the executives and staffs of health charities may believe that they are entitled to luxury hotel accommodations and first-class travel arrangements, it is difficult to argue that either donors or the needy are made better off by such arrangements.

What's the Bottom Line?

For most people, financial statements are confusing and difficult to comprehend. Aside from the problem of "audit fatigue," however, there is a more basic issue: Because of the nature of financial reporting, it is very difficult, if not impossible, to gauge a charity's efficiency or effectiveness merely by looking at its financial reports. Legal accounting loopholes permit even highly inefficient charities to show in their financial statements that most of their spending is for programs that benefit the public.

HEALTH OR WEALTH?

Solicitations for contributions to health charities are a prominent feature of contemporary American life. By mail, telephone, and volunteer door-to-door campaigns, urgent appeals for funds are buttressed by stories of the suffering of children, needless death, and the enormous costs of this or that malady to the nation's economy. Guilt seems to work well as a catalyst for generating charity income, and donors are exhorted mightily to dig deeply into their pockets to support the crusade against this or that killing, disabling, disfiguring, and psychologically or socially devastating affliction. Always, there is a faint light at the end of the tunnel that, though flickering, heralds the arrival of the long-sought breakthrough leading to The Cure. Only if each individual gives generously are the prospects for the future bright; otherwise, millions will suffer and the ever-elusive cure will not be discovered in the immediate future. Urgency and desperation are commonplace characteristics of charity appeals.

The financial facts for health charities, however, are far different from the fund-raising rhetoric: Health charities that routinely tell contributors about their precarious financial status are in many cases very wealthy. Each year, tens of millions of dollars collected to support critically needed programs and to fund research on the causes of and cures for disease are squirreled away. For fiscal year 1990, the NHC notes, the thirty-nine organizations that provided data for its report had total revenues of $3.22 billion dollars, but total expenses amounted to only $3 billion. What happened to the unspent $220 million? According to the NHC, "The difference between total revenue and total expenses represents acquisition of fixed assets, endowment investment, and support of future program services."[34]

Fixed assets? Endowment investment? *Future* program services? The use of donations for such purposes are never mentioned in fund-raising pleas to the general public. And for good reason: The public would not give generously for such purposes. The need is now, not in the future. How do endowment funds help alleviate today's agony? How do fixed assets aid disease victims and cure diseases? As explained below, endowments, fixed assets, and reserves for the future enhance the self-interests of the executives and staffs of health charities, but provide little or no benefit to the general public or to the afflicted. The ultimate goal of every health charity should be to put itself out of business as quickly as possible by finding a cure for or a vaccine to prevent its disease. If this were the aim, every cent contributed would immediately be committed to research and program services for the public's benefit. Every employee and volunteer should act as if *this is the year* the major breakthrough will occur. In essence, thinking and planning should be oriented toward short-term goals—why plan for the long haul if the organization succeeds and goes out of business?

Endowments, reserves, and fixed assets show that executives have a mind-set that is incompatible with the ultimate goal of a health charity: to conquer the disease and go out of business as rapidly as possible. Fixed assets—real estate and endowments in particular—reveal a psychology of long-term thinking and planning. Resources tied up in assets are not available for current activities and to some degree must retard the organization's mission. To use a sports analogy, health charities should always sprint rather than pace themselves for a lengthy marathon.

At the very least, if health-charity executives wish to increase their organization's assets, fund-raising appeals should state explicitly that contributions will be diverted from programs for this purpose. Anything less, including discreet silence, misleads donors and raises serious questions about the integrity of charity executives and staffs.

The sums involved are not trivial. The net worth or wealth holdings of nonprofit entities, by convention, are called "fund balances" in financial statements. At the end of fiscal year 1991, the ACS held fund balances of $491.7 million; the AHA, $264.6 million; and the ALA, $136.2 million. The net worth of these health charities has increased steadily over time. For purposes of comparison, the ACS's fund balances in 1981 were $232.4 million, so over the decade they more than doubled; the AHA had only $22 million in fund balances in 1981, so it stashed away an additional $244 million—a *twelvefold increase in wealth;* the ALA's wealth totalled $88 million in 1981, so its holdings rose by 54.7 percent over the 1981–1991 period.[35] Thus, a very high priority of health-charity executives is to use donations to enhance the wealth of their organizations. How—or, more to the point, whether—these investments benefit either the public or disease victims remains to be seen.

In 1991, fund balances for the ACS consisted of $398.8 million in cash and investments; $68.6 million in land, buildings, and equipment; $23 million in endowment funds; and $1.3 million in "life interest"— gifts to the ACS (such as real estate) that the donor uses as long as she or he lives. While actively soliciting financial support from the public, the ACS holds tens of millions of dollars in U.S. government bonds and notes, commercial paper, stocks, and bonds.[36] This is not unusual; the same can be said about the heart and lung associations and other health charities as well. The ALA's annual report for 1991 reveals that automobiles costing a total of $909,009 were purchased that year.[37] Thus, donations are used to acquire real estate and equipment (including autos) and to build large cash reserves.

Auditors tend to be conservative and, by accounting conventions, land and buildings owned by charities are carried on the books at historical cost—the price originally paid for the property. The current market value of the real estate may be much greater than reported because, even in a depressed market, property acquired some years ago may have increased significantly in value. Nowhere in the financial statements is the current market value of real estate reported.

To understand the wealth of health charities, it is useful to examine and compare the state affiliates. In a broad sense, each state affiliate is an experiment because each has its own board of directors and some discretion in conducting its business affairs. Thus, comparing and contrasting the actions and policies of different state affiliates provides useful insights.

Cash Reserves

Among the ten states in our sample of ACS divisions, the level of cash reserves varies widely. ACS-California had more than $36 million in cash and liquid assets; at the other extreme, ACS-Connecticut held just over $2.5 million. Such disparities are not surprising; the revenues and expenses of the California division are many times greater than those of the Connecticut division, so it is not surprising that California's cash hoard is many times larger than its counterpart's in Connecticut. A more reasonable way of looking at cash reserves across affiliates is to adjust for affiliate size. To do this, reserve holdings should be expressed as a percentage of expenditures. If reserves are equal to current expenditures, the percentage would be 100, indicating that the affiliate could operate for a full year at current levels without raising additional funds. The percentages for the states in the sample are: Arizona, 101; California, 127; Colorado, 309; Connecticut, 47; Florida, 128; Minnesota, 133; Missouri, 123; Ohio, 92; Texas, 88; and Wisconsin, 105. The average across all ten states is 125 percent, indicating that the average affiliate could operate for fifteen months at current levels without raising additional funds.

Why hold cash reserves that, on average, are sufficient to cover expenses for the next 15 months? The auditors for ACS provide the answer in notes to its audited financial statements: "To provide for continuity of programs and to permit effective budgeting, substantially all of the public support received during the current fiscal year is used to fund activities planned for the subsequent year."[38] In plain language, it is ACS *policy* to raise money in one year and hold onto it for expenses in the following year. This policy is not chiseled in stone; rather, it reflects a decision by management or the board of directors to hold one year's spending in reserve. Does this policy make sense, especially in light of the ACS's ceaseless fund-raising?

A Cushy Cushion

We acknowledge that no fiscally responsible individuals or organizations should reduce their cash balances to zero every week or month; it is not prudent to eliminate reserves entirely. But what large private firm keeps a cash cushion so large that expenses for the next year are already in the bank?

The level of reserves considered appropriate and necessary can be large if income fluctuates significantly from year to year so that predicting revenues becomes very difficult. Is this the case with the ACS? ACS affiliates have been raising funds from the public for decades; although much publicity accompanies the annual door-to-door Crusade conducted by volunteers each April, fund-raising events such as "jail-and-bail" benefits, flower sales on Daffodil Days, golf tournaments, and sponsored walks are held throughout the year. No special expertise is required to monitor how income from the various events in the current year compares with income from the same or similar events in prior years. From year to year, the American public has consistently and generously supported the ACS affiliates. Thus, predicting revenues for the coming year should not be at all difficult, within a small margin of error. The notion that the American Cancer Society can "effectively budget" only if it has one year's expenses in the bank cannot withstand close examination and raises questions about the effectiveness of ACS's fiscal management.

Many charities, most for-profit firms, and the vast majority of individuals manage—by choice or necessity—to operate with much smaller financial cushions without apparent drawbacks. Indeed, the Connecticut division of the ACS keeps only enough reserves on hand to pay its expenses for about five and a half months. Why is it that other ACS state divisions cannot follow the example of ACS-Connecticut? When asked this question as a guest with one of this book's authors on a radio talk show, John Henderson, executive director of ACS-Ohio, responded, "I don't know."[39]

If nothing else, ACS's policy of having a full year's spending in reserve reveals a serious inconsistency in ACS's logic—or at least a conflict with the organization's public pronouncements. Recall that the ACS attempts to explain the six-figure salaries, generous benefits, and perquisites of its executives by arguing that such compensation is required to attract highly qualified, talented individuals to the organization. Yet ACS's policy indicates that these well-paid executives apparently are not capable of preparing "effective budgets" unless they already have the funds in the bank. Little talent is required to produce budgets when the amount to be spent is known in advance to the penny. Either the ACS overpays its executives because they are not highly qualified and lack talent in managing organizations and their budgets, or the negative consequences of doing away with ACS's policy on cash reserves would be minuscule because the well-paid executives are highly qualified and can competently cope with much smaller cash reserves. The ACS can't have it both ways.

If all ACS affiliates reduced their cash reserves so that six month's expenses were covered rather than a full year's (or more), tens of millions of dollars would immediately be available for the battle against cancer. These funds could be used *now* to help thousands of cancer victims not currently receiving assistance, provide tens of thousands of mammograms for women with a high risk of contracting breast cancer, or perhaps to fund research grants that might make the breakthrough in finding a cure for this dreaded disease. Large cash hoards make life comfortable for ACS executives by increasing income, but the goal of the ACS should be to help those in need as much as possible and as quickly as possible, not to enhance the comfort of ACS executives. The organization's current level of cash reserves is difficult to justify.

ACS's policy encouraging its affiliates to hold next year's spending in reserve invites excesses. Note that ACS-Colorado had enough cash in the bank to run its operations for more than three years without raising additional funds from the public. What's going on? The Colorado division's audited financial statement for fiscal year 1990 shows an endowment fund (the Horace H. and Jeanette D. Brooks Memorial Trust) valued at $3,318,795. In a note in the financial statement, the auditors explain that

> in April 1986, the Division received an endowment to be known as the Horace H. and Jeanette D. Brooks Memorial Trust (the "Trust"). At August 31, 1990, the Trust assets had a carrying value of $3,318,795. The corpus [these assets] *may be used if the Division elects to erect and equip a building* in the State of Colorado *or as the Division's Board of Directors so designates.* . . .
>
> During fiscal year 1990 the Trust assets realized $224,955, which is reflected as investment income in the current Unrestricted Fund. The unrestricted fund balance *available for future programs* includes $589,423 of cumulative income from the Trust. [Emphasis added.][40]

In April 1992—six years after ACS-Colorado had received the Brooks trust—nothing had been done with the money other than let interest and investment income collect in an account designated "future programs." For all intents and purposes, the Colorado division was awash in money, but it decided not to use the Brooks' largess to help Colorado cancer victims, to fund cancer research, or to provide programs benefiting Coloradans. A great deal of good could be accomplished for the needy with more than $3 million, but ACS-Colorado's board of directors and executives hoarded the Brooks trust—and the income it generated—rather than put it to use.

The primary beneficiaries of this endowment were ACS-Colorado's executives, who could count on substantial annual revenue for the organization from these funds. Yet, after receiving the trust, fund-raising in Colorado continued with its usual ardor and zeal. It is difficult to understand how the Colorado division could continue to seek donations from the public when, year after year, it chose not to use the Brooks trust for cancer services.

Land, Buildings, and Automobiles

Consider the physical assets owned by the Texas division of the American Cancer Society:

> The Texas Division's audited financial statements for 1990 show that it owns buildings valued at $8.8 million and land worth $2.4 million. The Texas Division owns 17 office buildings, which provide working space for staff members, and leases nine others for the same purpose. . . .
>
> Officials in Texas say 14 parcels of land valued at $1,446,361 and eight office buildings worth $3,518,849 were purchased with money that donors earmarked for those purposes. Two pieces of land worth $911,077 and 8 buildings worth $4,883,334 were bought outright by the Division.
>
> The Texas Division owns 56 Ford vehicles worth a total of $847,206, including 11 Crown Victorias for senior staff members, 15 Tauruses, 25 Tempos, and 5 vans and trucks. Each of the cars is assigned to an individual staff member, while the vans and trucks are used by various employees.[41]

Is ACS-Texas a cancer-fighting charity, a real-estate management and holding company, or a Ford dealer?

How do officials at ACS-Texas justify using charitable contributions to purchase property? Stephen Tucker, the division's vice-president for administration, claims that "it is often cheaper to own rather than to rent. . . . When it [ACS-Texas] rents, it is usually charged an amount that is intended to cover a landlord's property taxes, interest fees, insurance costs and profit."[42] At first glance, this beguiling logic is appealing, but Tucker's reasoning is wrong because he ignores the basic economic laws of supply and demand. The rent or lease payments received by a building owner are determined not by the cost of the building, nor by the interest charges, nor by insurance fees, but by the supply of and demand for office space. Property owners do not set rents on a cost-plus basis that guarantees them a profit; they charge what the market will bear.

If Tucker were right—if every property owner not only covered his or her costs but also earned a profit by setting rents high enough— hundreds of failed savings and loans would never have gone out of business. In many areas of the nation, the vacancy rate in commercial buildings (the supply of office space) is so high that developers have not been able to cover their costs, let alone earn a profit. The resulting wave of defaults has caused massive problems for savings and loans and other financial institutions that hold mortgages on these properties. It is true that charities are exempt from property taxes and that those that own buildings do not pay "profits" to shareholders. But because rents are determined by supply and demand and not by a cost-plus-profit formula, Tucker's explanation for why owning is cheaper than renting does not withstand even casual scrutiny.

In any case, the "owning is cheaper than renting" argument cannot possibly be applied to the landholdings of any ACS affiliate. Land ownership does not in any way lower program costs, and funds used to purchase land are not available for the fight against cancer. If donated, land should be immediately sold to generate income for programs. The purchase of land is unjustifiable; every dollar spent on land is a dollar less for aid to disease victims.

Besides, if it were true that "owning is cheaper than renting," an important question arises: Why do many ACS state divisions choose to rent rather than own buildings? Divisions in Oklahoma, Louisiana, Nebraska, North Dakota, Wyoming, and Alaska, for example, own no real estate. If there are significant cost savings from ownership, why haven't the executives in other states recognized and exploited the advantages of ownership? If ownership is less costly, those divisions still renting are not operating as efficiently as they should. Of course, one might argue that because the real-estate market is very different from state to state, renting is cheaper in some states and ownership is less costly in others. But this explanation is more contrived than convincing: There is little evidence that the laws of supply and demand that govern the real-estate market differ significantly across states.

The value or price of a commercial building is determined by the annual income generated by rent or lease payments. So when rents are low, buildings sell at low prices; conversely, when rents are high, buildings command high prices. Rents and purchase prices move together; thus, a building purchased "cheaply" can also be rented "cheaply." But ACS executives would have donors believe that when rents are dear, the ACS can purchase buildings cheaply. If this were the case, the buildings could be acquired and immediately sold at a profit and the proceeds applied to the battle against cancer.

In general, real-estate ownership is economically justified because of the tax advantages resulting from the deductibility of expenses—such as mortgage interest, depreciation, property taxes, and maintenance—from income. But charities are tax-exempt, so they have no tax advantages. In addition, property can be acquired and held as an investment to make a future profit. But the mission of the American Cancer Society is to fight cancer, and the ACS solicits donations from the public *exclusively* for that purpose. If ACS national headquarters and many of its affiliates want to operate as real-estate holding companies that earn profits from property speculation, they should at the very least inform donors that their contributions may be used for that purpose. Donors are misled when their contributions, donated to fund research or to help cancer victims, are used instead to purchase real estate.

ACS officials also use the "edifice complex" to rationalize their real-estate holdings: Some contributors are willing to donate for bricks and mortar but not for less "concrete" purposes, such as research. This edifice complex is not uncommon; other institutions, such as colleges and universities, also find it easier at times to raise money for buildings than for equally worthy but less permanent and visible purposes, such as scholarships. In many cases, however, the edifice complex is initiated and encouraged by the ACS affiliate itself rather than by donors. Funds earmarked for buildings adds fuel to the flames of the edifice complex.

The bias for bricks and mortar shown by some contributors can easily be exploited by health charities by acquiring or constructing buildings that benefit disease victims. The ACS's Hope Lodges are outstanding examples of how the edifice complex can be harnessed to fight cancer (see chapter 7). These hotel-like buildings provide overnight accommodations near hospitals or treatment facilities for cancer patients and their family members or friends. But only a few

ACS state affiliates have Hope Lodges. ACS-Texas, despite its extensive real-estate holdings, has yet to provide a Hope Lodge for Texans suffering from cancer.

ACS real-estate holdings that are not uniquely tied to cancer programs—that is, property other than Hope Lodges—have the potential to negatively affect an affiliate's programs in several ways. Not only are funds diverted from the primary mission of combating cancer and helping cancer patients, but ACS executives must also expend time and energy on managing these properties rather than concentrating on cancer-related services. In addition, the purchase of a building is an all-or-nothing decision; once acquired, there is an impetus to utilize the space rather than leave it vacant. With office space, this implies hiring more staff, so there is an incentive to expand the bureaucracy beyond ACS's immediate needs. Alternatively, part of a building might be sublet to other tenants in order to recoup expenses. But this increases the landlord role of managers and raises questions about ACS's top priority: Is it combatting cancer or property management?

Finally, if owning property (other than Hope Lodges) is cheaper than renting, it is because the property is held for a long period of time. Once again, the ultimate goal of every health charity should be to conquer its disease and then disappear. To achieve this objective, every available dollar should be devoted to research and programs *now* and should not be tied up in real estate. Ownership of real estate detracts from rather than enhances a health charity's ability to achieve its basic goals.

With regard to automobiles, no reference to automobile ownership appears in the glossy annual reports of ACS state affiliates; in most cases, the audited financial statements make only vague references to "equipment, including automobiles," if that. Never is there an explanation of how the vehicles are used in the fight against cancer.

Transporting cancer victims from their homes to medical facilities for treatment is an important and highly worthwhile service to the afflicted, as are visits made by volunteers (see chapter 7). But volunteers use their own cars and can take a tax deduction based on mileage.

In an interview, senior officials from ACS national headquarters in Atlanta attempted to explain the purchase of vehicles by ACS divisions by noting that purchasing may be less costly than leasing. But many other ACS divisions—including Idaho, Minnesota, Montana, Nebraska, North Dakota, Oregon, Washington, and Wyoming—do not own vehicles. If purchasing is less costly than leasing, why is it that many ACS divisions do not buy autos? Donors should be told how the ownership of vehicles, especially top-of-the line models, contributes to the affiliate's mission. This disclosure is vital, for in its absence, there might be a suspicion that automobiles are a perquisite for executives and staff that diverts funds from cancer programs.

WHERE DOES THE MONEY GO?

It is easier to answer the question asking where health-charity donations go than it is to determine what health charities actually do. First and foremost, a solid chunk of health-charity revenues—half or more at the state and local levels—pays the salaries, fringe benefits, and payroll taxes of executives and staffs, this despite the oft-repeated refrain that health charities are "volunteer" organizations. Some ACS officials have claimed that the executives and staffs of their affiliates are no different than schoolteachers. To operate a school, one must have teachers; teachers must be paid; and their salaries are included in the cost of the service provided by the school. There's no question that schools require teachers and that teachers are paid—but no one pretends or claims that the school system is a volunteer operation. Put another way, a great deal more good could be accomplished with health-charity donations if the charities used volunteers as effectively and as often as their public pronouncements suggest they do.

Another slice of health-charity revenues are diverted from program services each year to increase asset holdings: financial reserves, land, buildings, automobiles, and equipment. There has been a determined effort by the ACS, the ALA, and the AHA to increase organizational wealth, which serves the self-interests of executives and staffs at the expense of programs that benefit the public.

Substantial sums are spent on overhead expenses, such as postage, supplies, telephone, and travel—far more than is spent on direct services (see table 4.1 for definition). Among the ten ACS state divisions in our sample, the percentage of expenditures going to direct services ranged from a low of 8.6 in Missouri to a high of 22.5 in Texas; over all ten states, the average was less than 16 percent. By including the cost of providing the service in the amount spent on the service itself, even highly inefficient charities can appear to be paragons of public service on their financial statements.

Although the secrets of the philosopher's stone always eluded the alchemists of old, they have not evaded the health charities' auditors and accountants, who have divined these secrets with a vengeance: Fund-raising expenses are transmuted into "public education services"; excessive salaries and lavish perquisites are reported as expenditures for "program services" that benefit the public in some fashion; and entities that use half or more of their expenditures on staff and executive compensation call themselves "volunteer" organizations.

TOOTHLESS WATCHDOGS?

It is not possible to determine whether a charity is good, bad, or indifferent merely by looking at its financial statements. Many prospective donors rely on independent charity rating services to determine which of the tens of thousands of nonprofit groups clamoring for contributions from the public are worthy of support. Unfortunately, these watchdogs are typically toothless, and their activities may do more harm than good.[43] Two organizations are widely regarded as the arbiters of the worthiness of charities: the National Charities Information Bureau (NCIB) and the Philanthropic Advisory Service (PAS), part of the Better Business Bureau. These self-anointed charity watchdogs are frequently cited in the popular press as fonts of both information and truth about charities.[44]

In 1975, NCIB began publishing and regularly updating a publicly available *Wise Giving Guide,* which lists organizations that the NCIB reviewed and that either (1) met NCIB standards, (2) did not meet one or more standards, (3) had not supplied adequate information, or (4) were having reports updated.[45] In addition to publishing the guide in February, June, and October of each year, NCIB provides the public, on request, with detailed reports on selected individual charities. *Give . . . But Give Wisely,* published bimonthly by the PAS, is similar in content and objectives to NCIB's guide.

No one questions the motives of these charity rating services. There is a great need to separate the wheat from the inevitable chaff in the charity world, and few donors have the time, expertise, or inclination to tackle this formidable task themselves. Although the evaluators' intentions are undoubtedly beyond reproach, the rating process itself may create unforeseen negative consequences.

Consider first the sheer weight of numbers. With hundreds of thousands of organizations active nationally, vast resources would be required to gather and analyze information on even a small fraction of the total. By any standard, NCIB is a small organization, with a research staff of four analysts and a 1989 budget of $870,000, two-thirds of which came from foundations and corporations.[46]

Both the NCIB and the PAS limit themselves to national organizations and to charities that generate a relatively large number of inquiries. The *Wise Giving Guide* provides summary information on only about 400 national charities, although NCIB has "files on more than 2,300 organizations . . . on which we receive relatively few inquiries—too few to justify preparing full-scale reports."[47] Even many highly respected and well-known groups, including UNICEF, the Salvation Army, and the Marine Corps' Toys for Tots, do not appear in the *Wise Giving Guide.*

Although the practical need for limiting the scope of research on charities is understandable, this policy has drawbacks. Concerned contributors may be discouraged from giving to charities that are not evaluated by NCIB or other groups, even though the *Wise Giving Guide* tells readers that "it is important to note that omission from the enclosed listing has no negative significance." A donor who takes the time and effort to request information from a charity watchdog is likely to prefer donating to a group that has been evaluated and approved rather than to a group that has not been approved. For this reason, national charities that have been approved have an advantage over local charities and those that have not been approved or even reviewed. For the same reason, large charities are favored over small ones, if only because a large charity is likely to elicit more inquiries.

A second reason for negative consequences is that, even in the best of circumstances, mistakes are inevitably made in evaluations. Consider Covenant House, an organization offering shelter to runaway youth across the country. As one of the nation's most rapidly growing charities, Covenant House saw its contributions increase by 51 percent between 1987 and 1988 to more than $80 million annually.[48] NCIB had approved Covenant House in March 1990, but less than a week later Covenant House's founder and head, Reverend Bruce Ritter, resigned amid allegations of sexual misconduct and financial irregularities involving a secret trust fund that made loans to members of the board of directors, to Ritter, and to Ritter's sister.[49] And both the NCIB and the PAS repeatedly approved the United Way of America.

Third, the most important approval criterion is an arbitrary one. From the perspective of donors, the critical issue is the proportion of the charity's expenses that are used to carry out the charity's programs. The NCIB requires that at least 60 percent of a charity's expenses be spent on programs; in contrast, the PAS stipulates a standard of only 50 percent. Differing standards can cause confusion. The Paralyzed Veterans of America, for example, is in compliance with PAS's guidelines,[50] but was disapproved by NCIB because it failed to meet the 60 percent standard.

Obtaining approval is far more difficult for new groups than for existing ones. The fund-raising costs of start-up groups are likely to be high, reflecting the lack of a volunteer network or corporate sponsors in the formative stages. Moreover, even older groups that address controversial or less-popular causes may be forced to spend substantial sums to raise money. Thus, the evaluation guidelines disproportionately favor older, established charities and especially those that deal with widespread, noncontroversial health problems, such as cancer and heart disease. To the extent that the rating system performs its intended function of directing contributions to approved groups, newer charities that are held to the same standards as long-established organizations are penalized because they are less likely to meet the guidelines due to higher fund-raising costs. Thus, the evaluation process itself makes it harder for groups to form to meet new needs or to fill gaps that traditional charities have not addressed.

Other differing standards also can create confusion. The PAS approves Boy's Town (Father Flanagan's Home for Boys) but the NCIB doesn't because the charity has more than five years' of assets on hand to cover its spending; the NCIB guidelines mandate that additional fund-raising is not necessary if assets are sufficient to cover two years' expenses.[51] The NCIB has questions about the governance and financial accountability of the Humane Society of the United States, but this group was approved by the PAS. The PAS claims that the Epilepsy Foundation of America, the National Kidney Foundation, and the National Audubon Society, among others, did not "conduct fund-raising without undue pressure," and disapproved them,[52] but all of these organizations met NCIB's guidelines. In fact, none of the 398 charities listed in the October 1990 *Wise Giving Guide* failed to meet NCIB's standard 5a: "Fund-raising practices should encourage voluntary giving and should not be intimidating." Apparently, what constitutes intimidation and undue pressure is subject to considerable interpretation.

A fourth way that the rating process creates negative consequences is that evaluations by the NCIB and the PAS can mislead the public in the case of "national service centers." Many organizations' national headquarters act as service centers to their affiliates by providing such services as "leadership training, research, consultation, program development, and liaison with other organizations."[53] In these cases, the NCIB evaluates the national headquarters, or service centers, rather than the individual affiliates. However, by approving the national head-quarters as a service center, a strong "halo" effect implies endorsement of the affiliates. Consider, for example, the ALA, the nation's oldest health charity, which has been approved by both the NCIB and the PAS as a service center. Nationwide, there are 135 affiliated state, regional, and local ALA groups incorporated in their respective states that operate under the guidelines and policies set out by the ALA national office in New York. All fund-raising is done by the affiliates, each of which then remits about 10 percent of its revenue to national headquarters, the service center.[54] No effort has been made to evaluate the various affiliates because only the national headquarters is rated as a service center. Since most of the real work of health charities is carried out at the state and local, and not the national, levels, evaluating the effectiveness of the service center provides little useful information for donors interested in programs that aid their local communities. The NCIB merely suggests that "contributors interested in specific affiliates should request information directly from them."[55]

Unlike the ALA, which is evaluated as a service center, the ACS and the AHA are each evaluated as a single organization; that is, "NCIB's report covers the national *and its affiliates*" (emphasis added).[56] Thus, the NCIB looks at the consolidated financial statements for the national headquarters and all the affiliates *combined*. Although highly undesirable, this approach is necessary to keep the volume of work at manageable levels. Unfortunately, a multitude of sins can be hidden by aggregating, or adding up, the figures in this way. The donor who looks at NCIB's *Wise Giving Guide* finds that the ACS meets all standards and may believe that all affiliates of the ACS have also been given NCIB approval. But recall that ACS-Colorado held three years' worth of expenses as cash reserves and that NCIB standards permit only two years' worth of expenses held in reserve. When this information was brought to the attention of Kenneth Albrecht, president of the NCIB, he stated that the Colorado division of ACS "appears not to meet the standard" for cash reserves.[57] Thus, another weakness of charity evaluations is that they may mislead rather than inform donors.

A last, but by no means least, cause of negative consequences is that a major input used by the NCIB and the PAS in judging a charity is the charity's own audited financial statements. As explained in detail earlier in this chapter, even under the best of circumstances, the financial reports of nonprofit organizations can conceal as much information as they reveal and may contain as much fantasy as fact.

Inefficient, ineffective, and fraudulent charities have been a persistent problem in the United States, in part because of the ease with which the nonprofit status can be obtained from the Internal Revenue Service. The assistant attorney general of Missouri has stated that "you can probably get your dog [exempted] as a charity under IRS rules."[58] Despite the repeated and well-publicized advice given to the public about the availability of information on charities and the need to investigate how donations are used, few donors heed this advice. Tens of millions of Americans give regularly to charities, but the NCIB reported that in 1989 "we provided information and materials in response to more than 38,000 requests from the general public. This number was slightly higher than the number of requests in 1988."[59] Apparently, only a minuscule proportion of donors takes the effort to check out charities to which they contribute. Under such circumstances, it is not surprising that charity scams are lucrative—the unscrupulous can flourish in a no-questions-asked environment.

Arguably, the NCIB and PAS ratings of charities do more harm than good. Their evaluations clearly favor older, larger, and national charities at the expense of newly formed, small, and local organizations. These ratings might have a chilling effect that hampers the formation of new groups attempting to fill vacuums left by existing charities or to address new social problems or diseases, such as AIDS. Another weakness of the ratings is that they may give a donor a sense of security about an approved charity that is unwarranted because of the inherent problems encountered in assessing the performance of charities, particularly in deciphering their expenditures. The negative effects of charity ratings, however, are likely to be very small because the vast majority of donors apparently ignore the ratings.

Overall, however, a persuasive case can be made that charity rating services accomplish a great deal by imposing uniform standards that charities must meet in order to be approved. The NCIB demands compliance with nine standards—six concerned with governance, policy, and program fundamentals and three with reporting and fiscal fundamentals. The PAS guidelines have the same general content, but differ in the details. In brief, the NCIB standards require an active, involved, accountable, and volunteer board of directors; a formal statement of purpose; programs and fund-raising activities consistent with this purpose; at least 60 percent of expenditures go toward programs; net assets at less than two years' worth of expenses; and public disclosure—audited financial statements, a formal budget, and annual reports available to the public on request.[60] None of these requirements is unreasonable or burdensome to a legitimate charity, but they could cause problems for "charities" set up by con artists.

When all is said and done, little progress can be made in answering the four basic questions, presented in the introduction to this chapter, that potential donors are likely to ask about a charity's programs by analyzing the organization's financial statements. The financial statements do, however, reveal two very important truths. First, health charities could do much more with their revenues if they made better use of unpaid volunteers in every aspect of their operations—far too much is being spent on salaries, fringe benefits, and payroll taxes. Second, financial reserves and real-estate holdings are excessive for many ACS affiliates; many charities place far too much emphasis on these assets. The simple expedient of more careful fiscal management and a policy requiring that land and real estate—other than Hope Lodges, which benefit cancer victims—be sold would release tens of millions of dollars for the fight against cancer, heart disease, and lung disease for the ACS, the AHA, and the ALA.

Still, no amount of financial analysis can possibly reveal whether various programs accomplish their objectives, reach the appropriate audience, and are appropriate charitable activities. An in-depth analysis of each program is the only way to shed light on these issues.

5

PUBLIC EDUCATION OR PUBLIC CONFUSION?

Public education has become the toxic dump of charity accounting.
—Kenneth L. Albrecht, President, National Charities Information Bureau,
quoted in *Forbes*, October 26, 1992

Too much and too little education hinder the mind.
—Blaise Pascal, *Pensées* (1670)

In the minds of Americans, education ranks close to the flag, mother-hood, and apple pie. The old saws stressing education seem endless: "A mind is a terrible thing to waste." "Knowledge is power." "The pen is mightier than the sword." Since society so universally accepts education as "good" and so widely regards diseases as "bad," it is not surprising that health charities report spending a significant fraction of their pro-gram-services budget on public education. For fiscal year 1990, the National Health Council reported that, on average, 37 percent of its members' program expenditures went to public education.[1]

There are several important considerations about education pro-grams that must be investigated in order to evaluate their effectiveness. First, the value of the content of the educational program must be assessed: Is the information useful in protecting the public against dis-ease? If not, public education programs might do far more harm than good. It is important to emphasize that there is no such thing as harm-less information in health matters. Suppose that, as part of an educa-tion campaign, the public is told that eating oat bran provides protec-tion against horrible disease X. Some might think that even if oat bran were later discovered not to protect against disease X, no harm was done because oat bran is "good for you," or at least it isn't harmful. But the no-harm-done logic is false, for it ignores human nature. If people believe that oat bran helps protect them against disease X, they could be lulled into a false sense of security. As a result, they might not take precautions that they would have taken before being misinformed: Thinking that oat bran offered protection, for instance, they might not seek medical attention as quickly when the symptoms of disease X first appear. For some diseases, early detection can mean the difference between life and death, so a supposedly harmless and, indeed, even a well-intentioned public education campaign can cause needless deaths.

Second, to take this logic one step further, assume that a charity's education program is not effective; that is, it does no real good. But also assume that it could be proved beyond a shadow of a doubt that the information provided to the public caused no *medical* harm of any sort. In this case, there would be no negative medical consequences, but problems now arise from an *economic* perspective. The resources of all health charities are limited, so funds spent on education programs are not available for other programs and activities, such as patient or community services. It is not enough for an education program to do no harm; it must also do good, or the funds spent on education are wasted and should be shifted to more worthwhile activities.

A third important issue is *who* is being educated. The very essence of charity is that efforts are directed first and foremost to the most vulnerable in society. Charity must help those who, for one reason or another, cannot help themselves. Invariably, the most vulnerable are the poor; the well-off and the wealthy can take care of themselves. Donors expect their contributions to aid those who have less financial wherewithal than they have. No one gives to a charity in the expectation that the wealthy will be the primary beneficiaries. There are millions of medically indigent people in the United States; the need is great. Thus, health charities should direct their education and other efforts to the poor.

HOW MANY ARE EDUCATED?

The Certificate of Incorporation of the American Society for the Control of Cancer (predecessor of the American Cancer Society) states, "The particular objects for which the corporation is to be formed are as follows: To collect, collate and disseminate information concerning the symptoms, diagnosis, treatment and prevention of cancer; to investigate the conditions under which cancer is found and to compile statistics in regard thereto." Thus, the American Cancer Society (ACS) has been actively involved in educating the public about cancer for at least a half-century. How many individuals have been reached by these efforts? If the American Cancer Society's numbers are credible, just about everybody is being informed—or already has been informed—about cancer. Consider the following statements from recent *Annual Reports* of the ACS:

1988: "American Cancer Society Public Education Programs reached a record 50 million—24 million adults and 26 million youth."

1989: "Public Education programs reached 55 million people last year, an increase of approximately 5.5 million. Over 28 million youth were reached compared with 26.5 million adults."

1990: "More than 62 million people were reached with Public Education programs last year. More than 31 million youth and 31 million adults received the Society's health messages."

1991: "This year, nearly 71 million people participated in Public Education programs, a 12.6% increase over last year. More than 35.2 million youth and 35.7 million adults got our cancer prevention messages."[2]

Keep in mind that the total population of the United States is about 250 million, including babies and senior citizens. From this viewpoint, the number of Americans educated about cancer by ACS programs is nothing short of phenomenal, both in absolute terms and in terms of the rate of growth. Between 1988 and 1991, the total number educated increased from 50 million to 71 million—a 42 percent increase in only four years! During the same period, the ACS reported that total expenditures for public education rose from $57 million in 1988 to $66 million in 1991. Thus, an increase of only $9 million in expenditures permitted an additional 21 million Americans to be educated about cancer! If we adjust these figures for inflation—a dollar bought less in 1991 than it did in 1988—the ACS's education feats are even more impressive.

What do such numbers mean? Two thoughts come immediately to mind. First, given that the ACS has been hammering away at public education for decades and is reaching such a high proportion of the population each year, surely almost everyone capable of being educated about cancer already has been. Common sense and economic logic both suggest that it's time to cut spending on public education and move on to more urgent problems, such as helping cancer victims. Why do ACS executives insist on education overkill? Why continue to spend vast sums to educate a public that is already educated?

The second thought is that such extensive public education should help us win the war against cancer. Once virtually everyone has been educated about what they can do to prevent this dreaded disease and to recognize the symptoms so that treatment can be sought early, the payoff from these massive expenditures on public education should be a declining number of cancer victims and deaths from cancer. But that's not the case. Each year, the ACS issues *Cancer Facts and Figures,* a book of statistics on cancer. In the 1988 edition, the total number of new cancer cases in the United States and Puerto Rico was estimated at 991,000; for 1992, the number of new cases was 1,138,300. Between 1988 and 1992, then, the number of new cases rose by 14.9 percent! We are losing the war on cancer. The ACS's own numbers raise serious questions about how effective its education campaign has been in preventing cancer. The news on the number of cancer-caused deaths is a little more encouraging, but not much. The death rate from cancer did not fall between 1988 and 1992, but it rose by "only" 5.3 percent—from 497,500 deaths in 1988 to 524,100 deaths in 1992.[3] Surely, an *effective* education campaign reaching tens of millions of people year after year would produce more promising outcomes. Yet cancer remains a killer on the rampage.

Clearly, something is amiss. There are three plausible explanations for the discrepancy: (1) the numbers reportedly educated each year are overstated, so that the ACS's education campaign reaches only a fraction of the number reported; (2) the numbers are correct, but the content of the education messages are not very helpful; or (3) both (1) and (2) are correct, and exaggerated numbers of Americans receive dubious information about cancer.

THE NUMBERS GAME

Let's examine the 1991 numbers carefully. The ACS claims that a total of 70.9 million people (35.2 million youth and 35.7 million adults) learned about cancer through ACS's programs. The 1991 *Statistical Abstract of the United States* reveals that the nation's total population is 248.2 million. We can safely exclude about 18.8 million people who are under the age of five (surely, no one can seriously suggest that preschool children can fully appreciate or understand cancer information). Although the ACS does not give its definition of the age brackets for its youth category, those between five and seventeen years of age seem appropriate, since eighteen-year-olds are of voting age. In 1991, there were about 45.3 million youth between the ages of five and seventeen, so *in one year* the ACS managed to educate 77.7 percent—

three out of every four—of the youth in America about cancer. This statistic suggests that you should be able to walk up to any group of four teenagers in any mall in America, and three of them will tell you that they have been educated about cancer by the American Cancer Society *during the past twelve months.*

What about adults? After subtracting everyone who is seventeen years or younger from the total, roughly 184.1 million Americans can be counted as adults. But some adjustments are necessary, because around 2 million Americans are institutionalized as inmates in prisons or in long-term detention centers, such as mental hospitals and nursing homes. It is doubtful that ACS volunteers routinely provide education programs in such facilities, not only because of the difficulty in obtaining access to prisons and mental hospitals but also because senile residents in long-term nursing homes have enough worries without adding cancer education to the list. Thus, the adult population is approximately 182 million. So, in 1991 alone, the ACS educated 20 percent—one out of every five—of all American adults about cancer.

One explanation for the huge disparity between the proportion of American youth reached in 1991 (77.7 percent) and the proportion of adults reached in the same year (20 percent) is that the youth form captive audiences. Much of the youth education is carried out in the nation's schools. Many of the youth reached in one year will also be educated again next year. This is not necessarily bad, for knowledge can be like fertilizer: Several applications are needed before it is absorbed. Even so, such high percentages reveal that the need for education will be greatly reduced in the span of a few years—with the exception of the children who enter the category each year, the pool of uneducated youth will shrink rapidly.

There is evidence, however, that the ACS's numbers are vastly inflated. Karen Packer, who has served on the board of directors of the Marshalltown unit of ACS-Iowa, explained the method by which school students are counted as having received cancer education:

> In a recent [1989] example during the Great American Smokeout, the ACS claimed in a newspaper article to have provided on-going education on smoking to our entire student population (several thousand students educated). Interviews of high school students from all grades revealed [that] their only education was an announcement over the school intercom that "those wanting Smokeout stickers and pins may come to the nurse's office."

The ACS tries to get key individuals on its board, such as education coordinators in the school system or community college. If the school text has a discussion of cancer—because the coordinator is on the ACS board—the ACS has educated every student that uses the text. If the community college has a continuing education course for nurses that includes a cancer topic, the ACS has educated umpteen professionals. Our district school health coordinator sits on the boards of the AHA [American Heart Association], ALA [American Lung Association], and ACS. It is my understanding—but I only have direct knowledge of the ACS—that all three organizations count the same way.[4]

A photograph in the Marshalltown *Times Republican* carries the caption: "Great American Smokeout—American Cancer Society's Great American Smokeout material is explained by Opal Fagle, director of health services.... Over 2,500 students have been exposed to this material."[5]

To illustrate further how the numbers game can be played, Packer relates that, as an ACS volunteer, she staffed a booth for the American Cancer Society at a Career and Health Expo held in 1986 by the Marshalltown Community School District. During the course of the day, a total of "eight students asked for information or brochures." Yet health-services director Fagle sent a letter to the public education chairperson of the Marshalltown unit of the ACS stating: "On behalf of the Marshalltown Community Schools I want to personally thank you and American Cancer Society, Iowa Division for providing an exhibit at our recent Career and Health Expo '86. Approximately 2,000 attended this event."[6] Somehow, eight students who showed a passing interest in the ACS's exhibit and educational materials became inflated by a factor of 250 to encompass all the students who attended the event—and perhaps some absentees as well.

To obtain the truly astounding public education numbers reported by the ACS, a great deal of exaggeration must occur. The national figures are derived by adding together the numbers submitted by the state affiliates, which conduct most of the public education programs. The tendency to overstate the numbers is understandable. The paid staff members who are responsible for public education programs have both a financial and an emotional stake in their work. The volunteers who conduct these programs undoubtedly are also proud of their accomplishments. Since no one is hurt by embellishing the numbers, why not do it? Both the staff and the volunteers want to look good and be recognized for their contributions to the organization. Thus, an interest group forms around the public education activity and lobbies for its share of the program budget. But if embellishment gets out of hand, the ACS numbers become absurd. Does anyone seriously believe that within five years almost every American will have been educated about cancer and, in the case of youth, educated multiple times? In sum, one reason that public education programs haven't been successful is that the number of people who have been reached may be grossly overstated.

DISEASE EDUCATION

A powerful argument can be made that the notion of educating the public about cancer and similarly devastating diseases embodies a contradiction in terms. The argument is straightforward: How can the public possibly be educated when even medical professionals do not fully understand these diseases? Little is known about cancer's causes and even less is known about its cures. In fact, the disease is so complex that a 1983 textbook on cancer, published under the auspices of the ACS, states that "various definitions of cancer have been put forth over the years. None is an all-encompassing or entirely satisfactory conception." The textbook adds, "There is no unanimity among scientists on some basic facts of cancer."[7] In other words, the medical profession has yet to agree on what exactly cancer *is*. Indeed, "no longer is cancer perceived as one monolithic disease. It is recognized as a loose coalition of hundreds of different types of malignancies, each with its own brand of virulence. It is now understood, for instance, that even breast cancer is not one but many diseases."[8]

Anyone who doubts the complexity of cancer and how little is known about the disease should read *The Transformed Cell: Unlocking the Mysteries of Cancer* by Steven A. Rosenberg and John M. Barry.[9] Dr. Rosenberg, a leading researcher at the National Cancer Institute, has sought a cancer cure for more than twenty years. This highly readable and fascinating account of Rosenberg's work explains that cancer is a generic term for different diseases that affect different organs and parts of the body, grow at different rates, affect different individuals in myriad ways, and respond, if at all, in a variety of ways to different treatments. Cancer is a mystery, an enigma, to the finest medical minds in the world. *The Transformed Cell* is a testament to what is not known about cancer. Much the same can be said about dozens of other diseases that, thus far, have eluded all determined attempts to unlock their secrets so that a cure can be found.

Yet the American Cancer Society has for decades spent a significant proportion of its annual expenditures to educate the public about cancer. Worse, the ACS tells donors that funds are desperately needed for cancer research because virtually nothing is known about the disease, while simultaneously claiming that it is cost effective to spend tens of millions of dollars to teach the public all about it! Health charities can't have it both ways.

The ACS's Cancer Education

What, precisely, are the facts that health charities believe are so important? The content varies from charity to charity, but there are remarkable similarities. According to the ACS, for instance, its major educational focus is in "(1) primary cancer prevention which includes smoking control and the relationship between diet, nutrition, and cancer; and (2) the importance and value of periodic cancer-related checkups and specific cancer tests. Prompt action in the event that one of cancer's seven warning signals occurs is also encouraged."[10]

Consider first the ACS's highly publicized warning signs of cancer, which when introduced in 1919 numbered four but now number seven:[11]

1. Change in bladder or bowel habits
2. A sore that does not heal
3. Unusual bleeding or discharge
4. A thickening or lump, especially in the breast
5. Indigestion or difficulty in swallowing
6. Obvious change in a wart or mole
7. Nagging cough or hoarseness

For practical purposes, these indications of cancer are notably general and, for adults, apply to remarkably common ailments. For example, "according to a Gallup poll . . . an estimated 62 million Americans in any given month have heartburn."[12] The medical journalist Lynn Payer shows that if the ACS's warning signs accurately signal the onset of cancer, then most Americans may have it:

> When people are asked if they've had various symptoms within the past week, two weeks, or six months, an enormous percentage report that they've experienced some sort of ache or pain. One recent survey, for example, in which adults were asked about their present symptoms and complaints found the following:

Symptom	Percent Reporting	
	Men	Women
Headaches	39	56
Easily fatigued	33	46
Indigestion	26	29
Cough	34	21
Constipation	18	34
Dizziness	16	29
Shortness of breath	25	22

Other studies find essentially the same thing, with slightly different numbers.[13]

Given these numbers, the miracle is that the ACS's warning signs of cancer have failed to make hypochondriacs out of most adults.

When the warning signs of cancer were first introduced decades ago, there was severe criticism. An article in the *Journal of the American Medical Association* in the early 1920s stated that "to warn the public that 'moles, excrescences, fistulas, and warts are the first signs of cancer' is to erect a specter capable of shattering even a normal mentality. . . . To say that 'symptoms of indigestion' are 'signs of cancer' is so small a part of the whole truth that it is better left unsaid."[14]

More recent critics have been equally disdainful of the ACS's educational effort. Edith Efron points out in *The Apocalyptics: Cancer and the Big Lie* that the warning signs of cancer have "rendered most citizens incapable of differentiating between known and unknown hazards. And that, too, is the meaning of the fable of the boy who cried wolf: The ostensible protector of the community actually *disarmed* the community."[15] In other words, by suggesting that almost any physical symptom, regardless of how commonplace, can signal cancer, the ACS's warning signs may have done far more harm than good. The principal beneficiaries are those physicians whose incomes are enhanced by increased demand for their services from individuals who fear that any change in their physical condition may signal the onset of cancer.

The information conveyed about how individuals may protect themselves from cancer is also of very limited value because so little is known about the causes of cancer:

> Virtually every imaginable substance and practice, both man-made and natural, has been claimed by some representative of one of the major cancer research institutes to be carcinogenic. This list includes virtually all chemicals known to exist, all forms of energy generation (including

solar cells and solar heating and cooling systems), most major components of foods (including salt and sugar), and even numerous naturally occurring substances in the air we breathe (including oxygen itself). The majority of these claims are based on flimsy, very limited evidence or no evidence at all.[16]

How can individuals protect themselves from cancer when almost everything is viewed as carcinogenic? Even retreat to an underground bunker is fraught with danger: Radon gas causes lung cancer. Everything under the sun causes cancer, it seems, including the sun itself.

The information provided by the ACS regarding the relationship between diet, nutrition, and cancer is relatively new. "In 1984, for the first time in its history, the ACS issued specific dietary recommendations for the prevention of cancer. Following what it calls a 'common sense approach,' the ACS began advocating the following measures: (1) avoid obesity; (2) cut down on total fat intake; (3) eat more high-fiber foods; . . . (4) include foods rich in vitamins A and C in your daily diet; (5) include cruciferous vegetables (such as cabbage, broccoli, brussels sprouts, kohlrabi and cauliflower) in your diet; (6) eat moderately of salt-cured, smoked, and nitrite-cured foods; and (7) keep alcohol consumption moderate, if you do drink."[17]

In short, the ACS spends tens of millions of dollars each year to establish itself as the nation's health nanny. The ACS's diet advice is nothing more than common sense, which is defined as normal native intelligence independent of specialized knowledge or training. Should tens of millions of dollars be spent each year to teach the public common sense? Worse, much of the lifestyle advice given by health charities is incorrect and may even be hazardous to our health.

The American Heart Association's Public Education Programs

According to the 1988 *Annual Report* of the AHA, the organization

spent $37.5 million for public education activities in 1987–88. That endeavor focuses on providing health information at the workplace, schools, grocery stores and eating places, and health care sites. Public and professional education and community service programs emphasize the prime risk factors that can lead to heart attacks and strokes—poor nutrition, smoking and high blood pressure.[18]

The gist of the information offered to the public is summarized in the AHA's 1991 fund-raising brochure that tells about "lifestyles which prevent heart disease":

1. If you smoke, stop now. If you use oral contraceptives and smoke, you are 39 times more likely to have a heart attack and 22 more times more likely to have a stroke than a woman who does neither.
2. Know what your blood pressure and cholesterol are. If they are high, work with your doctor to bring them down.
3. Eat right—cut the fat and cholesterol in your diet and limit sodium intake to no more than 3,000 mg. daily.
4. Regular aerobic exercise is an important part of a healthy lifestyle too. Invite your family and friends to join you.
5. If you are a black woman, you are particularly at risk for heart attack and stroke; controlling your risk factors is vitally important.[19]

The AHA's lifestyle advice is similar to that offered by ACS. Curiously, the concern about fats in the diet originated not from the ACS, the AHA, nor from cardiovascular research or any other part of the medical profession. It came instead from the longevity specialist Nathan Pritiken. Pritiken not only authored a book on diet and health (*The Pritiken Promise: 28 Days to a Longer, Healthier Life*), but introduced Pritiken Foods, a line of low-cholesterol, low-fat, high-fiber, low-salt, and preservative-free condiments.

The AHA's commitment to public education about diet is dubious in any case, as evidenced by the AHA's HeartGuide Seal program.[20] Prior to 1988, the AHA's charter specifically banned the endorsement of products. But the AHA's House of Delegates amended the charter in July 1988 so that the organization could award its seal of approval to foods that it deemed healthy. Unlike the seals of other organizations, which are awarded free of charge or for a nominal fee, the AHA planned to charge significant sums of up to $640,000 per brand per year, for a minimum of three years, for its endorsement. This purported attempt to aid the consumer in selecting healthy foods drew widespread criticism from both industry and government. The food industry claimed that the high fees amounted to extortion. The government asserted that the seal program was fatally flawed because what is important is the total diet, not individual foods; it threatened court action against the AHA if the seal program were put into effect. On April 2, 1990, under pressure from the federal government, the AHA discontinued its controversial plan to endorse foods that it regarded as healthy.

Three important points about the AHA's ill-fated HeartGuide Seal program must be emphasized. First, although the purported goal of the program was to educate consumers about food and nutrition, the AHA kept its approval guidelines secret.[21] Second, "many of the products that had already received the heart association's endorsement were products that are 100 percent fat, such as cooking oils, or nearly 100 percent fat, such as margarines."[22] The *New York Times* editorialized that "the Heart Association has started by awarding its seal of approval to foods in categories like margarine, crackers and cooking oil, which are not particularly healthful."[23] Such endorsements cast doubt on the AHA's admonition about reducing fat consumption and on its stated concern about public health. Third, "the Heart Association refused FDA [Food and Drug Administration] demands to have the seal bear a message that it was obtained for a price."[24] Nanny can be flexible about what is good for you if large sums are at stake, but nanny doesn't want the public to know about it.

The stated goal of the AHA's public education campaign is bizarre. In its 1988 *Annual Report,* the AHA claims to "inform the public about the prevention and treatment of cardiovascular disease."[25] As is true of cancer, it is impossible to provide information on disease prevention when the cause of the disease is not known. Equally important, the complexities of medical treatment for cardiovascular disease (not to mention the terminology involved) are far beyond the comprehension of the general public. Thus, the AHA's public education campaign is fatally flawed when measured against the organization's own goals.

The American Lung Association's Public Education Efforts

The ALA's public education program centers on its "10 Rules for Lung Health," which are widely publicized in fund-raising appeals and other ALA publications:

1. Don't smoke.
2. If you do smoke, quit. Ask your American Lung Association for help to "Kick the Habit."
3. Avoid secondhand smoke, especially in crowded and poorly ventilated rooms.
4. If you have a persistent cough, frequent colds, or if you are out of breath after simple exercise, consult your doctor.
5. If you already have a lung disorder, ask your doctor about a flu or pneumonia shot.

6. If you have been in contact with someone who is sick with tuberculosis, consult your doctor.

7. Check for lung hazards on the job and in the home products you use—and try to eliminate them or protect yourself.

8. Keep small objects that can be inhaled out of the reach of small children.

9. Be sure your children have the proper immunizations and booster shots. Ask the doctor or nurse which ones.

10. Do your part in fighting air pollution. Keep your car well tuned and your heating plant efficient.

The essence of these ten pronouncements is: Don't smoke or associate with smokers; see your doctor when ill and avoid sick people; try to eliminate lung hazards from both the home and workplace; and take care of the kids, the car, and the furnace. This information is so simplistic that it is worthless.

The ALA promotes itself as the leading advocate of lung health in the United States. However, much of the information it provides to the public about the costs and benefits of programs to improve lung health is not only politically motivated, its validity is also highly questionable:

> If measuring costs is difficult, figuring benefits seems mystical. The American Lung Association has estimated the toll of automobile pollution at $4 billion to $93 billion annually. Even if scientists could determine how many asthma attacks come from pollution, they still have to estimate the medical-cost savings of partially cleaning the air. The ALA study includes estimates of a "cough day"—the amount of money someone would pay not to cough for a day. (Answer: $10) The value of an entire life according to the [ALA] study, was $3 million.[26]

Cost estimates ranging from $4 billion to $93 billion are so divergent that they are useless for policy purposes and difficult to take seriously. After nineteen years of promoting Clean Air Week, the ALA apparently doesn't know whether automobile pollution is a serious problem or a trivial one. Yet the ALA engages in political advocacy based on studies containing "mystical" estimates.[27]

While the ALA spends millions promoting its ten rules, lung disease rages. Because of AIDS, tuberculosis—a lung disease that the ALA was originally founded to fight—is staging a comeback. Rather than reassessing its spending priorities to battle the new TB epidemic, ALA executives decided to do the right thing. They went to Washington and

> asked Congress [on January 30, 1992] for at least $91 million to combat what it called a "looming epidemic" of tuberculosis. . . .
>
> "Today we again turn to the policy arena to pursue initiatives to address the resurgence of tuberculosis in the United States," Fran Du Melle, deputy managing director of the association, told a news conference. . . .
>
> She said Congress should also provide a minimum of $10 million for the National Institute of Allergy and Infectious Diseases to accelerate tuberculosis research.[28]

The ALA is apparently too busy raising money, purportedly for lung research and for disseminating its rules for lung health, to assume responsibility for fighting the emerging tuberculosis epidemic; that's the concern of the taxpayers.

THE LIFESTYLE CRUSADE

Over the past decade, the most prominent feature of health charities is that their incessant campaigns have become increasingly focused on saving us from ourselves by changing our lifestyles. Health charities have become paternalistic and, like nannies, want to tell us what to eat and what to do to stay healthy. At the least, donors and those who are the target of these admonitions have a right to expect the advice to be based on sound scientific evidence. There are indications, however, that the content of costly health charity public education programs do little more than belabor the obvious or misinform and confuse the public— sometimes with serious consequences. Their stances on diet and exercise amply illustrate the problems.

Diet and Disease

The American Heart Association is at the forefront of initiatives to change the eating habits of Americans. Its dietary suggestions have been endorsed by the federal government, which "has urged that all people over the age of two adopt the American Heart Association's 'Prudent Diet.'"[29] Cookbooks have also been published under the AHA's auspices.[30] The AHA makes the claim that its campaign for improved nutrition has reduced the likelihood of disease:

Many Americans have learned to enjoy a healthy life-style, one designed to lessen their chances of having a heart attack. They have heeded the advice from the American Heart Association to eat a low-fat, low-cholesterol diet, become more physically active, avoid smoking and have their blood pressure checked regularly and treated if high.

The results have been rewarding. Even though heart disease continues to head the list of causes of death in the U.S., the death rate has been steadily declining since 1968. While this cannot be attributed solely to changes in life-style, it's clear that they have something to do with it.[31]

In this context, it is noteworthy that the death rate from heart and other diseases in the United States and in other developed nations was declining before 1968. John C. LaRosa, the physician who heads the AHA's nutrition committee, was evasive in responding to an inquiry about the effect of lifestyle changes on longevity. First he posed a rhetorical question: "Is there some way that we can measure some impact of these [preventive measures] in terms of life span?" Then he said, "The answer is, we just don't know how to do that."[32] Part of the difficulty in determining whether changes in lifestyle lengthen life expectancy and reduce the risk of heart attacks is that "more than half of all heart attack deaths aren't connected with any risk factor."[33] Thus, the principal rationale for lifestyle alterations—increased longevity—is questionable at the outset.

Despite decades of research, knowledge about what causes cancer and cardiovascular, lung, and many other diseases is still limited. Even more troublesome is discovering what constitutes a healthy diet. Contrary to the confident claims of health charities, the link between nutrition and health is largely unknown, and the relationship between diet and disease is even more tenuous. Consider the statements of Dr. Suzanne Harris, deputy assistant secretary of the Food and Consumer Service of the Department of Agriculture:

"Although the science basis for establishing recommendations for total quantities of fat, saturated fatty acids, cholesterol and sodium is increasing," she says, "desirable levels are not known with certainty for any, and certainly not all, subgroups of the healthy population. Furthermore, there is no basis for setting rules for the amounts of these substances that should come from various food groups." She noted that consumers group foods differently, and serving sizes or portions differ by age, sex and physical activity. Because of all the variability, she concluded, "we [at USDA] do not believe it is possible or even desirable to establish such rules [as] applicable to the entire U.S. population."[34]

In light of the statements of Dr. Harris and Dr. LaRosa, the government-endorsed AHA claim that *all* Americans over the age of two would benefit from its specific diet regimen seems dubious. What are some of these recommendations?

Salt. Conventional wisdom, based on AHA advice, holds that high levels of salt consumption are related to high blood pressure (hypertension), which is linked to heart disease. The *American Heart Association Low-Salt Cookbook* claims that

> high blood pressure—hypertension—can be a significant factor in cardiovascular disease. Recent research has proven that when you reduce the amount of sodium in your foods and change the kind and amount of fat in your diet, you can lower your risk of heart and blood disease. Now, with *The American Heart Association Low-Salt Cookbook,* people with hypertension have an invaluable guide to the lowering of blood pressure through sensible diet, developed by experts on matters of the heart, the American Heart Association.[35]

The authors of the AHA's *Low-Salt Cookbook* make an even more sweeping statement about the need for reducing salt consumption: "Actually, research is beginning to show that *most* of us—not just hypertensives—would benefit from reducing the sodium in our diets."[36]

Salt has been an integral part of the human diet for centuries. Unsalted food is often regarded as tasteless and unappealing, and adopting a low-salt or no-salt regimen requires a major change in eating habits. But there is little evidence that a low-salt diet will produce significant health benefits. According to a science reporter for the *Rocky Mountain News,* "Millions of dollars have been spent on dozens of research studies. But far from proving that salt is bad, the question has never been murkier. In fact, there is no convincing proof that eating salt is an important cause of high blood pressure."[37] The same view is expressed by Dr. Harriet Dustan, a former president of the AHA, who "is not convinced of the salt link [to high blood pressure, although] . . . she would advise less salt for a person who is already hypertensive or who has a history of high blood pressure in his family."[38]

The notion that reducing salt consumption will do no harm and perhaps some good is also suspect: "A controversial study [by Dr. Brent Egan, director of the Hypertension Unit at the Medical College of Wisconsin] has found that some people's blood pressure rises when they severely cut back on salt."[39] There is more than one type of hypertension, and people suffering from high blood pressure should not automatically cut back on salt consumption. The avoidance of salt by patients with "squeezing" hypertension, for example, will *elevate* their blood pressure, not lower it. Dr. Bruce Charash, professor of medicine at Cornell University Medical College, a fellow of the American College of Cardiology, and author of *Heart Myths: Common Fallacies About Prevention, Diagnosis, and Treatment,* concluded that "these patients may be better off eating as much [salt] as they want."[40] At best, the evidence regarding the benefits of a low-salt diet is mixed; at worst, this diet may be a potential health risk.

According to one researcher, the evidence regarding the health benefits of a low-salt diet is not convincing:

> Nearly two decades after limiting salt became synonymous with healthy living the relationship was convincingly demonstrated to be mostly a mirage. A major international research project in 32 nations showed that while the incidence of hypertension varied widely, salt intake had little to do with it. Only if salt was almost totally eliminated from the diet was there a useful effect. The lifestyles and habits of millions of Americans had been changed to little or no purpose.[41]

Despite such results, the AHA stubbornly advocates low-salt diets:

> About half the . . . men with high blood pressure who ate a low-salt diet in a month-long study had no change in [blood] pressure, while some actually had an increase. . . . That result tallies with other studies, but the heart association says it won't change its recommendation that salt intake be limited to 7.5 grams—about 1.5 teaspoons—a day.[42]

The federal government also prefers to ignore the evidence and recommends a low-salt diet:

> "We do take in more sodium than we need," said Dr. Michael Horan, chief of the hypertension branch of the National Heart, Lung and Blood Institute in Bethesda, Md. But evidence that it is an important factor in high blood pressure "is not so overwhelming that we all ought to be running out and doing something about it."
>
> This is a striking statement at a time when, for instance, the National Research Council issued a massive report on Diet and Health that advises cutting back daily salt intake to 6 grams or less.

Most Americans consume around 10 grams of salt a day, but there are some authorities who think 3 or 4 grams is optimal.[43]

Nanny may be wrong, but nanny is consistent.

Alcohol. The American Heart Association's position on alcohol is at least as perplexing as that on salt. The AHA claims that "research shows that people who drink too much alcohol tend to have high blood pressure. To help control blood pressure, it's best to drink only in moderation or not at all." Despite this admonition, the AHA suggests that low-salt food can be made palatable by cooking with alcohol, advising that "you'll create new taste sensations with wines and spirits."[44] Cooking with wine and spirits is acceptable because the AHA *assumes* that "the alcohol evaporates during cooking, leaving only the flavor and tenderizing qualities."[45] But a U.S. Department of Agriculture study on nutrient retention of foods showed that 5 percent to 85 percent of the alcohol is retained, depending on the cooking method. "Dishes using distilled spirits had a significantly higher retention rate than those using wine. And preparations in which the alcoholic beverage was not subjected to direct heat had, predictably, higher rates again."[46]

Following the AHA's culinary advice can have serious consequences. Even small amounts of alcohol can be extremely harmful to some people. Minuscule amounts can trigger a relapse among recovering alcoholics, for example, and some people are allergic to alcohol. Antibiotics and other medications are made ineffective or less potent by alcohol. The central concern of the AHA, according to the organization's official pronouncements, is the health of the American public. Indeed, it claims to be the "expert on matters of the heart." But its information about the retention of alcohol in cooked foods and its advice to include wine and spirits in recipes to enhance the flavor lost by the exclusion of salt has the potential to cause serious health problems for some people.

There are other contradictions in the AHA's recommended low- or no-alcohol diet. If alcohol contributes to high blood pressure, which is linked to coronary disease and heart attacks, then why is the relationship not confirmed by studies conducted in other nations? Inserm, the French counterpart to the U.S. National Institutes of Health (NIH),

looked at 18 countries and found "a strong and specific negative association between heart disease deaths and wine consumption." Finland, the United States and Scotland were in a group that drank the least wine and had the most deaths from heart disease; Belgium, West Germany and Austria drank more wine and had fewer deaths; Switzerland, Italy and France drank the most wine and had the fewest deaths.[47]

Fat. Both the AHA and the ACS recommend low-fat diets. The AHA, as part of "a coalition of health organizations and scientists," has scolded fast-food chains for cooking french fries in beef fat.[48] But in 1988, the AHA allowed "Rax Restaurants Inc. to use a heart logo in an existing restaurant program to promote a Big Rax roast beef sandwich. But [the sandwich] contain[ed] 30 grams of fat—over half an average woman's entire daily allowance."[49] Low-fat diets supposedly lowered the risk of breast cancer, but "a major U.S. study suggests that eating less fat and more fiber offers no protection against breast cancer."[50]

Nanny is also distrustful of technological change. In February 1990, the NutraSweet Company received approval from the Food and Drug Administration to sell Simplesse, a fat substitute that would permit consumers to reduce their consumption of fat and still enjoy traditionally high-fat foods. Such breakthroughs should be welcomed by both health-conscious charities and government, but "Dr. Alan Chait, chairman of the American Heart Association's committee on nutrition, said Simplesse 'may do little but reinforce the country's taste for high-fat foods.' He urges more emphasis on having consumers change their dietary habits."[51] Nanny believes in the "no pain, no gain" theory of nutrition.

There are good indications that some health charities have a hidden long-run agenda of compulsory vegetarianism. Dr. John LaRosa, one of the AHA's leading experts on nutrition, has stated that "it is possible to construct a perfectly healthful vegetarian diet. . . . I think in terms of many chronic diseases, including heart disease and malignancy, vegetarianism is an attractive alternative to meat eating."[52] Meat consumption is also coming under attack by the federal government and the ACS. "The U.S. surgeon general, the American Cancer Society and other groups have advised Americans to eat less meat, but Dr. Walter Willett, a researcher, . . . said 'the optimum amount of red meat you eat should be zero.'"[53] Claims are being made that strict vegetarian diets, in conjunction with mild exercise and stress-reduction sessions, can even reverse blockages in arteries.[54]

The May 27, 1991, cover story of *Newsweek* reported on a dietary "revolution" that is being promoted by several health charities, particularly the Physicians Committee for Responsible Medicine (PCRM) and the Ralph Nader–like Center for Science in the Public Interest. PCRM wants Americans to abandon the traditional food groups—two servings of meat a day, two of dairy products, six of grains, and five of fruits and vegetables. If the PCRM has its way, meat, poultry, fish, eggs, and dairy products would "retire to the far fringes of the American diet." PCRM claims that the four food groups are a political scam perpetrated by the food industry. According to one activist, "The standard four food groups are based on American agricultural lobbies."[55]

But PCRM is not without its own political agenda. Neal Barnard, the president of PCRM and a strict vegetarian, is a scientific adviser to People for the Ethical Treatment of Animals, an animal rights group that opposes using animals for medical research. Because of such connections, the American Medical Association has charged that since "a close relationship between PCRM and the animal-rights movement is [apparently] behind the group's dietary recommendations," the Physicians Committee for Responsible Medicine is "neither responsible nor are they physicians."[56] It is worth noting that, as the AMA asserts, many members of PCRM are not physicians but political activists.

The alleged problems created by meat consumption are chronicled in Jeremy Rifkin's *Beyond Beef: The Rise and Fall of the Cattle Culture:*

> The ever-increasing cattle population is wreaking havoc on the earth's ecosystems, destroying habitats on six continents. Cattle raising is a primary factor in the destruction of the world's remaining tropical rain forests. . . .
>
> Organic runoff from feedlots is now a major source of pollution in our nation's groundwater. Cattle are also a cause of global warming. They emit methane. . . .
>
> While millions of human beings go hungry for lack of adequate grain, millions more in the industrial world die from diseases caused by an excess of grain-fed animal flesh, and especially beef, in their diets. Americans, Europeans, and increasingly the Japanese are gorging on grain-fed beef and dying from the "diseases of affluence"— heart attacks, cancer, and diabetes.[57]

To Rifkin, beef consumption is the cause of most of the world's problems: medical (physical and mental), environmental, ecological, and economic. The health charities may not be affiliated with fringe groups like the animal rights movement, but they still have a not-so-hidden political agenda: to use the coercive powers of the state to impose their own version of a "good" lifestyle on Americans. Their paternalistic campaign is often very loose with the scientific facts.

Cholesterol. Through the efforts of the AHA and the National Heart, Lung and Blood Institute at the NIH, concern about cholesterol has become a national pastime. The two organizations announced that "the evidence linking elevated blood cholesterol to coronary heart disease is 'overwhelming.'"[58] In 1990 the *Washington Post* reported that

> an estimated 60 percent of Americans have blood cholesterol levels above 200 milligrams—a level that the . . . American Heart Association and others say places them at increased risk of developing heart disease. . . . The National Heart, Lung and Blood Institute has joined other groups in leading a public education effort to encourage all Americans to "know their (cholesterol) number."[59]

There is no doubt that the cholesterol campaign waged by the AHA and the NIH has been highly successful. Between 1983 and 1988, the number of prescriptions for cholesterol-lowering drugs rose fivefold; in 1988 alone, nearly 13 million prescriptions for these drugs were filled.[60] The crusade against cholesterol has been an economic bonanza for the drug companies, blood-testing laboratories, and physicians, but where is the evidence that the American public benefits?

In *Heart Myths,* Dr. Bruce Charash dispels a number of myths about cholesterol. First, noting that cholesterol is an integral part of every cell in the human body, Charash observes that it is essential to human biological functions. Second, the notion that there is a "normal" level of blood cholesterol is fallacious. Charash states that "there is no simple 'normal level' [of blood cholesterol]. The government would like to see all people [have] levels below 200. . . . In some people a level as high as 300 is listed as 'normal.'" According to Charash, the *average* cholesterol level among American adults is approximately 215;[61] thus, the target of 200 is arbitrary. The foreword to *Count Out Cholesterol: American Medical Association Campaign Against Cholesterol* contains a message from the AMA:

> More than 50 percent of all American adults have blood cholesterol levels that are higher than the desirable range. Half of this group . . . have a level that more than doubles their risk of coronary heart disease compared to people in the desirable range. That's why the American Medical Association is focusing on the problem of heart disease that is due to high blood cholesterol.
>
> Though there are many things you should do for yourself with *Count Out Cholesterol,* your doctor can and should play an important

role in helping you lower your cholesterol. . . . Your doctor can also schedule repeat measurements of your blood cholesterol and explain the results to you.

If your blood cholesterol does not come down far enough with the measures recommended in this book, talk to your doctor about the other alternatives available.[62]

Setting the "normal" level of blood cholesterol arbitrarily so that *more than half* of all adult Americans have elevated cholesterol levels and are "at risk" of heart disease makes about as much sense as setting the "normal" body temperature at 98.4 degrees and then announcing that more than half of all Americans need medical treatment for chronic fever. Cancerphobia has apparently spawned cholesterol phobia, with physicians and drug companies getting rich in the process. Cholesterol is now the mother lode for the disease mongers.[63]

Third, the notion that "eating foods with less cholesterol is the most important way to lower blood cholesterol" is in error, for using cholesterol-free products can raise, rather than reduce, blood cholesterol.[64] For example, milk contains cholesterol, but many milk substitutes do not. Nevertheless, milk substitutes may be high in fat, which the body uses to produce cholesterol. Thus, cholesterol levels may be lower when milk itself is used rather than high-fat milk substitutes.

A fourth myth, according to Charash, is that

lowering your cholesterol has been shown to make you live longer. Although great emphasis has been placed on lowering cholesterol, there is *no* evidence that it will make one live longer. . . .

The government has urged that all people over the age of two adopt the American Heart Association's "Prudent Diet" in an effort to reduce our national cholesterol level. It has further stated that each of us should have our cholesterol level measured. If it is greater than 240, an even more strict diet is advised. If, after diet, it is still greater than 240, cholesterol-reducing medications are to be considered. But, based on the government's own study, making these changes is unlikely to be of much help. Less than 2 percent of relatively young men with the highest cholesterol levels had been spared a heart attack by aggressive drug therapy. And . . . the total number of deaths was unchanged.[65]

Put another way, years of research costing hundreds of millions of taxpayers' dollars and involving thousands of individuals have failed to produce convincing evidence of a close, causal link between cholesterol levels and cardiovascular disease for the vast majority of Americans. In addition, if such a link were found, it is highly doubtful that cholesterol levels could be reduced significantly by strict changes in diet, even over long periods of time. It may even be true that low levels of cholesterol are associated with cancer, stroke, and other diseases.[66] Furthermore, if the link between heart disease and cholesterol is as direct as the AHA and NIH indicate, it is curious that this fact is not confirmed in comparisons with other nations. Jacques Richard, an epidemiologist at Inserm, has shown that "even if they have identical levels of cholesterol and parallel risk factors, the Frenchman is only about half as likely to have a heart attack as is the American."[67]

A high level of cholesterol for an individual may not be indicative of health problems. According to the *Journal of the American Medical Association*, "cholesterol levels can vary not only by the accuracy of the test used to measure them, but also because of differences in weight, diet, alcohol intake, smoking, season of the year, and exercise."[68] To that list, add the following factors, which have also been shown to influence the measurement of cholesterol levels: "whether a person is sitting up or lying down, whether a person has been exercising or losing weight, and whether or not the finger is squeezed during the procedure to get the blood out."[69] So many factors affect the measurement of cholesterol levels that one might reasonably ask whether it even makes much sense to set a "normal" level.

In *Balanced Nutrition*, Frederick Stare, Robert Olson, and Elizabeth Whelan observe that heredity also influences cholesterol levels.[70] Moreover, diet may not be successful in reducing blood cholesterol. Using drugs to reduce cholesterol may do more harm than good to the patient because there are often serious side effects (although drug companies always benefit from the sale of the drugs). Some side effects are merely annoying, such as stomach upset, hemorrhoids, rashes, and itching. But others can be life-threatening. More than one study has linked "cholesterol reduction with violent behavior. . . . The death rate from suicide, homicide or accidents for people on a cholesterol-reduction program turned out to be 1.76 times higher than that of people who did not adopt a cholesterol-reducing regimen."[71] Thus, "while the risk of mortality due to heart disease was decreased for patients on a low-cholesterol diet, this was offset by an increase in the number of deaths from accidents, suicides and homicides."[72]

Common sense dictates that violent behavior is linked in some way to stress, anger, and hostility, which can help cause illnesses. "Chronic anger is so damaging to the body that it ranks with, or even exceeds, cigarette smoking, obesity and a high-fat diet as a powerful risk factor for early death."[73] Duke University researchers have compared "the present cholesterol levels of 830 people [who were] administered personality tests in the mid-1960's." They concluded that "anger and hostility are the real causes of [heart] trouble. . . . Researchers at Yale, meanwhile, reported that people with strong emotions—whatever these emotions might be—are three times more likely to die of cardiac arrest than even-tempered people. . . . The heart can be damaged by adrenaline and other hormones the body pumps out when emotionally wrought."[74] The University of West Virginia clinical psychologist Kevin Larkin has claimed that there are "at least one hundred studies . . . showing that blood pressure and anger are related."[75] Some believe that emotional and psychological factors are also critically important in the treatment of cancer.[76]

Conflicting claims and contradictions on the cholesterol issue have produced confusion and chaos in people's minds. For example, an AHA press release stated that more than half of American women age 55 to 74 have elevated cholesterol levels that "pose a major risk of heart attack and stroke."[77] Yet Charash found that, "according to a large scientific study, those older than sixty years of age with very high cholesterol levels (greater than 260) do *not* have more heart attacks than those with lower cholesterol levels (under 180). A higher level of cholesterol was unrelated to the development of future heart attacks, and death, in these more elderly patients."[78] For senior citizens, the news is depressing: "Low cholesterol isn't necessarily a good thing. . . . Older men with low cholesterol are three times as likely to suffer from depression as those with normal or high cholesterol."[79] Only the medical establishment seems to unequivocally benefit from the war on cholesterol.

Whenever the interest in cholesterol seems to be waning or when findings that contradict the AHA and NIH view appear, nanny attempts to revive interest and silence the critics. "The American Heart Association and the National Heart, Lung and Blood Institute have issued a joint statement seeking to quiet doubts about the need for most people to lower their cholesterol."[80] The major reason for recurring doubt is the frequent recantations of earlier nostrums nanny has offered. Many of these episodes would be comical if coronary heart disease weren't such a serious matter. Consider the following examples:

Butter. Consumers were advised to substitute margarine for higher-fat butter, yet "a type of fat [was] found in margarine [that] may increase the risk of heart disease," according to a study published in the *New England Journal of Medicine.*[81] After the AHA and the medical establishment convinced millions of conscientious consumers to shift to margarine, an October 1992 *Washington Post* headline informed readers that "Margarine May Cause Heart Disease." Note that using margarine may do more than increase a risk factor; it may be a *direct cause* of heart disease: "The oils found in margarine . . . may *cause* heart disease, according to an Agriculture Department study" (emphasis added). The culprits in margarines are the oils used in making it; "foods such as cookies and chicken nuggets" are cooked using the same oils.[82]

Oat Bran. A health craze developed in the 1980s after it was announced that consumption of oat bran could reduce cholesterol levels. But further research showed that the reason oat bran appeared to lower cholesterol was that people tended to substitute oat bran for cholesterol-raising, high-fat foods.[83] So much for Cholesterol-Free Schmidt's Blue Ribbon Lite Oat Bran Diet Bread.

Olive Oil and Canola Oil. Scott Grundy, coeditor of the AHA's *Low-Fat, Low Cholesterol Cookbook,* was the first to report that olive oil could lower blood cholesterol.[84] The AHA's *Low-Salt Cookbook* claims that "olive and canola (rapeseed) oils . . . are low in saturated fatty acids and can be used to help lower blood cholesterol."[85] But "researchers at Columbia University report[ed] that . . . they found no evidence that mono-unsaturated fats—the principal ingredient in cooking oils like olive oil and canola oil—help to reduce cholesterol."[86] Olive oil and canola oil have suffered the same fate as oat bran.

Eggs. For decades, consumers were urged to start their day with a hearty breakfast that included eggs. But then cholesterol hysteria produced "the age of ovophobia—fear of eggs" because egg yolks contain cholesterol and so the AHA advised consumers to reduce their egg consumption to three per week. Between 1984 and 1988, egg sales plunged by $1 billion to $3.1 billion and the number of egg producers dropped by almost half. In response, the American Egg Board urged the U.S. Department of Agriculture to retest the cholesterol content in eggs. The new test found that "the average egg now contains 213 milligrams of cholesterol instead of the previously thought 274 milligrams. . . . As a result, the American Heart Association upped the allowable number of eggs per week to four from the previous three."[87] Why do eggs now have a lower cholesterol content? "The egg hasn't changed; testing has."[88] The AHA had issued its recommendation on egg consumption without using methods developed since the 1960s, when eggs were last analyzed for cholesterol.

Coffee. In terms of generating public confusion about healthy diets, almost nothing surpasses nanny's advice on coffee. Coffee contains caffeine, a stimulant that can jangle nerves. Because the medical establishment convinced many Americans that caffeine was "bad" for the heart, millions of consumers switched to decaffeinated coffee. Researchers then announced that the "consumption of decaffeinated coffee can increase cholesterol levels, increasing the risk of heart disease."[89] Suddenly, caffeinated coffee was better for the heart than decaf. To add to the confusion, a study conducted in the Netherlands reported that it is the way coffee is prepared that influences cholesterol levels, not whether or not it contains caffeine. "Boiled coffee—in which ground coffee is boiled directly in water—significantly increased cholesterol levels, but filtered coffee did not."[90] To be safe, one might give up coffee entirely, but researchers have also reported that "men and women over 60 who drink at least one cup of coffee a day had more active sex lives."[91] After all the vacillation about the health effects of coffee, Dr. Walter Willett of the Harvard School of Public Health has reported that "drinking coffee does not make people more likely to develop heart disease."[92]

Given these conflicting studies and the accompanying vacillations and recantations, one must wonder whether *any* of nanny's lifestyle guidelines are valid. Consumers have witnessed so many advice reversals and have been subjected to so many conflicting claims that disgust is a natural response. Even milk has come under attack. Millions of Americans were raised on cow's milk without ill effects, but nanny no longer seems to approve:

> Drink your milk to increase calcium. Switch from butter to margarine to decrease saturated fat. Just when you thought you had it figured out, two recent reports flipped the coins. But don't take them on face value.
>
> Late last month, the Physicians Committee for Responsible Medicine, advocates of animal rights and a vegan diet, joined forces with Dr. Benjamin Spock to denounce the consumption of milk.[93]

There are many other examples of claims and counterclaims about diet, disease, and health. Some of the claims—that baldness in men and television viewing by youth are linked to high levels of cholesterol, for instance—are simply bizarre.[94] One writer has suggested that "perhaps the soundest advice was given in a report by the U.S. Surgeon General in 1988: 'Definitive proof that specific dietary factors are responsible for specific chronic disease conditions is difficult—and may not be possible—to obtain, given the available technology. . . . Development of the major chronic disease conditions—coronary heart disease, stroke, diabetes, or cancer—is affected by multiple genetic, environmental, and behavioral factors among which diet is only one—albeit an important—component.'"[95] But if health charities admitted that little is known about the links among diet and disease and health, it would be difficult for them to act as the nation's nannies.

Exercise

As with other disciplines, both medicine and medical research are subject to fads. In the Victorian era, for example, masturbation was condemned by physicians who believed that it was injurious to mental health.[96] One of the latest fads is the belief that exercise is necessary to achieve and maintain good health. Until the first half of this century, exertion was believed to shorten life and people were advised to refrain from vigorous exercise. The human body was then likened to a machine: Too much use wore it out prematurely. The current emphasis on diet and weight control is a relatively new phenomenon and difficult to date, but the physician Kenneth Cooper helped launch the current fitness fad with his 1968 book, *Aerobics*.[97] At the first New York City marathon in the early 1970s, fewer than 200 runners participated; by 1990, more than 20,000 were running in the event. The health nannies have climbed on the fitness bandwagon:

> "Even the lightest activity is good for your health in general and your heart in particular," states the American Heart Association's *Cardiovascular Research Report* [CRR]. "People who avoid physical activity run a 30 percent higher risk of coronary heart disease than more active people," notes the CRR, citing a study reported in the February 1989 issue of *Circulation*. "Any kind of physical activity would probably protect against heart disease."[98]

But the AHA's sweeping claim that "any kind of physical activity would probably protect against heart disease" seems questionable. Andrew Selwin of Brigham and Women's Hospital in Boston has reported that "climbing out of bed in the middle of the night—or, for that matter, in the morning—causes strain on the heart. . . . Leaving our beds may cause dangerous pressure on our blood vessels."[99] Sadly, staying in bed may not help much either:

Now it looks as though even dreaming may be hazardous to your health. A new study has found that the periods of sleep when dreams occur kick the body into high gear. The heart speeds up. The blood pressure climbs. And stress hormones prepare the body to run and fight.

Researchers believe all this internal turmoil, which happens while the sleeper is tucked in bed, may trigger heart attacks.[100]

Yet physical stress produced by exercise is deemed essential to one's health: The primary goal of aerobic exercise is to increase the heart rate. "Exercise, long prescribed as a way of preventing cardiovascular disease, is gaining value as a way of treating the disease."[101] It apparently matters a great deal whether the heart rate is raised while in or out of bed, however. Although physical exercise is regarded as beneficial, mental stress seems almost deadly under certain circumstances:

Many studies in recent years have attempted to pinpoint activities that are especially risky for people with bad hearts, looking for instances in which the heart's own muscle fails to get enough blood [a condition known as *ischemia*[102]]. . . . Researchers have found that mental stress can be an especially powerful trigger of ischemia. . . . For instance, being asked to do simple math problems or to give a public talk can raise the heart's demand for blood or lower its supply.[103]

Shoveling snow can be healthy, but doing simple arithmetic may be fatal.

Should Nanny Be Humored?

It might seem that even though nanny's admonitions about lifestyle are of little value, the advice does no real harm. But evidence from medical research suggests otherwise:

The studies [of the effect of lifestyle improvement on health and life expectancy] constitute over a million subject-years of experience conducted at a cost of billions of dollars. Has intervention to "improve" lifestyle increased life expectancy? The answer is clear: In not one of the 19 studies is there any beneficial effect. On the contrary, in 3 of them there was a significant *reduction* in life expectancy. Since the thrust of recent campaigns aimed at changing our lifestyle is the elimination of premature and unnecessary death, it is evident that such campaigns are founded upon a false premise, or at least fail to take into account the inescapable conclusion of these studies so that the exhortations are quite misleading and pointless. If anything, so-called improvements in our lifestyle are deleterious, certainly with respect to life expectancy.[104]

Thus, the available evidence does not support nanny's claim that lifestyle improvements significantly increase longevity. In contrast to conventional wisdom, lifestyle changes may instead *reduce* life expectancy, at least for some people. Furthermore, if it's true that lifestyle changes have had little effect on health and longevity, then health charities are wasting their money on questionable public education efforts that urge the public to eat certain foods but not others and to engage in some activities and avoid others. There are many ways in which public health could have been improved through alternative uses of the funds now spent on questionable public education programs.

Following the lifestyle advice can even make things worse:

> Recently a well-intentioned but misguided campaign succeeded in having fast food restaurant chains switch from using beef tallow to vegetable oils for deep-fat frying. A healthful move? Don't you believe it!
>
> In tests, the FDA [Food and Drug Administration] and others have found that french fries cooked in beef tallow contain *less* fat than those cooked in vegetable oil. Thus, the shift to vegetable oil for deep-fat frying will *increase* fat consumption by 58%. Furthermore, this switch will increase the intake of saturated fat equivalents from the partially hydrogenated vegetable oils that are used. In addition, the amount of long-chain fatty acids—considered unfavorably by some medical researchers—plus the saturated fat equivalents will increase in the french fries from 5.7 grams per serving if tallow is used, to as much as 13.4 grams if vegetable oil is used. This switching represents a whopping 135% increase![105]

The good intentions of the health charities leading the campaign to substitute vegetable oil for beef tallow may cause far more harm than good.

The basic problem with the health charities' lifestyle advice is that the fundamental assumption underlying this advice is not necessarily true. Changing our lifestyle, the argument goes, will decrease the risk of disease. But lowering risk factors does not always reduce risk; the medical tests used to assess risk can be risky themselves—not to mention inaccurate; and doing something is always more expensive than doing nothing.[106]

Not only do the health charities vacillate from one dire warning to another, but the medical profession on which the health charities rely for information about diseases is also confused and uncertain about the facts:

> During the past fifteen years, evidence has been accumulating that much of medical decision-making is *not* firmly grounded in scientific evidence. Many medical practices are based more on anecdotal evidence than scientific evidence, and treatment of the same illnesses are very different among physicians. Some physicians are much more aggressive than others in providing what is increasingly very expensive medical care. Yet, there is little evidence of any significant differences in the outcomes of the varying styles of practice, even though such discrepancies lead to very large discrepancies in cost.[107]

Equally interesting, medical practice varies widely across countries. Because of differences in the definitions of disease, millions of Americans could "cure" their high blood pressure, their epilepsy, and their cholesterol problems simply by moving to Europe. American physicians are far more eager to treat diseases than their European counterparts, yet there are no significant differences in death rates between the United States and Europe.[108]

The scare tactics used by the health charities to increase public interest in and concern about their respective diseases (and to increase their donations) can do considerable harm. Lifestyle advice that leads people to believe that their current habits increase their risk of contracting this or that disease can itself be harmful. "Simply telling people their cholesterol or blood pressure is high can ... have negative effects on their life. ... Just telling people that their blood pressure was high caused an 80 percent increase in absenteeism from work."[109]

Nanny Spends Millions to Flog a Dead Horse

In fairness to the Big Three (the American Cancer Society, the American Heart Association, and the American Lung Association), there is one piece of lifestyle advice that is widely accepted as both accurate and important: Quit smoking. In this case, nanny's admonitions are on firmer ground. But should nanny continue to spend tens of millions of dollars every year educating the public about what, by nanny's own admission, is already widely known?

The heart, lung, and cancer societies all conduct anti-smoking campaigns to discourage the use of tobacco. But everybody already knows the dangers of tobacco. Consider the evidence. In 1985, then

Surgeon General C. Everett Koop, an ardent anti-smoking activist who views tobacco as the devil's curse, told the *New York Times*, "The smoker today is well educated about the health hazards of smoking."[110] Moreover, congressional testimony by Gerald M. Goldhaber, chairman of the Department of Communication at the State University of New York at Buffalo, clearly reveals the widespread public awareness of the risks associated with smoking:

> In [1985] . . . the nationally known consulting firm of Audits and Surveys, Inc. was commissioned to do a poll of the American public with respect to various smoking and health issues. When the pollsters asked whether, regardless of what they *believed,* people had *heard* that smoking was dangerous, an astonishing 99 percent responded in the affirmative. In that same year, the National Center for Health Statistics of the U.S. Department of Health and Human Services conducted a special survey on a number of lifestyle choices that Americans make with respect to diet, exercise, drinking and smoking to determine their degree of awareness of the possible risks involved with those choices. This government-sponsored survey revealed that fully 95% of the American public *believe* that cigarettes and smoking increase the risk of lung cancer; that 92% of Americans *believe* that the risk of emphysema is increased by smoking; and that 91% *believe* that the risk of getting heart disease is increased by smoking. Only 1% to 3% of Americans actively *disbelieve* these propositions.[111]

As a point of reference, Goldhaber also reported polls showing that only 89 percent of Americans knew the name of the nation's first president; that during the 1976 Bicentennial Celebration only 72 percent of Americans knew that the nation declared its independence in 1776; and only 38 percent of Americans can name their congressional representative. Goldhaber concluded: "The American public seldom, if ever, reaches on *any* matter the awareness level that it has reached on cigarette smoking."[112]

The American Lung Association also acknowledges the widespread public awareness about the health risks associated with tobacco use. Its 1987 *Annual Report* states:

> A 1987 survey conducted for the American Lung Association by the Gallup Organization shows that 75 percent of smokers are aware they risk getting lung cancer. In fact, public awareness in general has increased over the years: In 1954, just 41 percent said that smoking is a cause of lung cancer; in 1987, 87 percent—almost nine out of ten Americans—said they knew of this cancer risk.[113]

Given that the health risk associated with smoking is common knowledge, why do health charities continue to devote so much money to the anti-smoking campaign when their fund-raising appeals stress how much needs to be done and how critical the need is for resources to battle disease?

Another important point is the concept of duplication of effort. Each of the Big Three has extensive anti-tobacco campaigns. Does this make sense when the charities are constantly stressing the critical need for donations? Surely, common sense dictates that only one of these three organizations should carry the anti-tobacco banner while the other two turn to more pressing problems. It is odd, to say the least, that prior to 1973 the American Lung Association was known as the National Tuberculosis Association, but now the ALA does not wish to assume the responsibility for battling the resurgence of TB as a health threat—it is far too preoccupied with spending more than $25 million dollars a year educating the public about the dangers of smoking, which is already common knowledge.

DUMPING THE POOR

When the rich assemble to concern themselves with the business of the poor, it is called charity.
> —Paul Richard, *The Scourge of Christ* (1929)

Few, save the poor, feel for the poor.
> —Letitia Elizabeth Landon, *The Poor* (1853)

The ACS defines itself as "the national voluntary health organization dedicated to eliminating cancer as a major health problem by preventing cancer, saving lives from cancer, and diminishing suffering from cancer through research, education, and service."[114] Clearly, the ACS has noble and worthwhile aims. Note carefully the phrasing of this mission statement. The ACS claims to be *the* health charity concerned with cancer in the United States. It is not *one* of the organizations or *one of the major* organizations or even *an* organization concerned about cancer. Thus, all problems associated with cancer in the United States are the ACS's concern. There is little or no role for other players in the cancer field.

Conventional wisdom holds that, first and foremost, charity aids those who cannot help themselves—always and everywhere the poor. It is gratifying that the ACS seems to accept its obligation to the poor:

"A major ACS priority is helping people who are at greatest risk of dying from cancer. A recent ACS study confirmed that poor Americans—including economically disadvantaged whites, blacks, Hispanics, and American Indians—have higher rates of mortality from cancer than other income groups."[115] There are two reasons for the ACS's concern about the poor: First, they need help because they are poor and, second, the poor suffer disproportionately from cancer.

To determine how the poor were affected by and coped with cancer, the ACS sponsored a series of hearings held across the nation in the spring of 1989 "to better understand the dimensions of this problem and to identify possible solutions.... Hearings were held in Atlanta, GA; Jackson, MS; Newark, NJ; St. Louis, MO; El Paso, TX; Sacramento, CA; and Phoenix, AZ. People from throughout these regions presented testimony, with 47 states and territories represented." Based on the findings from these hearings, the ACS issued *Cancer and the Poor: A Report to the Nation,* as "part of a special ACS initiative to serve the disadvantaged."[116] What did the ACS conclude?

> Americans can be proud of the progress our country has made against cancer. ... For the nation's poor, however, there is little to celebrate. Millions of Americans living in poverty are not reaping the benefits of advances in cancer prevention, detection, and treatment. For these Americans, a diagnosis of cancer is most often a needless death sentence.
>
> This inequity is vividly conveyed by poor Americans and the people who serve them during a series of hearings ... in the Spring of 1989. Disadvantaged whites, blacks, Hispanics, American Indians, and older people described with passion their frustrations. ... They talked of their fears about cancer and the devastating impact cancer had on them and their families.
>
> We heard from many who had fought the system against all odds and won. They were survivors. But they paid a price which far exceeds that exacted from most cancer patients. Many of these hardworking Americans were driven into poverty by their treatment. They lost their jobs. They gave up their homes to pay for care. And in seeking help with little ability to pay for it, they sacrificed their dignity.[117]

Evidently, the ACS believes that the poor have not been provided cancer services. What other inference might logically be drawn from this grim assessment? Incidentally, those benefits of advances in cancer prevention, detection, and treatment the ACS referred to do not seem to be reflected in the cancer death statistics.

The ACS's report makes interesting reading. Two of its principal findings are especially relevant here. (1) "Cancer education and outreach efforts are insensitive and irrelevant to many poor people. . . . This problem is compounded by the lack of educational materials which appeal to different cultures and a lack of volunteers in poor communities."[118] "They are people who are not now reached by cancer education efforts."[119] (2) "Poor people endure greater pain and suffering from cancer than other Americans. . . . There is substantial evidence that the poor are more likely to be diagnosed with cancer when the disease is advanced and the treatment options are significantly more limited."[120]

The ACS's logic leaves much to be desired. It makes the following claims:

1. The ACS is *the* charity with national responsibility for all aspects of cancer;
2. The poor are a "major priority" of the ACS; and
3. The ACS spends tens of millions of dollars annually to provide cancer education to a large percentage of Americans.

But somehow:

1. The poor are not reached by these efforts; and
2. The education and outreach efforts that do get to the poor are "insensitive and irrelevant."

Cancer and the Poor is a remarkable self-indictment of the ACS's own programs, in which the ACS admits that it has failed to help the most needy with their cancer problems.

The tragic nature of this failure is amply documented in the personal testimonials summarized in the appendices of *Cancer and the Poor*. While the Michigan Division of the ACS held cash reserves of more than $5 million dollars, the poor in Detroit suffered:

> Neva Phillips, Detroit, Michigan. Ms. Phillips, who is black, was diagnosed with breast cancer. . . . She never had a mammogram and thought for one year that the pain in her chest was heartburn.
>
> Dorothy Jones, Detroit, Michigan. Ms. Jones' daughter, Belinda Pettigore, who is black, was diagnosed with cancer. She often does not have the transportation to get the medicine she needs.[121]

The testimony of Barbara Johnstone of Colorado is particularly moving:

[She] traveled 13 hours on a bus from her home in Aspen, Colorado to Denver to receive treatment for breast cancer.

"I'd be on a bus with millions of people and cigarette smoke and I would be absolutely hysterical and so sick by the time I got there for treatment. . . . There were so many times I just didn't want to go on and try any more. . . . Instead of battling the disease, I'm battling the whole system trying to figure out what I can do."

Ms. Johnstone, who lost her job and her home during cancer treatment, has moved to Grand Junction, Colorado to be closer to care.[122]

The report points out that "transportation is not covered by public or private insurance nor is the *cost of temporary housing for patients and family members who must travel long distances for care.* Such costs can be particularly substantial for cancer patients undergoing daily radiation therapy."[123] Indeed, temporary housing can be very costly. But why didn't ACS-Colorado use the $3 million Brooks trust "to build and equip" a building (see chapter 4)? A Hope Lodge to provide temporary housing for cancer patients undergoing treatment would have been a boon to Johnstone and many other Coloradans. Under the terms of the trust, the money could have been used for that purpose. Many similar incongruities can be found in the testimonials presented in *Cancer and the Poor.*

Having documented its own failures in serving the poor with cancer services and education, what does the ACS propose? The answer, provided by Kathleen J. Horsch, then chairman of the board of directors of the national ACS, is simple:

By calling attention to the problem, we hope to serve as a catalyst to change. We are asking the many organizations that are in a position to affect the health status of poor Americans to join with us in ending this needless discrimination and giving poor Americans an equal opportunity to survive cancer.

The leadership of the American Cancer Society is paying close attention to the findings of these hearings and will be developing specific programs to respond to the needs identified. We have already committed $2.8 million in seed funds for national demonstration programs to fund community services for the poor.[124]

Apparently, in the case of the poor, the ACS is no longer the one and only charity responsible for cancer services. Instead, "the many organizations in a position to affect the health status of the poor" are asked to join with the ACS. After revealing its own shortcomings in ignoring the needs of the poor with cancer education, detection, and services, ACS executives provide a budget of $2.8 million—less than *1 percent* of ACS's annual revenues—for "demonstration" programs. Relative to the size of the problem, this sum is insignificant.

What's the ACS's real agenda for the poor? To ascertain this, careful attention must be given to Horsch's statement—one must read between the lines and decipher a few code words. In her opening sentence, Horsch states that "for 76 years, the American Cancer Society (ACS) has been the *public's advocate* for cancer control."[125] No longer does the ACS function as a charity, for an advocate engages in advocacy—it undertakes lobbying and other activities designed to influence public policy. This role is made clear in the preface to *Cancer and the Poor:*

> We urge health *policymakers* [read: members of Congress], *advocacy groups* [read: lobbying groups], *professional societies* [read: American Medical Association, Pharmaceutical Manufacturers Association, and similar groups], employers, research institutions [read: National Cancer Institute and the other research centers] and others to help develop and implement comprehensive strategies for reform. And we pledge the commitment and resources of the American Cancer Society to make a meaningful contribution to this effort.[126]

Now the answer is clear. The translation reads as follows: The ACS will lead a lobbying campaign to provide cancer services to the poor, which will be paid for by the taxpayers.

PUBLIC EDUCATION: THE BOTTOM LINE

Although health charities spend substantial sums on public education, the content of these programs leaves much to be desired. How can charities pass the hat for research programs that are desperately needed because so little is known about disease while claiming to educate the public about what the medical pros don't understand? More is at stake than wasting scarce resources. Much of the information is wrong, and some of the health charities' advice can cause major health problems. Even well-intentioned advice can backfire. By putting out misleading and confusing propaganda, the health charities can disarm some people (if everything causes cancer, why bother changing lifestyles?), while other people may experience needless worry and anguish. A full-blown breast cancer hysteria has been "promulgated by the American Cancer Society and the National Cancer Institute." And "cancer risk specialists say that the recent torrent of publicity about breast cancer is unnecessaily scaring (and scarring) women. It has driven [some women] to take drastic measures such as having their healthy breasts surgically removed in the hope of preventing future cancer."[127] In short, some American women are so terrified that they are mutilating their bodies. If this is what can be expected from health-charity education, then the public might be far better off without these programs.

The worry and anguish about this or that disease serves the charities and members of the medical and drug establishments well. Induced phobias generate donations for the health charities, patients for physicians, and a ready market for prescription drugs, medical procedures and tests, and hospital stays. Thus, "public education" is about fundraising and disease mongering far more than it is about informing the public. This aspect of public education explains very well why the American Cancer Society, which its own report shows has failed adequately to serve the poor in the past, will likely continue to do so in the future—unless the ACS and its political allies can convince the taxpayers to pick up the tab. Otherwise the health charities and the medical establishment have little to gain from assisting the medically indigent.

Far more good could be accomplished if the money health charities now spend each year on dubious public education programs were used to help needy disease victims. In so doing, the health charities would help alleviate the nation's health care crisis and demonstrate the noble purpose of charity.

6

SUBSIDIZING PROFESSIONAL
EDUCATION AND RESEARCH

Physician, heal thyself.   —Luke 4:23

Medicine, the only profession that labours incessantly to destroy the reason for its own existence.
                                                      —James Bryce, 1914

There are some remedies worse than the disease.
                                             —Publilius Syrus (Maxim 301)

Nothing, it seems, captures the American imagination as much as medical research. In April 1992, Louis Harris and Associates conducted a public-opinion survey among voters about government-sponsored research. It found that "if voters could decide directly how research funds are spent, more Americans would choose medical subjects. . . . 91 percent favored more spending on medical research."[1] This statistic is amazing, for it is difficult to find such near-unanimity among the diverse American electorate on virtually any other issue.

Thus, there is a consensus that ending the suffering caused by disease is a noble and worthwhile social goal, and that research is the only way to achieve that end. Dr. Jonas Salk's conquest of polio, an illness that crippled children and imprisoned many in breathing machines, and the World Health Organization's elimination of the scourge of smallpox have whetted Americans' appetites for more victories in the war against disease. Cancer, cardiovascular disease, emphysema—all take an enormous toll on the victims and their families and friends. A study published in the *Journal of the National Cancer Institute* estimated the overall cost of cancer at $104 billion in 1990—$35 billion in direct medical costs; $12 billion for lost productivity; and $57 billion for mortality costs.[2] Add to that staggering sum the uncountable anguish experienced by everyone directly or indirectly touched by cancer, and

135

the consensus view of the immense value of medical research makes a great deal of sense. Medical research, conventional wisdom holds, is a wise investment in the future of mankind that can yield massive returns.

Health charities are well aware of the public's attitude toward disease research. John Garrison, managing director of the American Lung Association (ALA), stated in an interview with the *NonProfit Times* that "our marketing research [shows] that our donor would prefer to give money to research."[3] And because of its pull on the purse, research is emphasized in fund-raising appeals even though health charities play only a minor role, if any, in supporting disease research.

Professional education is also important to Americans. Every patient justifiably expects the medical professionals treating him or her to be up to date in their fields of specialization. The world of medicine is constantly changing due to new technologies, procedures, and products: Lasers made possible much more sophisticated treatments and exploratory procedures; computers permitted the development of scanners; and pharmaceutical research produced new drugs and diagnostic tests. To stay abreast of these innovations, continuing education is an essential part of the practice of medical professionals. The fruits of the research that Americans so strongly endorse would be worthless if medical professionals were unaware of them.

Given the obvious importance of research and professional education, it is tempting to conclude at the outset that health charities have an important role to play in advancing these activities and that their expenditures on research and professional education are therefore highly desirable. Case closed. But on close examination, this logic is faulty. The argument goes something like this: Most Americans agree that A and B are praiseworthy activities in the health field; most Americans also view health charities as praiseworthy organizations that do laudable things; thus, it logically follows that health charities should spend donors' contributions to support activities A and B. But it isn't that simple.

The central difficulty with this reasoning is that charities are no different from any other organization in society, private or public: Their resources are limited—no entity can do everything and be all things to all people. There are many worthy goals in the health field for charities to pursue, and because charities cannot do everything, choices must be made about which programs can be carried out most effectively. Thus, the questions arise: Are professional education and research appropriate activities for health charities? Should scarce funds be spent for these two purposes? We agree that both professional education and research are critical to public health, but whether health charities should be involved in funding such programs is another matter entirely.

PROFESSIONAL EDUCATION: ROBIN HOOD IN REVERSE

What exactly does professional education encompass? This question can be answered by statements from the annual reports of health charities. For example, the 1991 annual report of the American Heart Association (AHA) states that

> the AHA regularly informs physicians and other health care professionals about new developments in the prevention and treatment of heart disease and stroke. To that end, the association spent $30 million for professional education in 1990-91.
>
> A total of 25,414 physicians, scientists and others attended the 63rd Scientific Sessions in November 1990. The AHA's 14 Scientific Councils sponsored or conducted 10 educational conferences, which attracted 2,000 participants. Medical professionals are also kept informed of the latest developments through the AHA journals, including *Circulation,* the leading publication in its field.[4]

At the state level, American Cancer Society (ACS) affiliates report similar programs. For example:

ACS-Ohio: "In 1991, nearly 20,000 medical professionals . . . were provided with valuable cancer-related information through American Cancer Society conferences and programs."[5]

ACS-Wisconsin: "Information on up-to-date health care, cancer prevention, and the benefits of early detection [were provided] to 22,331 doctors, nurses, and allied health professionals."[6]

ACS-Colorado: "More than 7,700 medical professionals were also reached by professional education. By contacting 1,328 physicians, 837 dentists, 3,867 nurses, and 1,693 allied health professionals in 1989, Professional Education attained 84 percent of its medical goal, 232 percent of its dental goal, 110 percent of its nursing target, and 129 percent of its allied health goal."[7]

These statistics are most impressive, despite the fact that ACS-Ohio seems to have eased off in its efforts: "In 1988–89, [ACS-Ohio] reached an audience of 56,663 professionals statewide."[8] Tens of thousands of doctors, dentists, nurses, and allied health professionals are being informed about the most recent advances in medicine by health charities. What a wonderful service health charities provide for health professionals!

But let's look at professional education from another perspective—that of contributors. From the donors' point of view, the ACS's decision to spend $34.8 million in 1991 on professional education and the AHA's expenditure of $30 million in the same year for the same purpose might seem strange indeed. As a group, physicians who specialize in the diagnosis and treatment of cancer and heart disease, and health professionals in general, earn among the highest incomes in the United States. In May 1992, the *Washington Post* reported that the *average* income of full-time physicians (after paying all office and other business expenses and before taxes) was $164,300. Specialists earned more, with the average surgeon making $236,400.[9]

Physicians employed on a salary basis by hospitals and health maintenance organizations or in group practices also receive generous compensation:

> The average staff physician ... in 1992 received pay and bonuses totaling $139,732. ... The highest-paid group of salaried physicians ... was reproductive endocrinologists at $259,750. ... Salaried cardiothoracic surgeons were next at a median of $259,700; followed by radiologists, $183,150; anesthesiologists, $179,900; otolaryngologists, $178,700; obstetrician-gynecologists, $166,100; general surgeons, $145,300; pathologists, $144,550; and emergency physicians, $121,000. Other specialties include salaried psychiatrists, $108,150; family practitioners, $100,600; internists, $100,000; and pediatricians, $98,037.[10]

Even physicians in their first year of practice earn high incomes. For example, first-year internists earn between $80,000 and $90,000; neurosurgeons, $175,000 to $200,000; and family practice physicians, $75,000 to $120,000.[11]

Nurses also fare well. A nurse anesthetist can make $63,000 annually; a head nurse, $45,500; staff nurse (registered nurse), $34,500; and a licensed practical nurse, $21,900. Moreover, because of a recent shortage—50,000 new health care jobs are being created each month—salaries and fringe benefits are rising to attract personnel. To ease the shortage of nurses, which is more acute in some regions than others, "sign-on bonuses, incentive pay plans and higher starting salaries are being offered" by some employers.[12]

There is no doubt that the average health professional has a far larger income than the average health-charity donor. According to the 1992 *Statistical Abstract of the United States,* average per-capita personal income was only $19,082 in 1991. Thus, the revelation that "doctor salaries are far higher than average pay in the nation—$29,421 for full-time male workers in 1991" is a gross understatement.[13] The donor who responds to mail solicitations very likely has a lower-than-average income because "the typical mail donor, whether it's the American Lung Association, or Easter Seals or any organization is an older female." How much older? The average direct-mail donor to the ALA is seventy-two years old.[14]

Two important points can be drawn from the fact that the typical direct-mail donor is an older female. First, women on average earn less than men—as much as 40 percent less in comparable jobs—so that their incomes may be even lower than the national average and far lower than that of health professionals. Second, many donors are elderly and very likely have modest retirement incomes. Soliciting funds from blue-collar workers, retirees, and lower-income individuals to subsidize the education of high-income health professionals is nothing less than Robin Hood in reverse.

The sister-in-law of one of the authors was diagnosed with ovarian cancer in 1988. Her first surgery took nearly five hours, after which her husband received a bill for $13,000 from the lead surgeon. A statement from the assisting surgeon also ran into the thousands of dollars. How can such professionals allow charities to solicit contributions from people with lower incomes to pay for their continuing education?

Apparently, health professionals expect preferential treatment, along with high salaries, from the public. Most practicing professionals do not expect people who are less well-off to finance their education and training. To stay abreast of current developments in their respective fields, certified public accountants, attorneys, college professors, and other professionals subscribe to journals, purchase books, and attend seminars and meetings at their own expense. Of course, the costs of improving professional skills are deductible as a business expense. To ask donors who earn less to pay for professional education when so much needs to be done for the poor and the afflicted is inappropriate. How can the ACS justify subsidizing the wealthy through its professional-education efforts when its own report shows that it fails to adequately serve the needs of the poor?

Continuing education for health professionals is clearly important, but it should not be financed by charitable contributions, especially when those in the greatest need are suffering disproportionately. People donate to charity to help those who are less fortunate, not to pad the pockets of the well-heeled. In 1989, "a study conducted for Independent Sector, an organization that tracks trends in giving and volunteering, found that well-to-do people are more likely to give money to charity than the poor. But among givers, it turns out that the poorest give 5.5 percent of their family income while the richest give only 2.9 percent. 'It's a result of seeing need,' said Brian O'Connell, president of Independent Sector. 'When you're poor, you're going to see a lot of it.'"[15]

Physicians and other health professionals are the principal beneficiaries of continuing education, since it enhances their medical careers and their incomes. Thus, physicians should pay for the programs that benefit them directly; there is no role for charity in continuing education for health professionals. The biblical admonition, "Physician, heal thyself," might appropriately be rephrased to read, "Physician, pay for thine own professional education." And, on close inspection, a lot more of this may be going on than the health charities would care to admit. There is an alternative way of looking at health charities' reported expenditures for professional education. To understand what's going on, we must probe more deeply into the professional-education activities of health charities. A persuasive argument can be made that there is far less there than meets the eye.

PROFESSIONAL EDUCATION: PUBLISHING WHILE DISEASE VICTIMS PERISH

All charities have strong incentives to report high income and high program expenses: High levels of income indicate widespread public support and approval for their programs; high levels of program expenses supposedly show that the charity is doing a great deal of "good." Professional-education activities are an excellent vehicle for increasing reported revenues and program spending.

Health charities may not actually subsidize professional training and education nearly as much as their financial statements indicate. At least two activities considered part of professional education also generate income: publications, and conferences and meetings.

Each of the three major health charities publishes journals or magazines (see table 6.1). Some of these publications generate considerable subscription and advertising revenue; a one-page ad in one issue of the primary-care edition of the ACS's *CA: A Cancer Journal for*

TABLE 6.1
Publications of the Major Health Charities in 1992: Publication Frequency, Circulation, and Subscription Rates

Charity/Publications	Frequency (per year)	Ads?	Circulation	Subscription Rates (foreign rates in parentheses)	
				Individual	Institutional
American Cancer Society					
CA: A Journal for Clinicians	6	Y	400,000	Free	Free
Cancer	12	Y	20,000	$95	$150
Cancer Facts & Figures	1	N	500,000	Free	Free
Cancer News	2	N	240,000	Free	Free
American Heart Association					
Cardiovascular Nursing	12	N	54,000	$6 ($15)	$11 ($20)
Circulation	12	Y	25,000	102 (182)	133 (213)
Circulation Research	12	Y	3,750	152 (212)	207 (267)
Hypertension	12	Y	4,600	106 (144)	138 (176)
Arteriosclerosis and Thrombosis	6	Y	1,740	108 (128)	146 (166)
Stroke	12	Y	6,200	102 (136)	117 (151)
American Lung Association					
American Review of Respiratory Disease	12	Y	14,500	130 (170)	185 (225)
American Journal of Respiratory Cell and Molecular Biology	12	Y	NA	95 (115)	95 (115)

Sources: The list of publications for each charity, their publication frequencies, and whether advertising is accepted were taken from National Trade and Professional Associations of the United States, 1992, 27th ed. (Washington, D.C.: Columbia Books, 1992), pp. 47, 64, 71. Circulation and subscription rates for each publication were taken from Ulrich's International Periodicals Directory, 1992–93, 31st ed., vol. 2 (New Providence, N.J.: R. R. Bowker, 1992), pp. 3194–95, 3205, 3207–8, 3212, 3264, 3277.

Clinicians costs $3,255. Consider, for example, the subscription revenue that the American Heart Association obtains from its journals: The AHA's financial statements for 1991 report "sales of professional journals" at $8.52 million.[16] The ALA's financial statement for the same year indicates that "membership dues" brought in $1.02 million. The American Thoracic Society (ATS) is "the medical section of the American Lung Association,"[17] so that dues paid to the ALA for ATS membership may represent subscription income from the ALA's journals. The ACS does not report revenue generated from its publishing or other programs.

The ALA and the AHA both report income from programs. For 1991, the ALA recognized income from "service fees" of $3.55 million and from "sales of materials" of $3.90 million.[18] The AHA revenue statement for 1991 includes "program service fees and net incidental revenues" of $11.4 million and "sales of materials, *net*" of $8.2 million.[19] So, after deducting the cost of materials from the sales revenue, the AHA made a profit of $8.2 million. Where does this revenue come from? Charities are not as charitable as we would like to believe—or as the charities would like us to believe. They charge for things. There are registration fees for meetings, seminars, and courses that are paid by (subsidized) physicians, nurses, social workers, and others. Booths are rented to exhibitors; advertisers pay to appear in the meeting program. The ALA charges smokers to attend their "stop smoking" clinics. Books—the AHA's and the ACS's cookbooks, for example—are sold. The ACS's financial statements do not separately show revenue from these sources.

The point is that professional education activities can produce income—a lot of income. If the income were used to offset expenses, health charities would: (1) show a lower level of annual revenue; and (2) show far less spending for professional education. Aside from this, there is a much more significant issue: When they sell publications and sponsor meetings that generate income, charities are engaged in *commercial activities*. Commercial activities are the stock in trade of private, for-profit firms. Charities should do those things *and only those things* that for-profit firms and government *cannot* or will not do. In another book, *Unfair Competition: The Profits of Nonprofits,* we argued that commercial activity is not appropriate for nonprofit organizations such as health charities.[20] One reason that commercial activity is inappropriate for charities is that it takes attention and resources away from the organization's charitable mission. Far more important and far less understood, however, is the fact that health-charity control over major publications in the field can have serious negative consequences for disease research. As discussed in detail below, one of the reasons that disease research has produced so little in terms of determining causes and finding cures is that the health charities are suffocating innovative research.

HEALTH-CHARITY RESEARCH PROGRAMS

Health charities are inordinately proud of their research programs:

> The AHA provides money to support scientists and their projects. Since 1949 when it first began funding research, the AHA has spent almost $1 billion to find ways to prevent and treat heart attacks and strokes, this nation's No. 1 and No. 3 killers. From 1950 to 1990, U.S. age-adjusted death rates from heart attack have declined 51 percent and from stroke by 69 percent.
>
> . . . .
>
> At the 1988 Futures Conference in St. Louis, AHA leaders called for allocating a larger percentage of the AHA's publicly contributed funds to the support of promising research grants and fellowships. The AHA has met that goal. One result has been an increase in the AHA's research expenses to $95.1 million in 1990–91. That is 21.5 percent more money than was expended in 1989–90 and 45.6 percent more than the AHA expended in 1987–88 for research support.[21]

In a similar vein, the ACS touts its research efforts as follows:

> The American Cancer Society is the largest private source of cancer-research funds in the United States, second in total dollars only to the National Cancer Institute, an agency of the federal government.
>
> The Society's overall annual investment in research has grown steadily from $1 million in 1946 to approximately $94 million in 1991. This sum represents slightly over 25% of the total expenditures of the Society. To date, the Society has invested more than $1.4 billion in cancer research. The success of the Society's Research Program is attested to by the fact that twenty-five Nobel Prize winners received grant support from the American Cancer Society early in their careers.[22]

At first glance, health charities appear to be major players in disease research, and this research appears to be of high quality. But is this true?

First, let's talk dollars. Although it is true that the ACS is the largest private source of cancer-research funds, the sums that this organization devotes to research are trivial in comparison with taxpayer spending on cancer through the National Cancer Institute (NCI). In recent years, the NCI's budget *for a single year* has exceeded the total amount that the ACS has spent on research in its entire history. For every $1 spent by the American Cancer Society, taxpayers are currently spending about $15. One reason that the NCI's budget is so large is that the ACS has actively lobbied Congress for additional funds for its budget.[23] Similarly, the National Heart, Lung, and Blood Institute of the National Institutes of Health (NIH) spends more than $10 for every dollar spent by the AHA. And the AHA is a major lobbyist for congressional appropriations to NIH to fund research on cardiovascular diseases. Thus, in the overall scheme of things, health charities—even the big ones—are at most minor players in direct funding of disease research.

Second, let's talk about the goals of health-charity research grants. It may seem odd to raise questions about the ultimate goal of research grants made by health charities; it would appear obvious that the money is spent to find the causes of and cures for disease. But not necessarily. Often, what health-charity grant recipients are really searching for is money—usually government money. W. Virgil Brown, president of the AHA, has written, "What do Americans get when they give to the American Heart Association? Ask any of the thousands of researchers who have received *start-up grant money* from the AHA."[24] "Start-up grant money" is also called seed money, and seed money is used to develop a research proposal to obtain funds from other sources, primarily the American taxpayer through the National Institutes of Health.

The AHA reports that during 1990–91, a total of 2,805 grants-in-aid, fellowships, and student and other awards were made by both AHA headquarters and AHA affiliates. The total dollar amount of awards and grants for research in that year was $90.497 million.[25] Thus, the average award was $32,262.75—far too little to support a major research effort, since medical research is very expensive. Thus, much of the "research" being conducted under the auspices of the AHA is in reality a search for "real" research money, not for the causes of and cures for disease.

The American Lung Association is more forthcoming about its lobbying efforts to increase taxpayer funding of research and about the seed grants it provides to researchers. The ALA's annual report for 1990 states that testimony from ALA... leaders helped convince Congress to increase funding for the National Institutes of Health by $539 million. The 1990 funding includes:

- $1.1 billion (up $46 million) for the National Heart, Lung and Blood Institute.
- $1.7 billion (up $93 million) for the National Cancer Institute.
- $846 million (up $104 million) for the National Institute of Allergy and Infectious Diseases.
- $8.4 million (up $1.8 million) for the TB Projects Grants Program.[26]

The mail solicitations sent out by the ALA stress the need for research on lung disease, but the ALA apparently expects the taxpayer to bear the costs. The ALA's annual reports have become increasingly nebulous about its research grants. One reason for creating a low profile is that the ALA spends only paltry sums—less than 5 percent of its income—on research. However, the ALA claims that "since its inception in 1904, the American Lung Association has been an energetic advocate and supporter of research. . . . The ALA is a leading advocate of federal research funding for the National Institutes of Health."[27] To better understand what this means, replace the word *advocate* in these two sentences with the word *lobbyist*. Back in the ALA's 1981–82 annual report (before the ALA became much more circumspect about its activities), the seed-money nature of ALA research grants was made abundantly clear:

> During the past fiscal year [1981–82], 43 seed-money research grants—an investment totalling $548,814—were awarded to promising young researchers so they could begin projects related to the prevention and control of lung disease.
>
> Once a project is successfully launched with ALA seed money, the work will often become eligible for funding from other sources. In a recent survey, 101 former ALA grant recipients who responded had collectively received 151 additional grants—totalling $14 million—to continue their research.[28]

Here's how the seed-grant system works. Step 1: The health charity uses the "urgent need" for disease research in its fund-raising appeals to generate contributions. Step 2: The health charity gives out a large number of small seed-money grants to those researchers they favor so the researchers have an advantage in preparing proposals for government grants. Step 3: If anything comes of the "serious" research supported by taxpayers, the health charity can take credit for having "supported" it. Basically, that's how health-charity research works: Let the taxpayers pay the bills and the health charities take the praise, which can be used in future fund-raising appeals. Then the process starts all over again.

Third, let's talk about the quality of the research. Are these research funds being wisely spent? How is quality measured, anyway? The concept of measuring research quality seems vague but, fortunately, the health charities have already done it for us. The AHA, for instance, would like us to believe that the declines in the age-adjusted death rates from heart attack and stroke between 1950 and 1990 (cited earlier) are a direct result of its research efforts. But this will not wash. Death rates from cardiovascular disease and stroke would have declined even if the AHA had never spent a penny on research—and even if the organization itself did not exist. Many factors influence death rates, such as new drugs created by the pharmaceutical industry, improvements in diagnostic equipment, better monitoring equipment for patients, the development of trauma centers, the use of helicopters to transport patients quickly, safer medical procedures, and so on. The AHA cannot take credit for these developments.

Even if none of these changes had occurred, death rates still would have fallen. Between 1950 and 1990, the standard of living rose substantially for Americans; as incomes rise, individuals typically improve their diet; engage in more recreation (which reduces stress); and receive more and better medical care. There is a positive relationship between income and health that cannot be attributed to the research programs of health charities. It is not clear how much of a difference, if any, was made by the AHA's research grants. Moreover, if the researchers funded by the AHA had made major breakthroughs in medicine, why haven't they won any Nobel Prizes? Unlike the ACS, the AHA does not take credit for funding *any* Nobel Prize winners.

The ACS claims that the success of its research program is demonstrated by the number of Nobel laureates it has assisted since it began funding research in 1946: "The success of the Society's Research Program is attested to by the fact that twenty-five Nobel Prize winners received grant support from the American Cancer Society early in their careers." In absolute terms, this is an impressive accomplishment, but it tells us nothing whatsoever about whether the ACS could have done a *better* job of allocating its research dollars.

To better understand this issue, consider the Damon Runyon–

Walter Winchell Cancer Research Fund (DRWWCRF), a small health charity concerned exclusively with cancer research. DRWWCRF's total revenue in fiscal year 1990 was $4.2 million, or a little over 1 percent of the ACS's 1990 revenue of $332.6 million. In 1990, the DRWWCRF awarded $2.9 million in cancer-research fellowships—only 3.7 percent of the ACS's $78.6 million in grants and awards for 1990. Despite the fact that DRWWCRF has only a tiny fraction of the ACS's revenues, it was able to report that "all told the work of 36 Nobel laureates has received support from the Runyon-Winchell Fund since 1946."[29] Working with pennies relative to the ACS budget, the DRWWCRF was able to assist 44 percent more Nobel laureates than the ACS during the same time period, 1946–90.

By the ACS's own criteria of quality—the number of Nobel laureates supported—it has been outdone by a tiny health charity. Looked at in another way, the battle against cancer might have been waged far more effectively if the ACS had raised the money to support research and then turned the funds over to the DRWWCRF, which has been far more successful over nearly a half-century in identifying and funding distinguished scientists.

Promises, Promises

The ACS fares poorly relative to the Damon Runyon–Walter Winchell Cancer Research Fund in effectively allocating research funds to future Nobel laureates, the ACS's own criteria for research success. In absolute terms, the cancer establishment's research has also failed the American people. On December 9, 1969, a full-page advertisement was placed in the *New York Times* by the Citizens Committee for the Conquest of Cancer. Huge boldface type proclaimed: "Mr. Nixon: You can cure cancer." The members of the committee were not identified in this ad, but a knowledgeable insider claims that the members were "close to the American Cancer Society."[30] The ACS's connections with the committee is confirmed by the fact that Dr. Sidney Farber, past president of the American Cancer Society, was quoted in the ad. The ad's text reads in part as follows:

> Dr. Sidney Farber . . . believes: "We are so close to a cure for cancer. We lack only the will and the kind of money and comprehensive planning that went into putting a man on the moon."
>
> Why don't we try to conquer cancer by America's 200th birthday?

What a holiday that would be! Cancer could be then where small-pox, diphtheria and polio are today—almost nonexistent.[31]

The ad made bold promises: "There is not a doubt in the minds of our top cancer researchers that the final answer to cancer can be found."[32]

The ACS, likely the prime mover and shaker behind the scenes of this initiative, jumped into the congressional funding fray:

> Led by American Cancer Society forces, the Senate consultants argued for a great new targeted effort against the disease, like the successful efforts to harness the atom and land on the moon.
>
> . . . .
>
> The subcommittee will hear from cancer authority proponents today—and from the American Heart Association, which is expected to say that if there is a separate cancer authority, there should be a heart authority too.[33]

Thus, the ACS led the charge of the funding brigade and attempted to establish a separate cancer agency with taxpayers' dollars. The AHA was miffed: The "What about me?" syndrome is powerful among the health charities.

The political maneuvering behind the new cancer effort continued for two years and makes interesting reading, but is beyond the scope of this book.[34] In the end, a new cancer agency independent of the National Institutes of Health (NIH) was rejected, but the National Cancer Institute now submits its budget requests directly to the president rather than through the usual bureaucratic channels at NIH. Thus, the "war on cancer" was begun, and tens of billions of taxpayers' dollars have been poured into the campaign over more than two decades.

What have we gotten for our money? The nation's birthday came and went in 1976 and the cancer establishment failed to deliver the promised gift of a cancer cure. What's happened since then? Not much:

> Twenty years ago, the nation declared war on cancer, an enemy that was killing nearly 400,000 Americans a year. For President Richard M. Nixon, who signed the National Cancer Act on Dec. 23, 1971, it was a medical Apollo program, a scientific mission to match the triumph of landing astronauts on the moon.
>
> After two decades and $22 billion in federal funds, the enemy still claims nearly one life every minute, the same proportion of the

population [as] in 1971. Overall, there has been very little change in the death rates for the major cancers.

What all this means, and what all the generals and the soldiers know, is that the war on cancer is a long war. No one knows how long—a 30-year war? A 100-year war? There is no military precedent for fighting disease.[35]

The cancer establishment, "the war's generals—the researchers and government officials—remain optimistic."[36] This is not surprising. What else can they do? If there is no hope of a cure, why pour taxpayers' money down a rat hole? Why give in to the ACS's appeal for donations to support research?

The cancer establishment's claims that great strides have been made in reducing deaths from cancer must be viewed with serious misgivings. A cancer victim is considered "cured" if the patient survives for at least five years after the cancer is diagnosed. Thanks to modern scanners and more sophisticated medical tests, it is now easier to detect cancer, so diagnoses are made earlier. The likelihood of living for five years after a cancer diagnosis increases when the cancer is discovered at an early stage. In March 1985, the U.S. General Accounting Office (GAO) issued a report about cancer survival statistics:

> In recent decades, cancer incidence and mortality rates both increased. One hopeful sign of progress against cancer has been a steady increase in reported survival rates. Recently, however, questions have been raised as to whether this improvement in cancer patient survival is the result of advances in the detection and treatment of cancer or simply an artifact of the way survival rates are measured.
>
> Advances in the detection and treatment of cancer from 1950 to 1982 have extended patient survival in all but one of 12 cancers GAO examined. GAO concludes, therefore, that progress has been made. However, the extent of improvement in survival for specific cancers is often not as great as that reported. One reason is that biases artificially inflate the amount of "true" progress.
>
> GAO has determined that the improvements in patient survival have been most dramatic for the rarer forms of cancer and least dramatic for the more prevalent cancers. As a result, even though the absolute number of lives extended is considerable, this number remains small relative to all cancer patients.[37]

If you are diagnosed with cancer, pray that you have a rare form of the disease or you may be out of luck and time.

Two years later, the GAO issued yet another report about cancer survival—this time focusing exclusively on breast cancer. The GAO stated that

> as a nation, we continue to spend billions of dollars to discover, develop, test, and refine new medical technologies. However, little effort is exerted to determine if these technologies, once they are ready for public use, realize the potential they displayed during their development. The purpose of this report is to examine the extent to which one advance in the treatment of breast cancer has benefitted patients. . . .
>
> In the mid-1970's, great excitement was generated by reports from two separate clinical trials that chemotherapy administered following surgery (adjuvant chemotherapy) was beneficial for pre-menopausal women with breast cancer that had spread to the lymph nodes under the arm. Subsequent to these reports, the use of adjuvant chemotherapy increased considerably for this group of patients.
>
> The results of continued experimentation of the benefits of adjuvant chemotherapy led to a consensus that "adjuvant chemotherapy has demonstrated a significant reduction in mortality. . . ." In light of this consensus that adjuvant chemotherapy can increase survival, and given the increased use of this therapy, logic would indicate that the survival [rate of women treated with adjuvant chemotherapy] . . . should have improved.[38]

The logic was wrong. Although the percentage of women receiving adjuvant chemotherapy tripled between 1975 and 1983 (from 23 percent to 69 percent), the three-year, the five-year, and the seven-year survival rates did not measurably improve (see table 6.2). The GAO stated that "when these data are subjected to statistical tests, they show no statistically significant improvement in patients' survival. This finding was consistent across three analytic methods GAO employed to detect changes in survival."[39]

What's going on? Thousands of women were given chemotherapy after surgery because physicians believed that it increased the probability that the patient would survive. Chemotherapy is costly; it can also produce severe side effects that can cause both physical and psychological harm to the patient. Why were patients put to all the expense, pain, and anguish when the evidence indicated that the chemotherapy did not increase survival rates? The answer to this question is that clinical trials, or controlled experiments, "have shown that chemotherapy does extend survival for specific types of breast cancer patients." The GAO concluded, however, that "there have been problems in

TABLE 6.2
Survival Rates of Breast-Cancer Patients Given Adjuvant Chemotherapy

Year of Diagnosis	% Receiving Treatment	Survival Rate		
		3-year	5-year	7-year
1975	23%	0.82	0.72	0.64
1976	45	0.85	0.71	0.64
1977	46	0.83	0.71	0.64
1978	53	0.83	0.70	0.63
1979	55	0.83	0.71	0.65
1980	62	0.86	0.77	NA*
1981	66	0.83	0.72	NA*
1982	72	0.84	NA*	NA*
1983	69	0.85	NA*	NA*

*The survival rates provided assume complete follow-up only through the end of 1985. That is why the last year for the 3-year survival rate is 1983; for the 5-year rate, 1981; and for the 7-year rate, 1979.
Source: U.S. General Accounting Office (GAO), *Breast Cancer: Patient's Survival,* GAO/ PEMD-89-9 (Washington, D.C.: GAO, February 1989), p. 3, Table 1.

moving the treatment for breast cancer from the laboratory to the patients."[40] As the old adage goes, "There's many a slip 'twixt the cup and the lip."

DO HEALTH CHARITIES HELP OR HINDER DISEASE RESEARCH?

Even a sympathetic assessment of the progress made in finding the causes of and cures for disease over the past half-century must concede that the results are disappointing, especially in light of the vast sums that have been spent and the endless assurances that the answer is at hand. Something seems seriously wrong in disease research. Although the cancer establishment has repeatedly announced major advances in the war on cancer, real progress has remained elusive. Perhaps we are looking in the wrong places for cancer cures.

We believe that a persuasive argument can be made that health charities impede disease research by discouraging innovative approaches. This conclusion is not new, for it has already been made by others in connection with cancer. These critics have leveled a double-barreled attack on the research agenda of the American cancer establishment: (1) promising cures have been ignored; and (2) the establishment's emphasis on cures is misplaced because most cancers are caused by exposure to carcinogens in the environment, so cancer *prevention* must be stressed rather than cancer *cures*. These two criticisms are very different in their emphasis, but they share a common denominator: The economic self-interests of members of the cancer establishment—drug companies, physicians, medical researchers, health charities, and so on—lead to misdirected research.

Ignoring Promising Cancer Cures

The ACS is especially vulnerable to the charge that it obstructs cancer research because it publishes *Unproven Methods of Cancer Management,* a book that "exposes" unorthodox therapies in the treatment of cancer. According to the ACS,

> the Society monitors and maintains information on unproven methods of cancer management. Information on such questionable treatments is closely reviewed by a committee of volunteer health professionals, which periodically issues carefully researched position papers on these various "unconventional" treatments. These position statements are available to physicians, science writers, editors, and the general public.[41]

In *The Cancer Industry,* Ralph Moss claims that the ACS "maintains a blacklist on unconventional methods that is worthy of the Inquisition." Moss asserts that a number of "unproven" methods ("proven" techniques recognized by the cancer establishment are surgery, radiation, and chemotherapy) have shown promise in the past but have been discredited by the ACS and its allies: the National Cancer Institute, the pharmaceutical industry, and the medical profession. Why? "In my opinion," Moss explains, "the cancer field continues to be marked by political power grabs and economic selfishness."[42]

Many of the unorthodox methods are based on remedies that are not patentable, so there is little economic incentive to investigate these approaches. For example, Dr. Linus Pauling—twice a recipient of the Nobel Prize—claims that massive doses of vitamin C have proven useful in combating cancer; hydrazine sulfate has also shown promise. From the perspective of the drug industry, however, there is no money to be made from either substance because neither is patentable and both are very inexpensive to produce.[43]

There is fame and fortune for the organization that produces a cancer cure—that much is certain. Moss traces the interlocking directorates among the American Cancer Society, the National Cancer Institute, and the drug industry and concludes that

> the leaders of the top organizations . . . are certainly familiar with each other and interlock on many committees, panels, and boards. . . . What holds them together, however, is a community of interests and ideas. The top leaders generally see eye to eye on the major questions concerning cancer. They favor cure over prevention. They emphasize the use of patentable and/or synthetic chemicals over readily available or natural methods. They set the trends in research, and are careful to stay within the bounds of what is acceptable and fashionable at the moment.[44]

When all is said and done, Moss's highly detailed and carefully documented book suggests that a conspiracy has developed that has hampered research efforts in several promising areas, and that economic self-interest is the driving force behind the collaboration.

Cancer Prevention, Not Cancer Cures

The leading spokesperson for the prevention-not-cure contingent is Dr. Samuel S. Epstein, professor of occupational and environmental medicine at the University of Illinois Medical Center in Chicago. Epstein's 1978 book, *The Politics of Cancer,* was the opening salvo in a series of skirmishes between the cancer establishment and the prevention-rather-than-cure advocates that continues to this day. The book's central thesis was that "cancer is caused mainly by exposure to chemical or physical agents in the environment."[45] Early in 1992, according to the *Washington Post,* Epstein and a group of sixty-four other physicians and scientists claimed that

> two major institutions responsible for cancer research in the United States have paid little attention to environmental hazards, exaggerated claims in cancer diagnosis and treatment, and in some cases endorsed controversial medical practices. . . . In a wide-ranging indictment, the group called on the National Cancer Institute and the American Cancer Society to redirect their attention to research and education on preventable causes of cancer in the home and workplace.
>
> "The cancer establishment has grossly confused and misled the public into thinking we are winning the war on cancer. Nothing could be further from the truth. . . . The cancer establishment is fixated on

diagnosis and treatment, to the neglect of cause and prevention," and "has trivialized the risk of environmental causes," Epstein said.[46]

Why has the cancer establishment largely ignored environmental causes of cancer? According to Epstein,

> the [cancer-research] establishment is financially interlocked with giant pharmaceutical companies (grossing $1 billion annually in cancer drug sales) with inherent conflicts of interest. The establishment devotes minimal resources to research and education on cancer cause and prevention—only 5 percent of the $1.9 billion NCI budget. Furthermore, the establishment provides no scientific support for legislation and regulation to reduce avoidable exposures to industrial carcinogens. . . . As emphasized by critics of the cancer establishment, drastic reforms are needed.[47]

Thus, Epstein and his colleagues believe that greed and self-interest have sidetracked cancer research, and that cancer cures are stressed because the pharmaceutical industry can profit from anticancer drugs. There's no profit for the drug companies in prevention.[48]

Good Intentions Can Produce Bad Results

A dyed-in-the-wool cynic might suggest that the last thing ACS officials and NCI scientists and bureaucrats want is a cure for cancer—those highly talented people would then be out of their prestigious and well-paying jobs and the organizations would have no mission. We do not subscribe to this view. Cancer is such a horrible disease and its toll so devastating on the victim and family and friends that anyone who is in a position to do so, we believe, would do everything possible to conquer this disease. In contrast to these other critics, we do not impugn the motives of the cancer-research establishment leaders, nor do we believe in conspiracies designed to manipulate who gets money to do research in what areas. Indeed, we believe precisely the opposite: Disease research is being hindered by the very best of intentions. We are convinced that there is a burning desire on the part of everyone in the cancer establishment to find a cure. But funds for research are limited, so available funds are given to those who are regarded as the most able researchers. We also believe that the ACS's condemnation of "unproven" methods is a sincere effort to protect the public against what it perceives as medical "quackery." In other words, everyone involved in cancer or disease research is motivated by the best possible intentions.

The basic problem, however, is that good intentions do not always produce good results; indeed, they may actually hinder disease research. How can this be? For starters, it must be understood that the pursuit of science (medical, social, and physical) is a messy business. Relative to other sciences, modern medical research is still in its infancy. After all, a mere century and a half ago, barbers performed surgery, and there are Americans alive today who were born before the introduction of the first antibiotic (penicillin). There are lessons to be learned about research from looking at the history of science. Three major points are pertinent here:

1. Producers of major scientific breakthroughs are often scorned by their contemporaries; only later generations realize the importance of the discovery (the "20/20 hindsight" or "Monday-morning quarterback" syndrome).
2. Point 1 is not surprising because an important discovery may not be regarded as a breakthrough at the time, but rather as a curiosity or a toy; in addition, truly brilliant scientists may exhibit signs of insanity, and it's hard to take a madman seriously.
3. Every discipline has a culture, established by the elite leaders of the profession, that defines research excellence. If the elite controls the research funds and does not experience competition from other sources, misdirected research may continue indefinitely.

Today's Quacks, Tomorrow's Geniuses. Contrary to popular notions, science is often a rather sordid affair. The term *science* conjures up images of a modern, spotlessly clean laboratory where retorts, flasks, beakers, and test tubes filled with exotic concoctions and connected by a maze of glass tubing boil and bubble. The scientist is the epitome of objectivity: Having deduced some testable hypotheses from a theory, the scientist's goal is to collect empirical data that will confirm or reject the theory.

In reality, science is very different. For centuries, science—including medical science—has blundered along. In a great many cases, the scientist who makes great discoveries is ridiculed as a "quack" or a "kook" in his or her own time—only to be revered by later generations as a paragon of science. A few brief illustrations help make this point.

As most fledgling physicists/astronomers know, Johannes Kepler (1571–1630) discovered the laws of planetary motion long before the development of calculus, which permits the problems that occupied Kepler for decades to be solved in a matter of minutes. Why did it take Kepler so long? Aside from his astronomy, he spent considerable time trying to keep his mother from being burned as a witch, a fate which had already befallen his aunt.[49] His book, *Harmonice Mundie* (The Harmony of the Worlds), took matters literally: Kepler actually wrote the music each planet "sung" to glorify God as it whirled around the sun. When "several planets are simultaneously at the extreme points of their respective orbits," the result, Kepler said, "is a motet, where Saturn and Jupiter represent the bass, Mars the tenor, Earth and Venus the contralto, Mercury the soprano."[50] Orthodoxy held that the orbit was a circle, the "perfect" shape, but Kepler had proven that the planets moved in an elliptical orbit—a revelation that caused him to ridicule his own discovery:

> The oval [ellipse] lacks that archetypal appeal. It has an arbitrary, distorted form. It destroyed the dream of the "harmony of the spheres," which lay at the origin of the whole quest. At times he [Kepler] felt like a criminal, or worse: a fool. All he had to say in his own defense was: "I have cleared the Augean stables of astronomy of cycles and spirals, and left behind me only a single cartful of dung."[51]

Before his contemporaries could attack his findings, Kepler himself condemned them.

Galileo, a contemporary of Kepler (the two exchanged letters), ran into trouble with the Catholic Church, the most powerful institution of the time. In a nutshell, Galileo published *De Revolutionibus,* which claimed that the earth moves around the sun. The Congregation of the Index, a body of the Catholic Church, condemned the doctrine as "altogether against Holy Scripture" and banned Galileo's book on March 5, 1615. Unrepentant, Galileo published *Dialogue of Two Chief World Systems,* which defended his Copernican views, in February 1632. On June 22, 1633, after conducting a trial, church officials condemned Galileo "on vehement suspicion of heresy" and sentenced him to perpetual house arrest. Although Galileo's views were vindicated centuries ago, the Catholic Church did not officially acknowledge its error until 1992—more than three and a half centuries later.[52] For some institutions, admission of errors is painful.

Isaac Newton, revered as a father of modern physics, mathematics, and astronomy, was a mystic whose writings on religion might have raised more than a few eyebrows had his dog, Diamond, not upset a candle that destroyed virtually all of Newton's occult writings.[53] Apparently, Newton was as much a religious mystic as he was a scientist.

In *The Sleepwalkers: A History of Man's Changing Vision of the Universe,* a book about scientific discovery and the psychology of creativity, Arthur Koestler wrote, "The history of cosmic theories, in particular, may without exaggeration be called a history of collective obsessions and controled schizophrenias; and the manner in which some of the most important discoveries were arrived at reminds one more of a sleepwalker's performance than an electric brain's."[54] Koestler's biographer asserts that

> *The Sleepwalkers* is largely devoted to a chronological demonstration of theoretical ineptitude, stretching consistently from ancient Egypt to the age of natural philosophy, through Ptolemy, Copernicus, Galileo, Kepler, Newton, *and into the twentieth century where scientific confusion has reached increasingly grotesque proportions. Koestler demonstrates that . . . most scientific . . . theory has been more the result of accidental discovery than of cognitive, causal inductive processes.* [Emphasis added.][55]

The natural inclination is to nod wisely and admit that all this is interesting, but also irrelevant because we are far more sophisticated today than in the days when Kepler was defending his mother against charges of witchcraft and Newton was getting hit on the head by apples falling from the trees. Times have changed, but human behavior isn't all that much different. In *The Double Helix,* James D. Watson, one of the Nobel laureates honored for deciphering the structure of DNA (the fundamental genetic material), wrote, "As I hope this book will show, science seldom proceeds in the straightforward logical manner imagined by outsiders. Instead, its steps forward (and sometimes backward) are often very human events in which personalities and cultural traditions play a role. . . . There remains a general ignorance about how science is 'done.'"[56] *The Double Helix* is a saga of missteps, blunders, intrigue, arrogance, petty quarrels, one-upmanship, and serendipity, of discoveries made largely by accident and fortuitous circumstances.

But medicine must be different, right? Wrong. In *The Transformed Cell,* Steven Rosenberg relates the way in which one of his colleagues at the National Cancer Institute, French Anderson, "developed the technique of microinjection, in which DNA is physically injected into a single cell. He [Anderson] has said that even in his own lab the idea of microinjection was so ridiculed that he did the work at a microscope in his office, out of sight of others."[57] Anderson's work was essential to Rosenberg's research on immunotherapy, a promising avenue on the cutting edge of the battle against cancer. Ridicule is alive and well in medicine for those who attempt to accomplish breakthroughs.

Toys or Curiosities. According to Arthur Koestler, many discoveries of great significance are at first viewed as novelties or curiosities that have no practical application whatsoever beyond amusement:

> A number of discoveries in the history of science follow the same typical pattern: some "playful" performance or technique which has hitherto served no concrete purpose is applied to a task with which it had formerly no connection whatsoever. Examples are the invention of Dutch opticians . . . which Galileo later turned to astronomic use; the invention of the steam engine as a mechanical toy by Hero of Alexandria . . . ; the analysis of conic sections by Greek mathematicians in the fourth century B.C. as a pure mental exercise and their application to astronomy by Kepler and Newton 2,000 years later; the development of non-Euclidean geometry, of the theory of matrices, and other mathematical devices, which seemed to serve no earthly purpose until they were applied to the theories of relativity, quantum mechanics, etc.[58]

Little wonder that great ideas are not taken seriously if initially they are used as toys, riddles, or games. But who knows what may come of today's innocent horsing around 2,000 years from now? No one can foresee all the possible applications of a particular invention or technological change. At the outset, the laser wasn't designed as a new surgical device or as a bar-code scanner for supermarket checkout stations. Only twenty years ago, anyone who predicted that powerful computers would become so simple to operate ("user friendly") and inexpensive that even families of modest means could easily afford to have one in their homes would have been regarded as an impossible dreamer.

But where does medicine fit into the "toy" or "curiosity" category? How about the laetrile controversy of the 1970s? Briefly, laetrile is a drug made from apricot or peach pits that, some claimed, could cure some types of cancer. Twenty years ago, the notion that an apricot- or peach-pit concoction could cure cancer was, to say the least, far-fetched. It recalled images of the snake-oil salesman who traveled from town to town peddling nostrums that were long on promise (and often on alcohol) and short on demonstrated effectiveness. The cancer establishment condemned laetrile therapy after a long and acrimonious battle in the media and elsewhere. Ralph Moss claims that laetrile was not given a fair test, but dismissed out of hand, even though there was some evidence supporting its efficacy.[59]

How times change! Now the cutting edge of chemotherapy in the treatment of ovarian cancer is Taxol, a drug made from the bark of yew trees.[60] If yew bark can yield effective cancer drugs, why not peach and apricot pits?

Moss also lambastes the cancer establishment for initially attacking vitamin C and other nutritional approaches to cancer.[61] Nutritional and vitamin therapy, which the cancer establishment had labeled unorthodox and suspect, suddenly became "mainstream" and received the blessing of the ACS. The discussion of current research in the ACS's *Cancer Facts and Figures, 1989,* states that

> there is strong evidence that perhaps people can be protected from cancer by what they eat or drink, or by other substances or lifestyles that serve as defense mechanisms. Clues are being pursued by ACS researchers studying such agents as vitamin A; retinoids (synthetic forms of vitamin A); vitamin C; vitamin E; the chemical element selenium, found in the soil; and other naturally occurring substances in brussels sprouts, cabbage, and certain other foodstuffs. *This is a new and important area* which needs further research so that recommendations can be developed on how people should change their lifestyles to reduce their chances of getting cancer.[62]

Perhaps one of the reasons that the cancer establishment was slow to adopt nutritional approaches to cancer is that its chief proponent in the early days, Dr. Max Gerson, included in his daily regimen a coffee enema "to cleanse the body."[63]

All sorts of different approaches are now being explored in the search for cancer cures. The *Journal of the National Cancer Institute,* for example, notes that scientists are looking for "anti-cancer drugs in the ocean depths."[64] Apparently, some sea creatures hold promise in the battle against cancer:

> One compound, isolated from a sponge found in Canadian waters, showed activity against drug-sensitive and drug-resistant human cancer cell lines. It was effective in . . . [small] concentrations . . . and was more potent than Adriamycin, a common anti-cancer drug. Scientists are now trying to synthesize this class of compounds, because the sponge they come from is rare.[65]

The message seems clear: It is unwise and perhaps arrogant for the American Cancer Society or any other organization to attempt to discredit scientists or their approaches to cancer or any other disease. What may seem ludicrous at one point in time may become standard practice over the years. Had the ACS in the 1950s not been so critical of Dr. Gerson and his nutritional approach to cancer in the 1950s— critical to the point of having then Senator Claude Pepper (D-Fla.) hold congressional hearings about Gerson's claims—we might know a great deal more about the role of vitamins and diet than we know now. At the very least, it is hypocritical of the ACS to announce to the world in 1989 that vitamins and diet are a "new and important" research area after condemning the work of others in this field decades earlier.

Insanity. There is supposedly a fine line between genius and insanity. At times, path-breaking ideas are so very different from the prevailing orthodoxy that the individuals promoting them are viewed as madmen. Albert Rothenberg recognizes this in his *Creativity and Madness:*

> In view of such high achievement and honor in connection with genius, I was at one time extraordinarily puzzled and piqued about the fact that so many outstanding persons also suffered from some form of psychosis. Although absolute proof of the matter is hard to establish, the presumptive list includes the artists Hieronymus Bosch, Vincent van Gogh, Wassily Kandinsky, and Albert Dürer; the scientists Michael Faraday, Isaac Newton, Johannes Kepler, and Tycho Brahe; the composers Robert Schumann, Hugo Wolf, and Camille Saint-Saëns; the writers Johann Hölderlin, August Strindberg, Arthur Rimbaud, Edgar Allan Poe, Charles Lamb, Guy deMaupassant, Theodore Roethke, Ezra Pound, T. S. Eliot, Virginia Woolf, Hart Crane, Sylvia Plath, Jonathan Swift, Lewis Carroll (Charles Dodgson), William Blake, Ernest Hemingway, and Charles Baudelaire; and the philosophers Arthur Schopenhauer and Friedrich Nietzsche.[66]

There's something of a chicken-and-egg problem here. Perhaps insanity gives some gifted people a different view of the world that permits them to solve problems in ways that would not have occurred to the rest of us. Alternatively, gifted people who espouse radical ideas may run a far greater risk of being diagnosed as mentally ill simply because their ideas are so different from those in vogue at the time. Who knows which interpretation is correct?

The Culture of Cancer. Every profession establishes its own criteria for what constitutes good research. Good researchers are those whose work conforms to the profession's standards, and the good researchers are rewarded with financial support for their work. Medical research is little different from academic research, since many medical researchers are employed at universities or at clinics operated by or affiliated with these institutions. The precept of the researcher in every discipline is "publish or perish." Thus, a professional "proves" his worth as a researcher by having his or her papers reviewed by knowledgeable peers and published in the profession's journals. It follows that the people who control the professional journals effectively determine who is regarded as a good researcher and whose work will be financially supported.

Medical research is often costly, and it is not safe to bet large sums on "dark horses." Rather, the tendency is to award grants to those who are already working in established areas that academic peers regard as promising. Unfortunately, such an approach to research can result in a relatively small clique having almost complete control over the research agenda. Ralph Moss summarizes the situation well:

> To win a grant, an applicant must please the recognized experts in his field, and almost by definition must be working within the accepted framework of that field.
>
> To a certain degree, each person who approves an application [for a grant] has put their own reputation on the line in doing so. The safest and most politic thing to do is to give priority to those applications coming from the more conventional and established researchers at well-known institutions. . . . Should anything go wrong, the grant giver can justify his or her decision by the prestige of the recipient institution and the supposedly high probability of success.[67]

Prestige, of course, is measured by the number of publications. It is not accidental that Dr. Steven Rosenberg's credentials as a cancer expert are established on the jacket of *The Transformed Cell* by the statement: "A world-renowned authority on cancer and author of more than 500 publications."

The crux of the matter is that those who control the prestigious journals determine who publishes what and, thereby, who gets research funding. Control of the journals means control over the research agenda. Note in table 6.1 that the ACS, the AHA, and the ALA control major journals in the cancer, cardiovascular, and lung disease fields, respectively. So it is not at all surprising that "scientists thus must be responsive to the goals and thinking of the [American Cancer] Society if they expect to be funded."[68] The same may be said of researchers on cardiovascular disease with respect to the AHA and to researchers on lung disease with respect to the ALA.

The ACS looks after its own on the research-funding front. The

ACS's *Annual Report, 1976*, contains a statement on "Related Party Transactions" in the notes that is very revealing:

> The Society has adopted a policy whereby Board members are disqualified from voting with respect to any Board action affecting their affiliated organizations. . . . Awards and grants are approved by the Boards of Directors, after peer review to establish scientific priorities for funding. In 1976, such awards included approximately $26,000,000 to individuals or institutions with which Board members from the medical and scientific community were affiliated.[69]

In 1976, ACS awards and grants for research totaled $29,358,975. This means that 88.6 cents of each dollar for research grants went to individuals or organizations with which ACS board members were affiliated. ACS-supported cancer researchers are members of a close-knit club.

This ACS quote only appears in the ACS's *Annual Report, 1976*—there are no similar statements for earlier or later years, so year-to-year comparisons of the links between board membership and research funding are not possible. In fact, no statement of any kind about related party transactions appears in the annual reports issued between 1977 and 1991. Moreover, none of the annual reports for either the AHA or the ALA has a "related party transactions" statement. When questioned about the disappearance (or nonappearance) of the related party transaction statement from (or in) subsequent annual reports, Michael Heron, ACS's senior vice-president of communications, responded by letter that on February 13, 1976, a comprehensive policy on conflict of interest was adopted by the ACS Board that

> safeguards against allowing situations in which individuals could directly or indirectly control or significantly influence decisions regarding financial transactions.
>
> Our current audit team has also concluded that because of the policy, a related party relationship requiring disclosure in our financial statements does not exist.[70]

The ACS's policy on conflict of interest is, indeed, comprehensive: "All Directors, Officers, and Executives of the American Cancer Society shall scrupulously avoid any conflict between their own respective individual interests and the interest of the American Cancer Society, Inc. in any and all actions taken by them on behalf of the American Cancer Society, Inc. in their respective capacities."[71] Reference to this conflict-of-interest statement is made in the ACS's 1992 annual report.

So far, so good. But does this relieve the ACS's auditors of the task of reporting the links between board membership and recipients of research funds? We think not. There is no doubt that the ACS's policy statement is both comprehensive in coverage and well intended. But requiring board members, officers, executives, and others to sign this document guarantees nothing. Remember that everyone who obtains a license to operate a motor vehicle must sign it; by signing the license, the driver agrees to obey all traffic laws and regulations. If we apply ACS logic to the drivers of cars, truck, buses, motorcycles, and other vehicles, there would be no need for the police radar because there wouldn't be any speeding—after all, drivers had pledged not to violate motor vehicle laws.

ACS policies have been ignored in the past, so why should the conflict-of-interest policy be different? For example, the ACS states categorically that "the Society accepts no money from federal, state, or local government."[72] But the *Los Angeles Times* has reported that the ACS received a payment from a federal drought-relief program for farms.[73] (Aside from the fact of the payment, why is the American Cancer Society involved in farming?) In addition, via a freedom of information request, the authors have obtained evidence of payments from the Virginia Department of Health to the Virginia affiliate of the ACS.[74]

We have attempted to determine whether the ACS still awards large numbers of grants and a large proportion of its research funds to institutions with which ACS board members were affiliated (see tables 6.3 and 6.4). We matched the names of ACS board members—those for whom affiliations were given—with institutions receiving awards in ACS's fiscal years 1988 and 1989. In 1988, 287 awards worth $29.9 million went to institutions with representation on the ACS board; these figures represent 34.2 percent of the 838 grants and 35.2 percent of the $84.9 million in total 1988 research dollars. In 1989, a total of 769 grants worth $83.3 million were awarded; 295 (38.4 percent) of those grants and 32.9 million (39.5 percent) of those dollars went to institutions represented on the ACS Board. These figures, though impressively large, are smaller than those for 1976. Keep in mind, however, that affiliations are not reported for many board members, so our "rough and ready" approach may have missed many "related party transactions."

It is important to stress the purpose of this exercise. We are not accusing any ACS officer, board member, or executive of anything illegal, unethical, or immoral. Our aim is far less ambitious—and less titillating. What we have shown is that there are close, direct links between the institutions that receive ACS research funding and the individuals who control the ACS itself. And even a cursory examination of the grants made by the ACS over the years shows that the same institutions are regularly funded year after year.

In short, mainstream cancer research is conducted at a relatively small number of institutions and the cancer researchers at those institutions are members of a tightly knit group. It goes without saying—

TABLE 6.3

American Cancer Society (ACS) Research Grants to Institutions with Representatives on the ACS's Board of Directors, Fiscal Year 1988

Institution	ACS Board Member	Number of Grants	Total Amount
Baylor College of Medicine	David A. Sears, M.D.	8	$1,216,000
Beth Israel Hospital	Lowell E. Schnipper, M.D.	1	89,000
Case Western Reserve Univ.	Murray Stein, D.D.S., M.Sc.	4	424,000
Children's Hospital Research Foundation	Beatrice C. Lampkin, M.D.	1	47,000
Duke Univ.	R. Wayne Rundles, M.D., Ph.D.	9	1,045,000
Harvard Medical School	Harold Amos, Ph.D.	15	1,808,700
Howard Univ.	LaSalle D. Leffall, Jr., M.D.	1	113,000
Louisiana State Univ.	Winston H. Weese	4	457,936
Medical College of Wisconsin	Roland A. Pattillo, M.D.	4	279,030
Mount Sinai School of Medicine	Saul B. Gusberg, M.D.	8	828,088
Ohio State Univ.	Arthur G. James, M.D.	7	522,800
Roswell Park Memorial Institute	Curtis J. Mettlin, Ph.D.	11	1,003,465
Sloan-Kettering Institute	Dorris J. Hutchinson, Ph.D.	24	2,691,500
Temple Univ.	William P. Maier, M.D. Sidney Weinhouse, Ph.D.	3	397,000
Univ. of California	Helen G. Brown Philip DiSaia, M.D. William Griffiths, Ph.D. Sidney L. Saltzstein, M.D.	76	7,195,258

but it needs to be made explicit—that many of the researchers know their counterparts elsewhere and that all are aware of each other's work. In such an environment, a cozy club mentality can develop: "I'm okay; you're okay. The approaches taken by members of *our* club to find the causes of and cures for cancer [heart, lung, liver disease] are the right ones, but the work of 'outsiders' is ill conceived and unlikely to be fruitful."

A lot of mutual back-scratching goes on among the members of

TABLE 6.3, *continued*

Institution	ACS Board Member	Number of Grants	Total Amount
Univ. of Chicago	Francis H. Straus II, M.D.	10	$1,092,920
Univ. of Florida	Rodney R. Million, M.D.	2	70,000
Univ. of Illinois	Alvin L. Watne, M.D.	4	579,000
Univ. of Kansas	Jane E. Henney, M.D. Fredrick F. Holmes, M.D.	4	230,750
Univ. of Michigan	Nathaniel H. Rowe, D.D.S.	10	959,000
Univ. of Pennsylvania	Jonathan E. Rhoads, M.D. Willis P. Maier, M.D.	14	1,464,500
Univ. of Pittsburgh	Bernard Klionsky, M.D.	7	617,000
Univ. of Southern California	G. Denman Hammond, M.D.	5	701,000
Univ. of Texas	Charles A. LeMaistre, M.D.	20	2,136,000
Univ. of Utah	Harmon J. Eyre, M.D.	5	614,300
Univ. of Vermont	Roy Korson, M.D.	2	250,000
Univ. of Washington	W. Archie Bleyer, M.D.	7	754,500
Univ. of Wisconsin	Gary D. Gilmore, M.P.H., Ph.D. Gerald C. Mueller, M.D., Ph.D.	1	188,000
Yale Univ.	Marion E. Morra	20	2,079,320
Totals		287	$29,854,067

Sources: Board memberships were taken from the American Cancer Society's IRS Form 990. The number of grants and grant amounts were obtained from American Cancer Society, *Cancer Facts and Figures, 1990* (Atlanta: ACS, 1990), p. 28.

the cancer-research clique. When this psychology prevails, "incestuous" thinking can develop that effectively discourages the funding of unusual approaches. Research grants are difficult to obtain, and money is always tight; who needs an interloper coming in with some nonconformist ideas about cancer or whatever disease is at hand? The research clique will— through the peer-review process used to evaluate grants, social pressure, and other means—discourage unconventional approaches.

The methods used to discourage and discredit mavericks go far

TABLE 6.4

American Cancer Society (ACS) Research Grants to Institutions with Representatives on the ACS's Board of Directors, Fiscal Year 1989

Institution	ACS Board Member	Number of Grants	Total Amount
Baylor College of Medicine	David A. Sears, M.D.	5	$566,500
Brigham and Women's Hospital	William C. Moloney, M.D.	1	133,000
Case Western Reserve Univ.	Murray Stein, D.D.S., M.Sc.	5	681,184
Duke Univ.	W. Rundles, M.D., Ph.D.	9	1,095,500
Harvard Medical School	Harold Amos, Ph.D. David S. Rosenthal, M.D.	6	716,500
Howard Univ.	LaSalle D. Leffall, Jr., M.D.	2	132,623
Johns Hopkins Univ.	Raymond E. Lenhard, Jr., M.D.	26	2,572,800
Louisiana State Univ.	Winston H. Weese	2	290,000
M. D. Anderson Institute	Charles A. LeMaistre, M.D.	18	3,431,500
Medical College of Pennsylvania	Rosaline Joseph, M.D.	1	56,000
Medical College of Virginia	Walter Lawrence, Jr., M.D.	2	80,000
Medical College of Wisconsin	Roland A. Pattillo, M.D.	3	331,000
Memorial Sloan-Kettering Center	Genevieve Foley, R.N.	18	1,340,000
New Jersey Medical School	George J. Hill, M.D. William H. Knauer, M.D.	1	10,000
Ohio State Univ.	Arthur G. James, M.D.	8	661,500
Pennsylvania State Univ.	Robert B. Mitchell, Ph.D.	4	456,000

beyond the usual disparagement, snickering, and finger pointing. Consider David Raup's description of the treatment accorded Dr. Linus Pauling for his work on vitamin C:

> As a Nobel chemist with an almost unequaled record of achievement, Pauling is one of the world's truly great scientists. But to some observers, his research on vitamin C put him in the lunatic fringe. Attempts have been made to suppress some of Pauling's research papers, and some of his colleagues at the National Academy [of Sciences] see him as an embarrassment. On the other hand, the vitamin

TABLE 6.4, *continued*

Institution	ACS Board Member	Number of Grants	Total Amount
Roswell Park Memorial Institute	Curtis J. Mettlin, Ph.D.	10	$874,140
Temple Univ.	Sidney Weinhouse, Ph.D.	6	839,000
Univ. of California	Helen G. Brown Phillip DiSaia, M.D. William Griffiths, Ph.D. Sidney L. Saltzstein, M.D.	70	7,437,940
Univ. of Chicago	Francis H. Straus II, M.D.	9	907,396
Univ. of Michigan	Nathaniel H. Rowe, D.D.S.	12	1,553,000
Univ. of Pennsylvania	Jonathan E. Rhoads, M.D.	12	1,389,200
Univ. of Pittsburgh	Bernard Klionsky, M.D.	10	1,449,000
Univ. of Southern California	G. Denman Hammond, M.D.	5	566,000
Univ. of Utah	Harmon J. Eyre, M.D.	5	492,875
Univ. of Vermont	Roy Korson, M.D.	3	428,000
Univ. of Washington	W. Archie Bleyer, M.D.	10	912,480
Univ. of Wisconsin	Gary D. Gilmore, M.P.H., Ph.D. Gerald C. Mueller, M.D., Ph.D.	7	966,900
Vanderbilt Univ.	Benjamin F. Byrd, Jr. M.D.	6	578,300
Yale Univ.	Marion E. Morra	19	1,972,500
Totals		295	$32,920,838

Sources: Board memberships were taken from the American Cancer Society's IRS Form 990. The number of grants and grant amounts were obtained from American Cancer Society, *Cancer Facts and Figures, 1991* (Atlanta: ACS, 1991), p. 28.

C work constitutes a foray into nutrition and medicine where there exist strong paradigms that do not readily accept discordant ideas from a chemist. . . .

The lunatic fringe is an ever-present factor in science. It is loathed and feared, and inevitably, science protects itself. It is extremely difficult for a really radical idea to get a hearing, much less a fair hearing. And if the originator of the radical idea does not have normal credentials, getting a hearing can be virtually impossible.[75]

Ignoring or ridiculing a novel approach or idea is one thing; suppression of research is far more reprehensible and reveals a great deal about how much the in-group fears and loathes the maverick and his or her ideas.

There is nothing inherently wrong with research that is done by members of a club or clique—if it is on the right path and producing the desired results. The accomplishments of so-called mainstream cancer research, however, have been notably few and far between, according to the U.S. General Accounting Office and the critics of the cancer establishment. After the promises made that the cancer battle could be won by 1976, nearly two decades and more than $20 billion later there is little to shout about. Maybe what is needed is less cliquishness in the research arena.

But who cares if the ACS, the AHA, and the ALA have their research cliques that always get funded by the charity concerned with their pet disease? If the large grants come from government, isn't the National Cancer Institute and the other institutes at the NIH what really matter? These questions are very important, and now the significance of charity seed grants becomes readily apparent. By awarding seed grants, the health charities give members of their research cliques a definite advantage in the competition for funds from the NCI. Peer review is used to decide who gets federal tax dollars for disease research, and there are close links between the ACS and the NCI and between the AHA and the ALA and the National Heart, Lung and Blood Institute. So the same "group think" that prevails in the cancer, heart-disease, and lung-disease research cliques also dominates the grant-making process within the various components of the NIH.

What evidence is there of close links between the ACS and the NCI? There's plenty. Dr. Samuel Epstein, the frequent and vocal critic of the cancer establishment mentioned earlier, has charged that "the National Cancer Advisory Board and Cancer Panel have had close interlocking relationships with the leadership of the American Cancer

Society." The National Cancer Advisory Board exercises executive control over the NCI; the Cancer Panel "meets monthly and establishes NCI priorities and policies."[76] Examples of cooperation between the ACS and the NCI in research have been reported elsewhere.[77]

There are also long-standing and very cozy social relationships between NCI officials and ACS executives. According to Epstein, "The close links that have developed between the NCI and the society have been cemented by the personal relationships between members of the same lobby that supported both organizations. . . . These interlocking relationships have also helped create a fiscal pipeline from the NCI to clinicians in the American Cancer Society."[78] These social linkages became a source of concern to the staff of a congressional committee that held hearings in 1977 on the National Cancer Program. During the hearings, it was revealed that

> high NCI officials were invited by the American Cancer Society to attend banquets and scientific meetings. The officials were invited to bring their wives at ACS expense.
>
> Dr. [Frank] Rauscher, who was then director of NCI, was invited . . . to an ACS-sponsored scientific meeting in Montego Bay, Jamaica, West Indies. On his return from the meeting, he requested reimbursement for his wife's transportation, hotel bill, food, and other items.[79]

The ACS also paid for Rauscher's wife to attend several ACS banquets at the Waldorf-Astoria Hotel in New York City. All the VIP treatment received by Rauscher and his wife must have impressed him: "Dr. Rauscher went directly from the NCI—the National Cancer Institute—to the vice presidency of the American Cancer Society."[80] Links don't get any tighter than this, despite the disingenuous claim made by Walter Ross in his "official history" of the ACS that "the Society's board of directors and staff are entirely separate from and have no responsibility for National Cancer Institute policies or programs."[81]

At the same hearings, Irwin Bross of the Roswell Park Memorial Institute noted that

> the special administrative structure of the NCI that set it apart from the other institutes at NIH should be repealed. The superstructure was largely engineered and controlled by the American Cancer Society, a principal beneficiary of NCI funds. The liaison with the White House, Benno Schmidt, and the director of the National Cancer

Institute, Frank Rauscher, and many members of the National Cancer Advisory Board, such as Mary Lasker, all had close ties with ACS. This is also true, for that matter, for the proposed replacement for Frank Rauscher (who is now an ACS vice president). *What the superstructure did was to concentrate power in a tight little professional in-group which then proceeded to run the Conquest of Cancer program as a closed corporation with a total disregard for the public interest. In any other area of the federal government, this cozy set-up would have been regarded as very questionable or outright corrupt. . . . The American Cancer Society should be barred from getting any NCI grants or contracts.* [Emphasis added.][82]

In a similar vein, Rose Kushner, author of *Breast Cancer: A Personal History and an Investigative Report,* testified as follows:

Why is the National Cancer Institute so fearful of "confronting" the American Cancer Society? I don't know. Speculation has led me from the ridiculous to the absurd, because no rational explanation makes any sense. The NCI was charged by the Congress with the obligation of keeping us Americans—NCI's employers—aware of everything our tax dollars have bought. If the American Cancer Society wants to help the NCI, this is fine. But the NCI must be the parent, *not* the obedient child.[83]

The congressional hearings revealed that the ACS tail is wagging the NCI dog. Ralph Moss states that "ACS and NCI personnel interlock on many committees" and quotes the journalist Ruth Rosenbaum's claim that an "ACS-controlled clique . . . dominates NCI policy and funding decisions. . . . They've [the ACS has] turned it [the NCI] into a funding pump."[84] Therefore, the direction of cancer research at both the ACS and the NCI is determined by a small clique of NCI and ACS insiders. Members of a cancer-research club control the allocation of research funds from *both* the ACS and the NCI, and the same "group think" that dominates ACS research also prevails at NCI.

Social pressure to conform to group norms and prevailing wisdom about what constitutes good research are powerful forces shaping the disease-research agenda. Those who deviate from the norm are viewed as radicals and are ostracized, feared, loathed, and denied access to research funds. Thus, even without reference to the mundane notions of profit, self-interest, or greed, a scenario can be developed in which innovative disease research is stifled and impeded by the best of intentions. When the roles of profit and self-interest are also taken into account, additional evidence arises that health charities discourage new directions in research.

Greed, Profit, and Self-Interest in Disease Research

Moss believes that membership in the cancer-research clique includes other components of the medical establishment, such as the drug companies that have a substantial stake in chemotherapy. He devotes an entire chapter to revealing the interlocking relationships that form the cancer establishment and claims that

> in the United States today, the direction of cancer management appears to be shaped by those forces financially interested in the outcome of the problem. Distinct circles of power have formed which, while differing among themselves on many issues, are sufficiently cohesive and interlocking to form a "cancer establishment." This establishment effectively controls the shape and direction of cancer prevention, diagnosis, and therapy in the United States.
>
> There is a common belief that the doctors who administer cancer therapy and the scientists who perform laboratory research control the cancer field. . . .
>
> Within the cancer field, it appears that the major decisions are made at the tops of four or five major organizations. If a doctor or scientist exercises real control, it is as a result of his or her inclusion in one of these groups, rather than through professional expertise per se.[85]

Moss believes that the glue that holds these four or five organizations together is money. An effective cancer drug would be worth a king's ransom. The stakes are high, and it is only natural that the search is intense. Although the public might like to believe that the medical establishment is interested only in the public's health and well-being, the truth is somewhat different. Medical research is just like other endeavors: It has its share of misconduct and conflicts of interest.

Scientific misconduct is difficult to uncover and many cases undoubtedly go unreported, but so many instances were apparent by 1988 that the House Committee on Government Operations conducted an oversight investigation that focused on health research funded primarily by the National Institutes of Health. The committee concluded that scientific fraud and financial conflicts of interest were so extensive that its report concluded, among other things, that "the public may be misled and endangered by scientific misconduct and conflicts of interest."[86] In one instance, "although it was not publicly reported at the time, at least 13 of the researchers involved in the NIH-funded research [to evaluate a drug to dissolve blood clots] owned stock in Genentech [the company that developed the drug] or held options to buy the stock at a discount."[87] As another example, after giving a seminar at Cetus Corporation, Steven Rosenberg tells how he was

> asked to join the company, become actively involved in their decision-making and planning, and receive stock options. I refused the offer. The Stanford [University] scientists were a little surprised; private universities allow faculty such arrangements. . . . For me it would be a potential conflict of interest.[88]

Plagiarism and research fraud have also been growing, "and money and the very nature of the academic mind may be at the root of the problem." David Baltimore, a Nobel laureate who had received ACS funds, resigned from his post as president of Rockefeller University after a federal investigation revealed that a paper published under his and other researchers' names contained fabricated data.[89] The competition for research funding is so intense that investigators also occasionally claim more for their research than the actual scientific evidence justifies. Objectivity can be difficult to achieve—even from scientists—if they have a large financial stake in the outcome of their work.

Like Moss, Samuel Epstein argues that profit and greed motivate the cancer-research establishment to focus on cures and all but ignore prevention. But Epstein goes beyond the potential profits that the pharmaceutical industry could offer from a cancer-curing drug. He also claims that many of the cancer-causing agents in the environment are manufactured by large chemical companies that have a great deal of economic and political power. Reducing exposure to environmental carcinogens could only be accomplished by banning some products entirely or by requiring that often cumbersome and costly precautions be taken when using or handling these products. Such regulations would reduce the profits of firms producing carcinogenic materials. Epstein asserts that the ACS is tied in with industry: "By emphasizing individual responsibility for early detection, without providing information on environmental or occupational carcinogens other than tobacco, the American Cancer Society has implicitly created the impression that it endorses industry's 'blaming the victim' perspective."[90]

The last thing that the research clique wants is for critics such as

Moss and Epstein to raise questions about the direction of or motivation for disease research. But maybe it's time for the mavericks with radical ideas to be given a hearing. After decades and tens of billions of dollars, the establishment hasn't been able to strike pay dirt.

HEALTH CHARITIES AND THE MEDIA

One more topic must be explored before we attempt to unravel the various strains of argument in this chapter: the relationship between the health charities and the media. The health charities have positioned themselves carefully as brokers between the research establishment and the public. For example, the AHA states that

> magazines, newspapers, and radio and television stations rely heavily on the AHA for information to pass on to their readers and viewers. In 1990-91 the National Center [AHA headquarters] answered 3,730 national media inquiries. Additionally, local AHA offices fielded thousands of calls from their media. The AHA operated newsrooms during five national meetings, including the Scientific Sessions and the Science Writers Forum.[91]

In 1977, Lee Clark, then president of the American Cancer Society, told a congressional subcommittee that

> we coordinate, as best we can, the [media] pronouncements that have been made in regard to research. Actually, the American Cancer Society, in this very vein, has started an annual meeting for the science and medical writers of America. Researchers are *invited*, present new findings, and review with the writers what has been accomplished during that year so that they can truly be analyzed jointly.
>
> The Annual Science Writers' Seminar has done a great deal not only to bring the science writers together with the researchers, but to have research analyzed so that the incidence of misinformation is reduced.[92]

By inviting the speakers to the writers' seminars, the health charities can effectively control what the public is told about cancer research. These seminars are often held shortly before major fund-raising events. There is a general theme in each: A major breakthrough is just beyond reach.

Let's reminisce. The March 30, 1957, issue of *Business Week* (page 50) contains a headline that reads: "Cancer Research Nears a Pay-

Off." The story proclaims that "today, a fever of hope about cancer research is running high." Dr. John R. Heller, then director of the NCI, boldly announced: "Virus strains that can literally knock a hole in some forms of cancer have been developed." That "fever of hope" must have been the flu—when did you last hear about those virus strains? Three years later, *Business Week* was at it again. In the July 30, 1960, issue (page 101), the reader is told that

> much progress has been scored in the race to control cancer. This is the encouraging note sounded by people such as Dr. Kenneth M. Endicott, newly appointed director of the National Cancer Institute, and Dr. John R. Heller, newly appointed director of the Sloan-Kettering Institute for Cancer Research (New York).
>
> "Research is beginning to pay off," says Endicott.
>
> Sloan-Kettering's Dr. Heller looks for "exciting" results from virus studies within the next year or two. These might make it possible to prevent cancer at the source.

Note that Heller moved from the directorship at the NCI to the directorship at a leading cancer-research center, Sloan-Kettering. More than thirty-two years later, those "exciting" results from virus studies that were to take only "a year or two" have yet to materialize. Take any popular magazine or newspaper from five, ten, fifteen, twenty, thirty, or even forty years ago and you'll find some highly prestigious scientist or medical administrator announcing that a cure is imminent for some disease. Then check it out. This exercise might be humorous if it weren't for the fact that a cancer victim dies in this country every sixty-four seconds and heart disease kills far more people than cancer.

A cure or major breakthrough for various diseases has been heralded to the public so often that the announcements elicit little more than yawns. How does this happen when a primary function of the writers' seminars is to reduce misunderstanding? When all else fails, blame the media. The ACS's Lee Clark explained that "often, scientists are not responsible for the headlines that accrue from such meetings and, in some articles are not as precise as was intended. They [who?—the writers or the scientists?] tend to be overly optimistic. Overoptimism, I think, is a thing that is very disappointing to all of us."[93]

In *Health in the Headlines: The Stories Behind the Stories,* Stephen Klaidman explores the tangle of science, politics, economics, and the media's fascination with it all. With regard to reporting on health issues, Klaidman states that reporting on health risks is rarely simple and straightforward. Scientific findings are often complex and ambiguous. Even researchers may disagree on their import. Relatively few journalists have special training in science or medicine. Sources of information are often biased, and there is constant pressure to convert dry, technical material into compelling readable stories. No wonder reporters sometimes exaggerate or otherwise misinterpret the risks, or overemphasize the emotional side of scientific stories, or unwittingly introduce inaccuracies or make important omissions. All this leaves us—the newspaper reader or TV viewer—with many unanswered questions.[94]

The media deserves its share of the blame for building false hopes, but it still takes two to tango. Rare is the news report that points out all the conflicting lifestyle advice that health charities have given the public over the years; rarer still is the story that asks, "Where is that cure we were promised ten years ago?" The media do not wish to offend the health charities they rely on so heavily for news and information, nor are science and medical writers anxious to admit that when the "exciting breakthrough" (that never materialized) was announced, they fell for it. The news on the disease front is bad enough without the media pointing out the seemingly endless false promises and their role in publicizing them.

The media help health charities in a number of ways. The most important is by publicizing the activities of the charities and praising their work; rare is the discouraging word. This free publicity is a critical part of the constant propaganda campaign all charities conduct to polish their public image. Equally important, by bringing the latest lifestyle fad to the public's attention (eat broccoli; reduce salt consumption; go to the doctor if you sneeze; get this or that medical test), a "blame the victim" approach can be taken toward the afflicted. Examples: If a woman is diagnosed with breast cancer, she would have detected it much sooner if she had had regular mammograms (ovarian cancer: pap smears; cardiovascular disease: cholesterol tests). There is always some piece of advice the disease victim failed to follow that is the root cause of the problem. Never mind that the advice changes, is misleading, or is patently wrong. When people die from cancer or heart, lung, or any other disease, it's their own fault. Forget that the health charities have repeatedly promised the public imminent cures, vaccines for prevention, research breakthroughs, or anything else. But you rarely, if ever, see letters to the editor from health charities attempting to reduce the misunderstandings or correcting those misleading stories about research findings.

The science writers' seminars and the health charities' dealings with the media seem primarily to benefit the interests of the health charities rather than provide the public with information about progress on disease research. To date, the pronouncements have been long on promise and short on performance. Look at it this way: If the health charities can't get across accurately what is going on with disease research to the people who make a living writing about science and medicine, their efforts to educate the general public about disease is doomed from the outset.

WHAT DOES IT ALL MEAN?

The major health charities claim to spend millions of dollars each year offering myriad programs to keep health professionals up to date about developments in the battle against disease. If this is true, funds donated for charitable purposes are used to subsidize high-income professionals—it's Robin Hood in reverse. Clearly, given the needs of the poor, the money spent for professional education should be redirected to the most vulnerable in society—the poor the charities *claim* to serve. Charitable contributions should not be used for professional education: Doctors, dentists, nurses, and other health professionals should pay their own way, just as other professionals do.

Another and more sensible way of looking at professional education is to recognize that it is a commercial activity. It's true that charities spend large sums on publications and conferences, meetings, seminars, videotapes, and the like. But it's equally true that these activities generate income—a great deal of income—from individual and institutional subscriptions to journals, magazines, and newsletters; from advertising; from meeting registration fees; from exhibitor booth rentals; and from the sales of books and audiovisual materials. Thus, the reported costs are offset by revenues.

In fact, health charities, if they are highly cost conscious (a debatable point, as revealed in chapter 2), may make a handsome profit from their professional-education activities. Why don't their financial statements show the *net* cost or the *net* profit? There are two reasons. First, counting the income from professional activities increases the reported revenue and gives the impression that the charity is large relative to others. Revenue is an indicator of public support for the organization. By counting the costs as expenses, it appears that millions are being spent doing "good" things. Second, charities should not be engaged in commercial activities—they should do only those things that for-profit firms and government don't do or can't do effectively. A private firm could publish the journals and conduct professional-education programs and make a profit by doing so. In other words, there is no reason for health charities to engage in professional-education activities; by doing so, their efforts are diverted from their central purpose: charity.

With regard to research, health-charity involvement may hinder rather than help efforts to find the causes of and cures for disease. Health charities foster an "in-group" mentality that discourages novel approaches to disease research. There is nothing wrong with a clique controlling research activity if the clique produces results. But the record of accomplishment on the disease front is, to say the least, disappointing—even by the criteria the health charities themselves use to measure progress. Time after time, decade after decade, promised cures, vaccines, and research breakthroughs have faded into oblivion. The health charities have raised false hopes too often. Given nearly a half-century of disappointment, the time has come for health charities to abandon their involvement with and support of research. The funds can be put to better use, and alternative approaches that have been scorned in the past may yield promising results. We don't know whether alternative approaches will produce solid results, but the research avenues favored by the health charities do not appear to be achieving many victories in the battle against disease.

7

SWEET CHARITY: PATIENT
AND COMMUNITY SERVICES

Charity shall cover the multitude of sins.   —James 4:8

Volunteers are the lifeblood of all charities. Those who contribute only money are volunteers as much as those who give their time and energy to an organization, but there is an important difference: The former often have little information about or insight into how their funds are used (or perhaps abused); the latter are far more knowledgeable about the organization's activities. We emphasize here the functions that "true" volunteers—those who donate their time and energy to health charity programs in addition to or instead of their money—can perform to benefit the public.

As has always been the case, most volunteers perform their duties in the local communities where they live and work.[1] Their primary allegiance is to their neighbors, not to some distant bureaucracy at a national headquarters. People are more aware of those needs in their communities that can be aided by voluntary effort. Moreover, the personal satisfaction is greater at home, because a volunteer can directly observe the results of his or her efforts. Volunteers may also receive peer or public recognition for aiding the community: Annual awards events at which accomplishments are acknowledged with certificates or plaques are a staple of all charities.

Volunteers are important to the functioning of health and other charities not only because their uncompensated efforts lower the costs of fund-raising and labor-intensive programs, but also because their willingness to work without pay makes an important public statement about the organization itself. The willingness to give of oneself without expecting compensation or benefit in return is what makes charitable actions noble. A group that cannot obtain the commitment and allegiance of unpaid helpers is not a true charity in the pure and traditional sense of the term. Both its charitable mission and its goals must be suspect if compensation is required to recruit people to its cause. As a rough rule of thumb, the greater the number of volunteers associated with a charitable organization, the more important is that organization's role and mission in the eyes of the community. "Doing good" motivates volunteers to assist in a charity's chosen work. With more volunteers, more good can be accomplished.

For this reason, health charities widely publicize their volunteer armies and stress carefully that, even though the organization is national in scope, its roots are firmly planted in thousands of local offshoots. In fact, Walter Ross's book, *Crusade: The Official History of the American Cancer Society*, is dedicated to "the 2,500,000 volunteers of the American Cancer Society (ACS)—more than two of every one hundred U.S. volunteers."[2] The American Heart Association (AHA) states that "today the AHA is one of the world's premier health organizations with about 3.5 million volunteers. They are involved either nationally or with the association's nearly 2,000 state and metropolitan affiliates, divisions and branches."[3] Likewise, the ACS reports that "continuing close communication among the National office, our 57 Divisions and our 3,482 community-based Unit organizations, is critical to the performance of our cancer mission. We also highly prize the effective partnership of the American Cancer Society volunteers and staff in this process."[4]

The number of volunteers associated with each charity is self-reported, so the numbers may be somewhat exaggerated. They undoubtedly include tens of thousands of people who each spend one or two afternoons or evenings a year passing the hat during annual door-to-door fund-raising drives. Because of the pressures of work and family, many cannot do much more than this on a regular basis, but millions of others make a much greater commitment. In economic jargon, charities have a "comparative advantage" because of their unique ability to harness the energies of volunteers to solve social problems.

For health charities, volunteers (aside from those who are exclusively engaged in fund-raising) participate primarily in two types of activities: patient services and community services. The National Health Council (NHC) defines patient services as "activities performed or programs conducted for the purpose of providing physical, emotional, and other assistance to individuals afflicted with a disease or health impairment or to their families. Also included is the furnishing of medical care, hospitalization, equipment, drugs, and other tangible items to those in need." Community services, according to the NHC, are "activities such as the detection of disease or health problems, planning and improving health practices, supporting clinics or other public health facilities, [and] conducting rehabilitative or similar programs."[5]

Both patient and community services are community-based programs carried out in large measure by volunteers. So it would seem logical that patient and community services would be a crucial part of every major health charity's mission. After all, only hardened misanthropes might oppose aiding disease victims. But the fact remains that many health charities do not help individual sufferers at all, and others spend only token sums on patient services. Of the thirty-nine health charities participating in the NHC's fiscal year 1990 report, fourteen—including the AHA—spent *nothing* on patient services; another eleven spent less than $1 million each. Half of all reported spending for patient services in that year was reported by one organization: the National Easter Seal Society.[6]

It is also reasonable to expect that expenditures for community services would represent a significant proportion of total charity expenditures, but once again this is not the case. Only twenty-three of the thirty-nine members of the NHC reported *any* spending on community services for fiscal year 1990. The total spent by these twenty-three health charities was $1.073 billion, but the American Red Cross accounted for $910.2 million of the total, or 85 cents of each dollar. Ten of the twenty-three spent less than $500,000 each on community services. Among the four biggest spenders for this purpose are the AHA, the American Lung Association (ALA), and the ACS. In fiscal year 1991, these Big Three together spent more than $85.5 million on community services.[7]

But these numbers may overstate the assistance that actually reaches individual patients or members of the local community. Recall from chapter 4 that reported expenditures on patient and community services, just like all other programs, include the costs of providing those services. In any case, it seems rather odd that more health charities are not offering programs to patients and the local communities where they raise their funds, since these programs are central to the charities' ability to utilize volunteers.

PATIENT SERVICES:
CHARITY AT ITS FINEST

Health charities have a capacity unmatched by any other institution to offer newly diagnosed disease victims and their families help in overcoming the worry and mental anguish that inevitably accompany a diagnosis of serious illness. Volunteers could staff telephone hot lines to answer questions and reduce anxiety. Volunteers who have successfully recovered from a disease could be paired with patients who are beginning treatment for the same illness to provide moral support and information and to share experiences. Networks directed by volunteers could arrange social functions where families affected by disease could meet in a supportive environment. The attitudes and physiological state of the patient and the family are significant factors influencing the likelihood of recovery. Simply knowing a person who has recovered from the same disease can improve a patient's prognosis. These activities are important to patients and their families; they need not be costly or time consuming; and health-charity volunteers are ideally suited to provide such services.

The excellent programs offered to cancer victims by the ACS vividly illustrate the assistance that could be offered to victims and families of virtually any disease. The ACS's patient services have grown dramatically from their modest beginnings. "During the 1940s, the provision of bandages and other sickroom supplies *was* the original American Cancer Society service program."[8]

ACS Service Programs

No other health charity even comes close to the ACS in terms of aiding disease victims. The ACS offers an extensive array of service and rehabilitation programs designed to help cancer patients.

Community Connection program. The Community Connection is a service provided by local ACS units in communities throughout the nation. It offers information about cancer and referrals to the ACS's own services, and to other services available in the community, in order "to meet the social, psychological, and other support needs of cancer patients and their families."[9] In fiscal year 1991, this program accounted for about one-third of all services rendered by the ACS.[10] The "connection" at the national level is the ACS's telephone hot line (800-227-2345); only one telephone call is needed to tap the various patient services offered by the ACS.

The toll-free telephone number is called the Cancer Response System. The calls are brief (lasting about three minutes, on average); the information provided is broad-based and general; and there is no call-back system to provide more information or personalized assistance. In contrast, the Resources, Information, and Guidance (RIG) part of the program is located in local unit or division offices throughout the nation. The RIG supplements the Cancer Response System:

> Volunteers in unit or division offices or, in some states, their own homes, respond to questions, concerns, and requests for help from patients themselves, family members, or friends. The specially trained RIG volunteer acts as a personalized resource to callers, providing information unique to the structure, available services, and special needs of the community in which the caller resides. Callers receive the requested information either on the initial contact or in call-backs, and are often referred to other sources for additional information. RIG contacts have risen 43% to 656,000 since the early 1980s.[11]

Since 1975, the ACS has produced about forty pamphlets and brochures that emphasize helping patients, family, and friends cope with cancer.[12]

Road to Recovery program. In the ACS's Road to Recovery program, volunteers provide transportation to cancer victims when they travel for medical treatment—a critically important service for the poor, the elderly, and those who live alone. Because chemotherapy can make a cancer patient very ill, many patients would be greatly inconvenienced without transportation assistance. The ACS states that "transportation is 19 percent of patient services provided. More than 60,000 cancer patients received an average of ten free, volunteer, round-trip rides for medical treatment."[13] The Road to Recovery program is certainly praiseworthy. Although there are undoubtedly many who would have benefited from transportation assistance but did not receive it, the ACS has done a great deal of good for a large number of cancer patients through this program.

The ACS's 1991 annual report contains the following rather odd statement about the Road to Recovery program: "A national survey completed during the year [1991] showed the Road to Recovery program serves the poor, the elderly, and those living alone."[14] Why would the ACS need a national survey to determine who is being served? Doesn't it already know? What other groups *would* a health charity serve? The only interpretation of this statement that makes much sense is that the ACS is defensive, having been criticized for not serving these groups. Recall in chapter 5 that the ACS's own report admitted that it had failed to adequately serve the poor. To counter this criticism and shore up its reputation, the ACS apparently decided that a national survey was necessary.

Equipment Loans, Medicine, and Nutritional Supplements. In terms of tangible aid, many local ACS units loan equipment to cancer patients and provide limited amounts of dressings, some assistance with medications, and nutritional supplements. The ACS estimates that "more than 75,000 cancer patients were provided with 179,000 home care equipment items during the year [1991]."[15]

ACS Rehabilitative Programs

Look Good ... Feel Better program. Launched in February 1989, Look Good ... Feel Better (LGFB) is a program first developed by the Cosmetic, Toiletry, and Fragrance Association (CTFA) to teach female cancer patients how to improve their appearance and self-image during chemotherapy and radiation treatments.[16] CTFA, a trade association representing the cosmetics industry, provides makeup, materials, and financial support for the program. All cosmetics are made available at no charge to LGFB participants. Classes and demonstrations are provided by volunteers who are members of the National Cosmetology Association (NCA), which represents hairstylists, wig experts, makeup artists, and nail technicians. The ACS cooperates with the CTFA and the NCA by administering the program:

> The program unites the resources of these three organizations to provide: (1) patient education—through group or individual sessions—by volunteer cosmetologists and beauty advisers; (2) complimentary makeup kits for each patient participating in a group program; and (3) free program materials such as videos and patient pamphlets.[17]

The sessions are held in hospitals, comprehensive cancer centers, ACS offices, and elsewhere. In the fall of 1991, a Spanish version of the program was introduced to aid Hispanic cancer victims. Each year, the cosmetics industry donates hundreds of thousands of cosmetic items to the program.

The side effects of chemotherapy and radiation treatments can be devastating, both physically and emotionally. LGFB is based on the "lipstick theory" of recovery; that is, "the observation made by medical professionals that when a woman battling cancer starts to put on her lipstick, she is on the road to recovery."[18] An improved personal appearance helps restore the patient's self-image, confidence, and sense of control, all of which aid patients in their battle against cancer. The ACS has a toll-free telephone number (800-395-5665) that offers patients information about the LGFB program. Some 20,000 women were served nationwide in 1991; the toll-free telephone number received 5,421 calls in only ten months.[19]

Reach to Recovery program. The ACS's largest rehabilitative program, Reach to Recovery, was started in 1953 by Terese Lasser, whose book of the same title described her experiences after having a mastectomy. Incredible as it might seem today, the notion that breast-cancer patients would benefit by having former patients visit them in the hospital was strongly opposed by physicians:

> Indeed, from the time Reach to Recovery was begun in 1953 until it was embraced and adopted by the American Cancer Society in 1969, it had to overcome widespread resistance within the medical community, where physicians saw intervention by anyone who was not a medical professional as interference in the doctor-patient relationship.
>
> According to Arthur Holleb, MD, now-retired Senior Vice President of Medical Affairs for the American Cancer Society, it was not until knowledge of this one-to-one, woman-to-woman program had spread by word of mouth and women were demanding to be put in touch with Reach to Recovery volunteers that doctors began to realize that their care alone was not enough.[20]

The Reach to Recovery volunteer, who is called a "visitor," has herself recently undergone breast-cancer surgery and is trained to help others by being a source of information and inspiration. An effort is made to "match the visitor to the patient in terms of type of surgery, treatment, age, marital status, and socioeconomic level, so that she is most likely able to answer the patient's questions."[21] The visitors help "address the physical, psychosocial, and cosmetic needs of women. . . . [They] provide support and information. In addition, literature and services to help husbands, children, and friends of breast cancer patients are available."[22] In 1991, "thirteen thousand volunteers visited more than 85,000 women with breast cancer."[23]

Reach to Recovery has been so successful that, beginning in the 1970s, similar programs were established abroad. Today, there are Reach to Recovery groups in about thirty countries in Europe, South America, and Asia.[24]

CanSurmount program. The CanSurmount program was begun in Denver, Colorado, in 1973 by a cancer specialist and one of his patients who believed that cancer victims could benefit from emotional support provided by former cancer patients. In this program, trained volunteer visitors who have or have had cancer meet with cancer patients and their families and provide support and information. The program was immediately successful:

> In 1976, CanSurmount became a Service and Rehabilitation program of the Colorado Division of the American Cancer Society which enabled the program to reach many more cancer patients. In 1979 it became a National Service and Rehabilitation program of the American Cancer Society with emphasis on reaching those patients not already served by the existing breast cancer, laryngectomy, or ostomy visitor programs.[25]

CanSurmount is a "short-term visitor program for cancer patients and their families. Hospital and home visits are made with the approval of the physician. The one-to-one visit by a person who has experienced the same type of cancer offers functional, emotional, and social support."[26] Among the greatest benefits of the program is that the volunteer attempts to demystify the disease. A CanSurmount brochure states that the volunteer can "assist you [the patient] in drawing up questions to ask your physician, nurse, or other health professional so you can find out what you need to know about the diagnosis of cancer, its treatment, and the expected outcome."[27] The volunteer is trained not to interfere with the physician-patient relationship but to facilitate it. Volunteers may leave notes for the patient's physician about concerns and questions that the patient has raised. A patient may well be more comfortable in bringing up issues with a volunteer who has undergone a similar experience with cancer than with his or her doctor.

ACS's state and local affiliates play a central role in the functioning of this excellent program. Using various manuals and materials developed by the national headquarters, they recruit, screen, and train volunteers; publicize the program to medical professionals and the public; provide materials for the volunteers to distribute to patients, their families, and their friends; maintain records of visits; evaluate the program's effectiveness; and periodically recertify the volunteer visitors.[28]

The popularity of this program—about ten thousand patients participated in 1990—is ample testament to its value.[29] It should also be recognized that volunteers themselves also benefit by knowing that their own battles with cancer are helping others. Everyone comes out ahead.

ACS Programs for Patients with Specific Cancers

Cancer of the larynx. This cancer can require removal of the larynx (voice box). To help those who have undergone this procedure to adjust, the ACS offers pre- or postoperative visits. In this program, the ACS works in conjunction with the International Association of Laryngectomees (IAL), a voluntary organization composed of three hundred member clubs called either Lost Chord or New Voice, each of which has between ten and three hundred or more individual members. Originated by the IAL in 1952 and adopted by the ACS in 1959, this program is the first peer visitor program started for cancer victims. About five thousand patients were served in 1990.[30] The volunteer visitor program is coordinated through the clubs, and the thirteen thousand members receive the *IAL News,* a newsletter published three times a year.[31]

In the visitors program,

> well-rehabilitated laryngectomees call on laryngectomee patients in the hospital at the request of a physician. By example and experience, the visitor encourages the new patient to realize that return to a normal life is indeed possible. The spouses of laryngectomees in the club may talk with the spouse and family of the patient, assuring them that normal family life is possible again. They suggest ways to manage the patient's care and help him or her with speech retraining.
>
> The new laryngectomee is urged to attend meetings of the local laryngectomee club with his or her spouse. Associating with successfully rehabilitated laryngectomees and their families and observing different methods of communication [are] important step[s] toward total rehabilitation. Club meetings may involve a session in speech training, a speaker or film, and a social period. In many areas speech pathologists attend club meetings and assist in speech training sessions.[32]

In addition to the U.S. clubs, the IAL has six clubs in Australia, ten in Canada, and at least one each in Denmark, Germany, India, Jamaica, Japan, Panama, Singapore, Uruguay, and Venezuela.[33] The ACS also assists the IAL by providing publications and materials, such as the handbook entitled *First Steps: Helping Words for the Laryngectomee.*[34]

Ostomy patients. Special rehabilitation services are offered to patients with intestinal or urinary cancers that require surgically constructed openings for the elimination of body wastes. In cooperation with the United Ostomy Association, trained volunteers who have experienced the ostomy surgical procedure assist patients in their physical and psychological adjustment. There has been a decline in the number of patients served over time, from about 15,500 in 1983 to about 9,600 in 1990. This decline has occurred for two reasons: (1) better surgical techniques have reduced the numbers of patients who actually need the artificial opening; and (2) figures from early years included patients with both malignant and nonmalignant tumors, but more recently the malignant cases have been tabulated separately.[35]

I Can Cope program. This is a structured group-education program that provides information about cancer, cancer treatments, nutrition, resource availability, and other concerns to cancer patients and their families. Begun in 1976 in Minneapolis by the Minnesota division of the ACS, the idea of group education for cancer patients and their families was revolutionary at the time. Because of its immediate success in Minneapolis, I Can Cope (ICC) was adopted as a national program shortly thereafter by the ACS. Currently, there are more than nine hundred ICC programs throughout the nation. ICC consists of a half-dozen or so two-hour sessions, which address the following topics:

1. Learning about cancer
2. Understanding cancer treatments
3. Managing the effects of illness and treatments
4. Keeping fit in mind and body
5. Communicating concerns and feelings about cancer
6. Exploring self-esteem and intimacy
7. Mobilizing resources and support
8. Celebrating life

The purpose of ICC is to provide participants with the knowledge and skills they need for coping with the challenges that result from a cancer diagnosis.

ACS headquarters develops and updates training and program materials, which are then distributed to ICC facilitators—primarily nurses and social workers—by the local or state ACS unit. Typically, the program is cosponsored by a local hospital that provides the meeting space and publicity and obtains patient referrals from physicians and nurses. Videotapes, guest speakers, panel discussions, role playing, and question-and-answer sessions are some of the resources and techniques employed in the program. There is no charge to participants for the sessions or for the course materials.[36]

Hope Lodges. Hope Lodges are praiseworthy programs conducted by eight state ACS affiliates. Hope Lodges were established to help cancer victims living far from hospitals, clinics, and medical centers, which are usually located in large cities. Although cancer treatments may be performed on an outpatient basis, overnight accommodations are required if the treatments are administered over more than one day. Hope Lodges are hotel-like buildings that provide cancer patients and their families with accommodations during treatment. The New York state ACS division operates Hope Lodges in Buffalo, Binghamton, Rochester, and Poughkeepsie. There are also Hope Lodges in Maryland, Massachusetts, Michigan, Pennsylvania, South Carolina, Vermont, and in Miami and Gainesville, Florida.

Opened in 1987, the Hope Lodge in Baltimore is exemplary in its operations. Both lodging and transportation to and from treatment is free to all cancer patients, who are served on a first-come, first-served basis. The lodge accommodates about seven hundred patients each year by giving them and their companions a relaxed, homelike atmosphere in twenty-six guest rooms with private baths. There is a central kitchen where guests may prepare their own meals; a dining room; a library; a recreation room; an exercise room; a large family room; and a large enclosed garden. Hope Lodges do far more than lower the housing costs and alleviate the inconvenience of cancer treatments: They offer a setting that facilitates communication among cancer patients and their families. This social interaction helps patients overcome the fears and feelings of isolation that can haunt them and influence their attitudes about recovery.

Some ACS affiliates that do not have Hope Lodges ask hotels and motels near treatment centers to donate rooms. The Guest Room program, in which about twenty-three hotel chains participate, was initiated by the Washington state ACS division.[37] Although this approach serves the utilitarian purpose of providing convenient, subsidized shelter to patients, it does not offer opportunities for social interaction with other cancer patients in a congenial atmosphere. Hope Lodges are indeed unique facilities, and there is a great need for these facilities throughout the nation.

TALK IS CHEAP, BUT IT WORKS

Many people might justifiably be skeptical about the benefits of support groups and volunteer visitors for cancer or other disease victims. Cancer is a horrible disease, so what can sitting around and talking about it possibly accomplish, aside from making everyone even more anxious and depressed? Before dismissing such programs out of hand as ineffective hand holding, however, consider the findings of Dr. David Spiegel, professor of psychiatry and behavioral sciences and director of the Psychosocial Treatment Laboratory at Stanford University. In 1989, Spiegel conducted an experiment on eighty-six women with metastatic breast cancer; that is, breast cancer that has spread throughout the body. It is always fatal, killing most victims within two years. Spiegel wanted to test the "often overstated claim . . . that the right mental attitude will help to conquer cancer":

> The eighty-six women were randomly divided into two groups. Half were given standard medical care. The other half received that same care—radiation, chemotherapy, drugs—but were also asked to meet once a week in a group therapy session. Spiegel had hypothesized that they would show an improved quality of life. He was right; the women reported less depression, anxiety, and pain than those in the other group. What startled him some years later, when he was reviewing the study after all but three of the women had died, was the discovery that those who took part in the group psychotherapy had lived twice as long after they entered the study as the group that received only standard medical care.
>
> Spiegel had been extremely rigorous about the design of the study. He consulted with other scientists and with skeptics and showed them his findings, asking them to poke holes in his methods and conclusions. They couldn't.[38]

Spiegel's findings are extraordinary. Apparently, mutual caring and concern can greatly influence the both quality and quantity of life. This conclusion is buttressed by an analysis of medical treatments across countries, which found that there is wide variation in the definitions of diseases and in treatments within different developed nations. According to the medical journalist Lynn Payer, the chasm is so vast among physicians in different cultures that "one country's treatment of choice may be considered malpractice across the border."[39] Yet there are no significant differences among these nations in life expectancy![40] In the foreword to Payer's *Medicine and Culture*, Dr. Kerr White, retired deputy director for health sciences of the Rockefeller Foundation, explains how wide variations in diagnosis and treatment of disease among nations can produce the same life expectancies:

> Perhaps values would be of less importance if there were indisputable evidence that all interventions of all physicians were always of clear

benefit to all patients. . . . Although things are much better than they were a generation ago, it is still the case that only about 15 percent of all contemporary clinical interventions are supported by objective scientific evidence that they do more good than harm. On the other hand, between 40 and 60 percent of all therapeutic benefits can be attributed to a combination of the placebo and Hawthorne effects, two code words for caring and concern, or what most people call "love."[41] Although the placebo effect is usually dismissed as a "residual" outcome, and the Hawthorne effect as an inconsequential phenomenon restricted to industrial settings, these two ubiquitous responses still constitute the most powerful, all-purpose, therapeutic interventions available to the profession.[42]

Why isn't the importance of "caring and concern" much more widely known and acknowledged? After all, White provides evidence that the psychological aspects of healing are far more important than the various therapies that receive widespread attention. Rare is the week that the media are not touting some new drug or therapy for cancer or other disease, but little is ever said about the importance of support groups or other types of psychological therapy. Why? Bill Moyers answers this question in *Healing and the Mind:*

If a new chemotherapy for metastatic breast cancer had doubled survival time, it would be headline news. There would be a massive effort to find out if that was, in fact, the case. When a psychological intervention that costs almost nothing suggests in a carefully done controlled clinical trial that this may, in fact, happen, there's a replication effort, but because of our scientific orientation, nowhere near the same level of resources are committed to the effort.[43]

Thus, the reason that virtually no attention or publicity has been given to the benefits of support groups is precisely that they cost "almost nothing," so there is no profit in such programs for the medical establishment. "About 60 percent of the outpatient visits to primary care physicians are related to stress or mind/body interactions," but despite the enormous importance of the mind to health, healing, and disease, "Congress appropriated $2 million and the National Institutes of Health [NIH] opened an office to study unconventional medical practices, hoping to evaluate what truly works and to separate the quacks from the healers."[44] Two million dollars is a minuscule fraction of 1 percent of NIH's $11 billion annual budget.

Almost two years after its establishment, the NIH's Office of

Alternative Medicine was subjected to scathing criticism at a congressional hearing for its inaction. The appropriation required that the office have no fewer than five scientific investigators, but staffing was still not complete. Former Iowa Representative Berkeley Bedell, a member of the office's Advisory Committee, complained that committee members "have been like pygmies trying to get an elephant to go where it should." The *Washington Times* reported his charge that the office "needs a 'director willing to stand up to the forces' of pharmaceutical companies and NIH researchers hostile to funding for studies of nonconventional therapies." Even though the office has not even begun its mission, "some NIH and National Cancer Institute scientists have called the office a waste of money."[45] If funding is used as an indicator of interest, clearly the mainstream medical-research establishment has little interest in alternative therapies.

Nevertheless, there is evidence that a great deal of good can be accomplished by volunteers who merely listen, inform, and show caring and concern for cancer and other disease victims. Both the quality and quantity of life (and, perhaps, the prospects for recovery) can be markedly enhanced at little cost.

THE ACS: A ROLE MODEL FOR PATIENT SERVICES

The programs of the American Cancer Society illustrate well the ways in which health charities can use volunteers to aid individual disease victims. In total, the ACS reports that 696,817 patients received 3.4 million services in the 1990–91 fiscal year.[46] The ACS is justifiably proud of its accomplishments, and there is no doubt that it serves as a role model for other charities in providing patient services. Yet despite these notable accomplishments, much remains to be done. Table 7.1 shows the number of patients served over time by various programs (excluding the Hope Lodge and Guest Room programs), the total number served, and the potential number of patients that would benefit from ACS's assistance.[47]

Despite the ACS's best efforts, only about half of the potential patients are being helped by its programs. And even this may overstate the ACS's penetration. After all, there are more than 1 million newly diagnosed cases of cancer each year; in addition, hundreds of thousands of other cancer victims struggle for years with their disease and might well benefit from ACS assistance. If this is the case, even a smaller proportion of those who might benefit are being helped by the

TABLE 7.1
Patients Served by the American Cancer Society, by Program, 1983–84 to 1989–90 (in thousands of patients)

Program	1983–84	1984–85	1985–86	1986–87	1987–88	1988–89	1989–90
Reach to Recovery	70.8	70.9	77.8	81.6	90.9	87.5	85.1
Laryngectomee	4.8	4.6	4.9	5.2	4.8	5.5	5.1
United Ostomy Association	15.5	13.4	13.7	13.6	11.6	11.6	9.6
CanSurmount	5.3	5.8	7.1	8.4	9.1	9.3	9.9
I Can Cope	72.7	81.9	79.6	75.6	66.1	60.8	62.8
Community Connection/Resources, Information, and Guidance	457.8	486.1	529.6	559.0	585.9	645.2	656.0
Road to Recovery	46.4	45.8	51.3	50.9	48.5	51.6	52.8
Total Served	480.2	488.3	502.0	545.4	576.2	631.9	664.4
Potential Patients	1,180.4	1,181.2	1,178.3	1,243.9	1,243.7	1,234.7	1,245.9
Total Served as a % of Potential Patients	40.7	41.3	42.6	43.8	46.3	51.1	53.3

Source: Adapted from Constance Engelking, "American Cancer Society Patient Service Program: An Update," in *Continuing Care, Proceedings of the Sixth National Conference on Cancer Nursing, Seattle, Wash., July 25–27, 1991* (Atlanta: ACS, 1992), figures 1–7, 13, pp. 13–18, 21.

ACS. In the Society's defense, however, it must be recognized that many who are diagnosed with cancer do not *want* or seek help from the ACS, even though they might benefit from the assistance. The problem in such cases is that some people still regard cancer as a stigma and an embarrassment. The age in which we live is by no means as enlightened as we might like to believe.

One other point deserves mention: The ACS is widely regarded as the premier charity in the cancer field. No other organizations come close to matching its name recognition or its ability to raise revenue. One would think that the ACS would know more about the needs of cancer victims and how best to address those needs than any other organization in the world. Yet the ACS has apparently been slow to introduce new programs for cancer victims. Four of its most successful programs—Look Good ... Feel Better, Reach to Recovery, CanSurmount, and the International Association of Laryngectomees—were initiated by outsiders and then, once they became popular, were taken over by the ACS. Look Good ... Feel Better was conceived of and begun by the Cosmetics, Toiletry, and Fragrance Association; Reach to Recovery had been in operation for thirteen years before it was "adopted" by the ACS; CanSurmount was three years old when it was taken up by the Colorado division of the ACS, and three more years elapsed before it became an ACS national program; and the International Association of Laryngectomees was seven years old before the ACS became involved.

Without a doubt, ACS involvement has expanded and greatly improved all of the programs it has adopted. But it seems odd that the ACS, which promotes itself as *the* national organization concerned with cancer, had to rely so heavily on the inspiration of outsiders for innovative ways to serve cancer patients.

The AHA and the ALA Shun Patient Services

In contrast to the ACS's commitment to cancer patients and their families, the AHA spends nothing on individual cardiovascular-disease patients, and the amounts spent by the ALA on individual patients is minuscule. Yet the annual fund-raising appeals of the ALA routinely emphasize assistance to individuals. Consider the following statements from past ALA fund-raising appeals:

1984: Would you spend a few dollars to help a small child overcome the effects of chronic asthmas?

1987: By remembering the lung association in your Will, you can help us provide . . . patient care.

1989: If you could help save someone who was dying—would you? We're asking you to do just that.

1989: Your last gift to Christmas Seals helped little Amy. She's now six, and can control her tragic asthma. *Thanks to your gift, Amy is able to run and play* like other little girls.[48]

These statements insinuate to donors that their contributions will be used to help lung-disease victims. But the ALA's 1991 annual report shows that the national headquarters and all of the ALA's affiliates spent less than 1 percent of revenues on "assistance to individual patients."[49] Like research, aid to the afflicted apparently has a persuasive appeal for fund-raising purposes. It seems misleading, however, for the ALA to dedicate so little to programs that aid patients while touting "assistance" in its fund-raising appeals.

COMMUNITY SERVICES

The American Cancer Society's patient services (Road to Recovery, CanSurmount, Look Good . . . Feel Better, and similar programs) are national programs offered and administered by individual ACS units. Program content (printed materials, videos, and so on) is developed by national headquarters so that, subject to minor adjustments to reflect local conditions, these materials are uniform throughout the nation. In contrast, local units have more discretion in developing and offering community services. A variety of services is offered, including disease screenings and summer camps for children with cancer. The ACS's annual report says little about the content of community services.

The AHA is equally vague. "In 1990–91 AHA expenses for community services were $37.2 million. One of the most visible programs is the training of 5 million Americans in basic and advanced life-support courses. In addition, 1.3 million people took part in AHA cholesterol screenings and blood pressure checks."[50] Discovering the true content of the ALA's community services is all but impossible, because the ALA's reporting is based on categories of diseases and problems, such as "air conservation," "occupational health," and "lung disease," rather than on specific programs.[51] The ALA's *Annual Report, 1991,* for instance, describes its battles against asthma, infant lung disease, and air pollution. There are, however, asthma camps for children;

smoking-cessation clinics (for which the ALA charges participants a fee); and a radon "action" week, which is funded by taxpayers through the Environmental Protection Agency.

Disease Screening

One way that health charities' community services might make contributions to the nation's health care is by screening for diseases. Medical costs might be reduced dramatically if diseases were identified and treatment begun at an early stage. For example, high blood pressure can often be controlled. If left untreated, however, hypertension can lead to strokes, which can paralyze victims so severely that long-term intensive care is required. Early detection of cancer also increases the treatment options and the likelihood of a cure while substantially reducing costs. Breast cancer, for instance, may afflict as many as 10 percent of the nation's females. If detected early, treatment is relatively simple and inexpensive, and the prognosis for complete recovery is excellent. At advanced stages, however, the only option may be major surgery followed by extensive chemical and radiation therapies, which themselves have physically debilitating and potentially life-threatening side effects and can be psychologically demoralizing. Worse, this extremely costly and unpleasant regimen does not guarantee survival.

The nation's health charities are ideally suited for conducting large-scale disease screenings at the community level through their local units. A classic example of how disease screening can be conducted is provided by the National Tuberculosis and Respiratory Disease Association (NTRDA), which in 1973 became the American Lung Association. Until the late 1960s, many NTRDA affiliates sent vans equipped with X-ray machines throughout the community to screen for tuberculosis. Chest X-rays were provided at no charge. This practice was discontinued because tuberculosis was no longer considered a major health problem, and the association changed its name and objectives to encompass all lung diseases. The mobile equipment made tuberculosis screening convenient for the public and was very effective, for the vans could be sent into high-risk areas to screen high-risk individuals. A similar approach might be used for mammograms to screen for breast cancer.

Recent advances in medical technology permit volunteers with little or no formal medical training and a minimum of on-the-job experience to screen for diseases. Although formal training may be needed to take accurate blood-pressure readings with a sphygmomanometer (the blood-pressure cuff commonly found in physician's offices), inexpensive hand-held devices are now available that provide this information in digital form almost instantaneously when a finger is inserted into the device. With minimal training and at modest expense, one AHA volunteer could screen dozens of individuals for hypertension at any location in a matter of hours and inform each person tested on the spot whether their blood-pressure readings indicated a potential health problem. ACS volunteers could explain and distribute a simple, inexpensive test for colo-rectal cancer that only requires the test taker to mail in stool smears. After processing, the ACS could notify those whose tests were positive to seek medical care. Trained volunteers could offer classes on self-examination for breast cancer, one of the most effective means of early detection. Health charity volunteers involved in screening for disease could also refer those in need of medical care to appropriate clinics or other sources of treatment. The world of medical care can be an impenetrable maze, and knowledgeable volunteers could provide both information and assistance to overcome a reluctance to seek care.

A Mixed Blessing

The benefits of disease screenings are not as obvious as they might appear. Not everyone accepts the idea that screening for disease is useful or economically advantageous—that the benefits exceed the costs. In *Disease-Mongers,* Lynn Payer points out that many medical tests are inaccurate and, worse, if treatment is started to lower a risk factor (such as high blood pressure), the treatment may cause more problems than it cures. For example,

> it was logical for the medical profession to assume that if high blood pressure and high cholesterol increased the risk of stroke and heart attacks, lowering both would reduce the risks. This worked for stroke, particularly for people with very high blood pressure: when people with high blood pressure were treated, their risk of stroke was lowered as much as their blood pressure.
>
> But when the rate of heart attacks in the treated groups was studied, observers were disappointed: bringing blood pressure down to normal didn't seem to cut the risk of heart attacks very much. In fact, the use of some types of blood pressure medications in some patients actually raised the death rate: a 1991 study performed at the Joslin Clinic in Boston showed that diabetics who also had high blood pres-

sure had a higher death rate if given diuretic drugs for their high blood pressure than if their hypertension went untreated. Nobody knows quite how this happens, but diuretics tend to raise cholesterol, thus raising one risk factor in the process of lowering another. Another study published in 1991 showed that people taking any type of medication for hypertension increased their risk of becoming diabetic.[52]

Evidently, treatment of high blood pressure through medication is a mixed blessing. Although the risk of stroke is reduced, the evidence on lowering the risk of heart attacks is not encouraging—and is discouraging for diabetics. Nor are the benefits from mammography screenings an unmixed blessing. Payer contends that

> the way mammography is being promoted ... often leaves the impression that if only women would get annual mammograms, they'd never get breast cancer, or at least not die of it. Such promotions don't emphasize that mammography lowers the death rate from cancer only by about one-third, and then only in some age groups. The focus on mammograms may cause women to neglect routine physical examinations, which may be more important in women under the age of 50, and seems to give some doctors the dangerous idea that they can give drugs that may increase the risk of breast cancer with impunity as long as they order mammograms.[53]

Payer's work concentrates on the medical aspects of disease prevention and treatment. A book by Brookings Institution senior fellow Louise B. Russell entitled *Is Prevention Better than Cure?* emphasizes the economic issues—the costs and the associated benefits—surrounding prevention. As Bruce MacLaury, president of the Brookings Institution, makes clear in the foreword, these are important issues:

> The beneficial effects of prevention on health are increasingly well known, but its costs and risks are not clear. These dimensions, too, need to be assessed. Making good choices in health, as in other fields, requires consideration of the full range of outcomes—health benefits, health risks, and resource costs. . . . We need better evaluations of prevention to ensure that it receives a reasonable share of resources [and] that those resources are allocated to the most effective prevention programs.
>
> Louise B. Russell examines the policy debates about several preventive measures—the smallpox and measles vaccines, drug therapy for high blood pressure, and exercise—to demonstrate the many com-

plex factors in evaluating them. For these and other preventive measures, *the evidence indicates that they rarely reduce medical expenditures.*[54]

Russell herself frames the prevention issue in the following way:

Some people have argued that, in addition to its obvious benefits,
prevention costs less than cure. The cost of many preventive measures . . . is rather small. . . . When disease is prevented, the costs of
treating it are also avoided, so there are savings to be balanced against
any costs of prevention. Many people believe that these costs are so
great that more attention should be given to prevention simply on the
grounds that it saves money.

In reality, the situation is more complicated than these expecta-
tions, which are reasonable on their face, would suggest. Preventing
disease involves risks as well as benefits, although the risks are usually
low. And even when the financial cost of the preventive measure
looks small, careful evaluation often shows that the full costs are
rather large, larger than any savings. In fact, prevention usually adds
to medical expenditures.[55]

Russell is not alone in her assessment that disease screening as a
preventive measure is not cost effective. Milton Weinstein and William
Stason have shown that the costs of treating mild or even severe hypertension are at least four times the savings.[56] An in-depth discussion of
Russell's analysis is beyond the scope of our study, but when her con-
clusions are taken together with Payer's, only the medical establishment
clearly benefits from disease screening. The phrase "prevention usually
adds to medical expenditures" is equivalent to saying that the incomes
of physicians, pharmaceutical companies, testing laboratories, and diag-
nostic-equipment manufacturers are higher with prevention.

Thus, from both health and economic perspectives, the gains to
society from screening individuals for risk factors, such as cholesterol
tests for cardiovascular disease and mammograms for breast cancer, are
at best a mixed blessing. The evidence to date does not confirm the
widely accepted notion that early diagnosis and treatment necessarily
reduce medical costs or even help individuals. Part of the problem is
that so little is known about how specific risk factors influence the
health of different individuals that more harm than good may sometimes result from prevention. Moreover, the cost side of the cost-benefit
calculation is unfavorable because screening and treatment typically
require the services of highly paid health professionals.

The use of volunteers to screen for disease reduces labor costs and makes the cost-benefit ratio more favorable. But because most volunteers are not health professionals, they are limited in what they can accomplish. Far more could be done if health charities and their volunteers teamed up with health professionals and offered free medical care to the indigent. But what evidence is there that health professionals—doctors, dentists, and nurses—would be willing to undertake such efforts? Although health professionals earn high incomes, they have the same motivations as the rest of us—they are willing and able to donate their services to those in need. Indeed, a great deal could be done to resolve the nation's health care crisis if health charities worked in tandem with volunteers who are medical professionals.

HEALTH CHARITIES AND THE HEALTH CARE CRISIS

The need to help the ill, and especially the medically indigent, is rapidly growing, and this need drives the nation's health care crisis. There is a widespread belief that the nation's health care system needs major reform. The quality of care is not the primary issue, for the U.S. health system is envied throughout the world. Rather, the current debate is driven by rapidly escalating costs (expenditures have risen 60 percent more rapidly than the rate of inflation over the past twenty years) and access to care (more than 30 million Americans do not have health insurance; millions more lack adequate coverage).[57] Numerous policy options have been proposed, ranging from tax credits and vouchers (which would help those without insurance to obtain coverage from private firms), to a national health care system similar to Canada's, which guarantees universal coverage funded by federal tax revenues. Because of the apparent magnitude of the problem, the options that generate the most interest are those that would expand the role of government in health care provision—either directly via financing or indirectly through mandates and regulations on private employers. But if history serves as a guide, more government involvement in health care would likely produce a system with the efficiency of the Postal Service, the compassion of the Internal Revenue Service, and Pentagon prices.

Although small in number and relatively unknown and unheralded, dozens of free community clinics in the United States marshal the volunteer efforts of health professionals. These clinics first appeared in the 1960s and are, like the local units of health charities, community based. Writing in the August 14, 1991, issue of the *Journal of the*

American Medical Association, Kevin Kelleher, a physician who volunteers at the Bradley Free Clinic in Roanoke, Virginia, dismisses the notion that government action is the only or even the most appropriate solution to the nation's health care difficulties:

> The whole idea of approaching the crisis of over 30 million uninsured Americans with a basically volunteer program may at first seem ludicrous. We are all overwhelmed by the enormity of this problem and therefore have a tendency to dismiss anything but sweeping proposals. . . . The first objection is that voluntarism on such a scale is unrealistic. [But] the one thing that is consistently missing from the discussion of health care planners is mention of the altruism of physicians. . . . The volume of unreimbursed care, the willingness to be available at all hours, and even the depth of emotional attachment is matched by no other profession.
>
> The second most common objection is that free clinics represent a two-tiered health care system and therefore inferior care. There is no system that is not two-tiered. Under nationalized health care systems, the wealthier have access to fee-for-service. . . .
>
> There are many reasons to expect voluntarism to work. By centralizing indigent care, no one physician carries the majority of the burden of unreimbursed care. Bad-debt patients are fewer and practice overhead is lowered. Abuse of emergency departments is lessened. . . . Volunteers are recognized and honored by their communities. The patients themselves recognize the effort, and they are less likely to abuse resources than under an entitlement.[58]

The Bradley Free Clinic is one of about 140 free, community-based clinics currently operating throughout the nation. The Roanoke facility is staffed entirely by volunteers, who treated 3,115 individual patients in 6,469 patient visits in 1991; more than ten thousand prescriptions were filled at no cost to the patients; and the estimated value of services provided was $611,310 at an operating cost of $317,038. About 30 percent of Roanoke's physicians and dentists give their time and professional services annually; dozens more make financial contributions to or take referrals from the clinic for specialized care. The clinic's operations are supported by contributions from individuals, churches, civic groups, foundations, and the United Way; modest aid is provided by local governments—a total of $26,528 in 1990—and no federal support is sought. Patient contributions cover about 1 percent of operating costs. There is never a shortage of health professionals willing to offer their services, and no eligible patient is turned away.[59]

Because it serves patients from the local area, a clinic's operations can be tailored to meet community needs with a minimum of the bureaucratic procedures and paperwork that are inevitable in a government-mandated program, especially a federal program. During its eighteen years of operation, the Bradley Free Clinic has been so successful that it created the Free Clinic Foundation of America, Inc., a charitable organization that promotes the establishment of new free clinics around the country. Through this effort, eight new clinics have been started and an additional twelve are now in the organizational stage. The Free Clinic Foundation—a charity to promote charity—provides at no cost a manual for and advice to those who wish to start a free clinic.

Public policy, at little cost, could do much to encourage the formation of new community clinics and help them flourish. For example, tax credits might be offered to pharmaceutical companies that contribute medicines and to companies that donate equipment or services, such as utilities, to community clinics. A federal "good samaritan" law that exempts volunteers at free clinics from liability would encourage volunteer participation (Virginia, North Carolina, and other states already have such laws). And, as a result of the savings-and-loan debacle, the federal government now owns thousands of properties throughout the nation, many in areas that would benefit greatly from the services of a community clinic. Legislation permitting a group seeking to establish a clinic to obtain one of these properties at low or no cost would help overcome a major obstacle to the formation of new clinics—the capital cost of a building. Over time, a network of community clinics spread throughout the nation could contribute much to the solution of the nation's health care crisis by mustering the energies of volunteer health professionals to treat the medically indigent in concert with the efforts of health-charity volunteers. Free clinics are the front lines in the battle against disease for those who are already ill and lack access to the health care system.

CONCLUSIONS

Charities are unique institutions in that only they can organize and direct the energies of volunteers to alleviate society's problems. Although most volunteers work in the communities in which they live and many do little more than collect donations during periodic fund-raising drives, the wide range of excellent services offered to cancer patients by the American Cancer Society illustrates what can be accomplished when volunteers assist individual disease victims. Patients and their families can receive information, psychological support, services, and various forms of tangible assistance that the ACS offers through its national network of volunteers directed by local units. These programs undoubtedly do a great deal to ease the suffering of cancer victims and their family and friends and help win the patients' battle against cancer.

The American Cancer Society's programs should be adopted by and adapted to other diseases by their respective charities. Many health charities offer no patient assistance at all (as with the AHA) or only token amounts (such as the ALA) and thereby fail to effectively utilize their volunteers to maximum advantage. Society could be made much better off if health charities refocused their efforts on helping disease victims. The needs are almost limitless. The ACS's programs to help cancer victims, as commendable as they undoubtedly are, only address the tip of the iceberg. The range and effectiveness of services offered to disease victims could be significantly expanded if health charities worked in tandem with free clinics, which mobilize health professionals as volunteers. By aiding in the establishment of free clinics, which serve the poor in local communities, and helping in their operations, a great deal could be done to solve the nation's health care problems.

Many health charities offer community services, particularly disease screening. Although these services might seem highly beneficial, there is considerable evidence that prevention can cause more medical problems than it cures and that the costs of prevention exceed the benefits. Thus, screening for disease and other prevention programs, such as immunization, despite their intuitive appeal, are questionable on both medical and economic grounds. A critical issue that health charities should be addressing is whether the funds now spent on community service activities could be more effectively used in other ways, such as helping disease patients. The only clear beneficiary of prevention efforts is the medical establishment. However, the goal of charity is not—or at least should not be—to benefit the medical establishment, but to benefit the needy.

There are many suffering from disease who need and deserve charitable assistance but are not currently being reached or served in any way. The old, established health charities would be overwhelmed by the task. Indeed, some charities use this as an excuse for not making *any* attempt to aid individual patients. Long ago, for example, the ALA decided to strictly limit its assistance to individuals because the large number of sufferers would drain the ALA's economic resources. Helping those in need would divert the ALA "from more remunerative

tasks."[60] If a charity is more interested in tasks that are "more remunerative" than helping the needy, perhaps a new definition of "charity"
is needed. Although the well-established and well-known health charities have by design or necessity left wide gaps in the charitable services
that they provide, they vehemently oppose the formation and development of new organizations that attempt to fill these voids, as we will
discuss in the next chapter.

8

HEALTH-CHARITY
LOOK-ALIKES

I was here first! Leave me alone!   —Petulant three-year-old to sibling

Imitation is the sincerest form of flattery.
    —Charles Caleb Colton, *The Lacon* (1823)

Despite the vast sums spent over many decades by the major health charities, little progress has been made in the wars against cancer and other dreaded diseases. Moreover, the needs of individual patients for assistance are virtually endless. In short, a great deal remains to be done, and nature, as it's said, abhors a vacuum. So it is not surprising that many newer, and therefore smaller, health charities have been formed to help fill the very large service gaps left by the old-line charities.

Given the size of long-established health charities and the seriousness of their missions, common sense suggests that they should welcome aid from any source. But the Big Three (the American Cancer Society, the American Heart Association, and the American Lung Association) have been anything but hospitable toward the newcomers. Instead, they view these recently formed groups as interlopers that pose a major threat to their own power, prestige, and—most importantly—their budgets. Monopolists in the charity arena, as elsewhere, do not relish competition. Rather than welcoming the new troops in the battle against disease and viewing them as additional sources of aid to disease victims and their families, the Big Three have enlisted the help of federal and state governments to harass the newcomers. Indeed, the hostility goes far beyond simple harassment: The Big Three have urged government to use its powers to eliminate the new charities altogether by claiming that their activities are not only inappropriate but also illegal. The Big Three are still actively engaged in a political vendetta to label new health charities as "deceptive" fund-raisers and unscrupulous "look-alikes."

Although there may be some similarities between the major health charities and the newcomers—they both utilize door-to-door fund-raising methods, for example—the disparaging phrase *look-alike* is itself deceptive and misleading. It is precisely because of the failures and inadequacies of the older health charities that the new ones have been formed. Undoubtedly, some deceptive fund-raising exists—there's at least one bad apple in every barrel—but the old-line charities have indiscriminately and unjustly associated all newcomers with a few isolated cases of questionable and misleading behavior, something that the major health charities are not entirely innocent of themselves, as revealed in previous chapters. The pot is calling the kettle black.

ELIMINATING COMPETITION

The Big Three obviously see new charities as undesirable competition—for donations, government grants, and domination of the disease-research "industry." Otherwise, the major health charities would welcome the newer organizations as allies and appreciate their efforts in the battles against cancer, heart disease, and other ailments. Instead, they have instigated congressional inquisitions and smear campaigns.

Such a response is not unusual. Throughout America's history, organizations of all kinds have responded to competition not by competing but by lobbying the government to eliminate competition by legislative fiat. American automobile, steel, and textile manufacturers have for decades lobbied to keep foreign competitors out of their markets. Cable TV companies lobby for, and receive, monopoly franchises in most cities, and they have also used their political clout to prevent telephone companies from entering the cable TV business, which fiber-optic cable now makes technologically feasible.

Many occupation-based groups, whether engaged in taxi driving or the practice of medicine, have procured laws that make it difficult for newcomers to enter the field and compete with those already there. One of the most egregious examples of this behavior is the New York City requirement that taxi drivers must purchase a license (a taxi "medallion"), either from the city government or from an existing license holder, that costs almost $150,000! Needless to say, most citizens cannot afford such a license. By limiting the number of outstanding licenses, city regulators guarantee an artificial scarcity that makes taxi fees higher than they would otherwise be. The quality of service is also undoubtedly lower, as it always is whenever competition is stifled.

In a comprehensive study of occupational licensing in America, S. David Young concluded that

> occupational regulation has served to limit consumer choice, raise consumer costs, increase practitioner income, limit practitioner mobility, deprive the poor of adequate services, and restrict job opportunities for minorities—all without a demonstrated improvement in quality or safety of the licensed activities. The evidence with respect to medicine, law, dentistry, and other highly visible professions is consistent with these findings. Indeed, some of the most blatant and indefensible abuses of licensure have been committed by the most revered professions.[1]

American consumers pay a heavy price indeed for monopolistic occupational licensing laws, especially in health-related professions. In an early study, Milton Friedman and Simon Kuznets found that the reason physicians make so much more money than dentists is that the number of medical schools in the United States declined by almost one-half between 1900 and 1950, and the number of physicians per 100,000 population fell from 157 in 1900 to 130 in 1938.[2] Fewer physicians means more costly medical care for patients.

In another study, William D. White found that hospital laboratory personnel earned 16 percent higher wages because of strict occupational licensing in that profession.[3] That extra 16 percent comes out of the pockets of those who pay the hospital bills, which consumers pay either directly out of pocket or indirectly through higher insurance premiums.

Lawrence Shephard discovered that in states where there are government-mandated competitive barriers in dentistry, the mean income of dentists is 15 percent higher than in other states, costing consumers approximately $700 million in 1976 (over $1 billion in current dollars).[4] Similar results have been obtained in other countries as well. Timothy Muzondo and Bohumir Pazderka studied advertising, fee setting, and mobility restrictions in twenty occupations and found that these elements "enhanced earnings by nearly 27 percent." The aggregate cost in 1970 to Canadian consumers was found to be almost $350 million (over $1 billion in current dollars), not counting the additional costs of entry restrictions.[5]

There are additional, and more insidious, costs related to restrictions on competition. Government-mandated entry restrictions channel the time and energy of some of the most talented and educated people into less productive pursuits, thereby reducing social efficiency. This is particularly true of the medical professions. As the economist Mancur Olson has written, "Professional associations and public policies that largely control the practice of law and of medicine are no doubt . . . costly to the society, because it is the time of some of the most highly educated and energetic people in the society that is being misallocated; yet few areas of modern society are so rife with cartels, anticompetitive rules, and other redistributions as are the law and medicine."[6]

Nowhere is the antipathy toward competition more prevalent than in the opposition voiced by public-school teachers' unions to "school choice" policies that would allow parents to send their children to alternative schools if they are dissatisfied with their public schools. As a rough measure of the cost to parents and taxpayers of the public-school monopoly, researchers have found that private schools that serve children with socioeconomic backgrounds similar to those in public schools spend about half the money that public schools do while providing a higher-quality education. Unencumbered by bureau-cracy and union work rules, many private schools can provide parents and children better education at half the price.[7] Members of teachers' unions, however, have enormous political clout, reportedly comprising almost one-half of all the delegates at the 1992 Democratic National Convention. They use that clout to maintain their monopoly power over the nation's school systems.

Large corporations are notorious for supporting costly government regulations, not because they think the regulations are a good idea—they rarely are—but because they know the regulations will impose dis-proportionate burdens on smaller businesses, many of which may be driven from the market. The cost to consumers of this reduced com-petition are hard to document precisely, but it is very real nevertheless. This is especially true of protectionism—the use of tariffs and quotas to stifle international competition. Economists have estimated that pro-tectionism in international trade costs consumers as much as $100 bil-lion per year, or approximately $1,700 for every family of four. The cost of a compact car, for example, is at least $2,500 higher because of protectionism.[8]

Whenever an organization succeeds in eliminating its competitors, consumers are inevitably the losers, suffering from lower-quality prod-ucts and services and higher prices. In the context of health charities, weaker competition will likely encourage the kind of questionable activ-ities and dubious or useless programs discussed in detail in earlier chapters. The losers in this process are the donors, the disease victims, and the public, all of whom suffer from slower progress in the war against disease.

In sum, there is a long history of organizations responding to competition by using their political clout to seek legal prohibitions of or reductions in competition. As a rule, whenever an organization complains about its competitors, its carping should be taken with a very large grain of salt. The complaints may have some merit, but more often than not they are an expression of sour grapes—or worse.

THE DECEPTIVE FUND-RAISING CHARGE

In 1989, representatives of the Big Three all testified at congressional hearings that their organizations were being harmed by deceptive or fraudulent fund-raising by look-alike organizations.[9] Clear-cut examples of deceptive fund-raising were commingled with whining about "illegitimate" fund-raising by look-alikes. "Fund-raising by the look-alike organizations . . . ought to be stopped," said Keith A. Greiner, chairman of the American Cancer Society, at the hearings. "The best interests of the public are not being served by what look-alikes do, and therefore, some legislation ought to be in order."[10]

This blanket condemnation and call for legislation assumes that government should put *all* so-called look-alikes out of business. But a closer examination of some of the specific complaints made by the Big Three reveals that their claims are motivated more by a desire to have the government grant them monopoly status than to advance the cause of public health or the public interest.

Greiner argued that government should eliminate look-alikes because "their fund-raising costs are extremely high in comparison to our fund-raising costs" and "typically exceed 50 percent."[11] But it is not unusual for an organization that has not yet established the kind of name recognition enjoyed by the American Cancer Society (ACS) to have higher fund-raising costs. Because of its reputation, the ACS can rely heavily—and at very little cost—on a loyal donor base from which it can expect many more or less "automatic" donations each year. Besides, who knows for certain how much the ACS or any other charity actually spends on fund-raising? As explained in chapter 5, many fund-raising expenses are passed off as public education costs, and it is possible that some community-service expenditures may also be fund-raising costs in disguise.

It is common knowledge among economists that a new business trying to enter a market dominated by an older, established firm must usually advertise more intensively than the established firm if it is to succeed. The new business may have good products or services, but consumers must be persuaded to switch brands. Similarly, a relatively new charity might have to advertise heavily to announce its programs and purposes to potential donors, and heavy advertising, of course, increases fund-raising costs.

There are also economies of scale in fund-raising. Once the initial heavy investment in a fund-raising apparatus is borne, the cost of raising additional funds is relatively low. In building a large donor base and developing name recognition, the ACS and the other established health charities have already incurred many such costs, but because newer organizations may not have, their fund-raising costs are higher, at least temporarily. Thus, it is not surprising that fund-raising costs as a percentage of total expenditures might be higher in newer charities than in older, more established ones.

In a truly remarkable case of the pot calling the kettle black, Greiner indignantly accused look-alikes of having higher fund-raising costs because much of their revenue is allegedly used not for cancer research, education, or patient assistance, but for salaries and perquisites for management and employees. "In our case," Greiner boasted, "at least 25 cents of every dollar is spent on bona fide, qualified research projects."[12] But, as discussed in chapter 5 and elsewhere, this claim is highly questionable, to say the least. Greiner knows plenty about perquisites—the ACS provides perquisites to its national executives and to the managers of its state affiliates. It is interesting that the Big Three pointedly omitted wealth accumulation from their litany of complaints about the newcomers. Undoubtedly, this omission is by design: The newcomers lack the vast holdings of real estate, cash, and automobile fleets that raise so many questions about the operations of the Big Three.

Another complaint the ACS lodged against its competitors is that look-alikes supposedly "use a name which is similar to our name" and "typically use a topic like cancer . . . that gets the public very excited."[13] But one wonders just what name might be chosen by a cancer-research organization if the term *cancer* were not included. And besides, the ACS also gets the public "very excited" with its own fund-raising appeals, which typically include stark and scary statistics about projected cancer deaths. Why is this tactic not equally legitimate for the ACS's competitors? Apparently, what's good for the goose is not good for the gander.

IMAGE BUILDING

The Big Three spend considerable time and resources on self-praise. "No other private organization can match the reputation the American Cancer Society has earned," says the ACS's *Manual for Dealing with Look-Alike and Sound-Alike Organizations* submitted as evidence at the congressional hearings.

Although much of the American public appears to accept these self-serving claims, they reek of smug self-satisfaction. Most other institutions would not be taken seriously if they were to make such claims. It would sound absurd if a member of the House of Representatives, for example, declared that "no other organization can match the reputation for honesty, sobriety, and intelligence that we in the Congress have earned." Or if a manufacturer declared that "none of our competitors can even come close to duplicating the quality of our product." Such statements would rightly be viewed as self-serving nonsense, but are somehow taken seriously when made by the major health charities.

Whenever private businesses or politicians make such claims, they are typically regarded with a hefty skepticism. A business must always pass a market test to back up its advertising rhetoric; if consumers disagree with the firm's puffery of its product or service, they will avoid the company's offerings in the future. The politician must eventually run for election or reelection, at which time the voters judge his or her credibility at the polling booth.

But in the nonprofit sector, both marketplace and political constraints are very weak, if they exist at all. There is no bottom line, and neither health-charity managers nor the members of their boards of directors ever have to run for election. Consequently, the health charities have great latitude to make self-serving claims that, being cloaked in the word *charity,* are accepted as accurate by most citizens. Never having to prove their claims in a competitive marketplace or by facing an electorate, the health charities invest heavily in public-relations campaigns designed to substitute rhetoric for actual performance. Such self-serving claims should be met with at least as much skepticism as they would be if they were made by a business or politician. The phrase "caveat emptor"—let the buyer beware—might more appropriately be rephrased as "caveat contributor." A healthy skepticism is just as valuable to a charity's donors as it is to a business's customers.

GANGING UP ON LOOK-ALIKES

The American Lung Association's Complaints

Joyce Waite, deputy managing director for administration at the American Lung Association (ALA), also warned Congress of look-alikes "who would deliberately mislead and deceive the American public" and that should be dealt with by Congress "in an aggressive manner" because "our country's entire system and spirit of voluntarism is at stake."[14]

These are certainly alarming statements. Is America's much-vaunted "spirit of voluntarism" really at stake? Is charity in America really at risk? When given the opportunity to substantiate her claims to the congressional committee, Waite could offer only three trivial examples: a North Carolina stop-smoking hypnosis group that allegedly used the ALA's address in its fund-raising; a New Mexico organization whose name was "too similar" to the ALA's because it contained the words *lung association;* and "several" unnamed organizations that allegedly committed the "crime" of using names, slogans, or fund-raising methods similar to the ALA's.

Although the first case might be one of deception or fraud, the second two could just as easily be construed as signs of healthy competition. Any organization involved in research on lung disease or in assisting afflicted patients would have to have the word *lung* in its title, along with the term *association* or *organization.* The ALA does not have a trademark on these words, nor does it own a patent on mail solicitation or door-to-door fund-raising methods that are routinely employed by thousands of nonprofit organizations.

If look-alikes were as heavily involved in deception as Waite claimed, one would think that more than three isolated and rather minor examples would have been uncovered and reported to her by the ALA's 132 local and regional affiliates, by its thousands of volunteers and employees, and by its many friends in the media. The media love a good scandal, and fund-raising fraud is prime scandal material. Such illegalities are always good for a newspaper headline or the lead story on the local television news. If there were a genuine scandal of serious proportions, the media would surely have exposed it long ago. Either the ALA has not bothered to bring such scandals to the media's attention, or the scandals do not exist. Given the ALA's intense interest in this issue, it is likely that it did as much as possible to interest the media in the look-alike issue. Clearly, the ALA exaggerates the alleged misdeeds of the newer health charities.

After making her remarkably weak case against the newcomers, Waite further argued that the public should rely exclusively on the ALA's advice about which organizations deserve financial support. But wouldn't this be similar to, say, the Chrysler Corporation arguing that the car-buying public should rely exclusively on its assessment of which automobile to purchase? Wouldn't its assessment ignore Ford, General Motors, Toyota, and its other competitors? Who could possibly take such advice seriously?

In case the public did not want to rely on the ALA's advice, Waite also urged the public to seek information from independent sources, such as the National Charities Information Bureau (NCIB). But as discussed in chapter 4, the NCIB relies on *self-reported* financial data from the ALA and other charities. And according to NCIB President Kenneth Albrecht, "There's vast misrepresentation of expenditures going on right now, and it's growing."[15] Since the NCIB's data comes from the charities it monitors, using the NCIB as a reliable guide for donations is akin to relying on the American car manufacturers' trade association as an "unbiased" source of information when choosing between American- and foreign-made automobiles.

The American Heart Association's Complaints

The American Heart Association (AHA) expressed similar alarm at the congressional hearings. Board Chairman William Van't Hof warned that deceptive fund-raising is a national problem that "is clearly growing in size and one that may require a national solution" in the form of federal legislation and regulation.[16]

Like the ALA, the AHA has over one hundred local affiliates and claims over 2.5 million volunteers. Yet despite the massive size of his organization, the best Van't Hof could do to convince Congress of the supposedly urgent need for a "national solution" was to offer two notably undistinguished examples: (1) a handwritten note by a potential contributor in Idaho who claimed to have read of a competing heart-research association, confused it with the AHA, and discovered that the competitor allegedly spent almost 90 percent of its revenues on fund-raising; and (2) an organization that raised money for heart research and had the audacity to call itself a heart fund!

Shocked and dismayed by the heart fund's "impropriety," Van't Hof announced that "we have written this sound-alike organization asking them to cease and desist." Does it not seem reasonable, however, for an organization involved in fund-raising for heart research to include the words *fund* and *heart* in its name? Van't Hof's complaint is analogous to General Motors complaining that Ford produced an Oldsmobile look-alike, writing Ford a letter urging it to "cease and desist" production, and lobbying Congress to pass a law outlawing all Fords. In short, Van't Hof's reaction seems exaggerated.

Van't Hof condemned profit-seeking organizations and praised his own organization, whose activities are supposedly conducted "without intention of seeking profit." "The problem we face," he said, "is trust." Look-alikes supposedly violate the public trust because they are less efficient and effective than the AHA, which "spends approximately 23 percent of its income on . . . fund-raising and administrative expenses, leaving more than 75 percent . . . for the specific purposes of the organization, including 32 percent which goes to research, more than 25 percent to public and professional education, and more than 15 percent to community service."[17] Again, as explained in chapters 4 through 6, such percentages are highly questionable.

As the oldest and largest heart charity, the AHA has for years been a virtual monopoly. It is not surprising, therefore, that its "product," like the product of any monopoly, is not of the highest quality. Nor is it surprising that some of its top executives appear to be detached from reality or overreact when faced with even a hint of competition from so-called look-alikes. Van't Hof's condemnation of "profit seeking" by look-alike organizations and his contention that the AHA operates "without intention of seeking profit" are bizarre in light of the AHA's efforts to sell its HeartGuide Seal for a profit—even to producers of foods that were 100 percent fat!

Encouraging Deception

In its *Manual for Dealing with Look-Alike and Sound-Alike Organizations,* the ACS encourages its state and local affiliates to use deception themselves. The manual contains numerous sample letters to the editor written by ACS public-relations specialists. The manual instructs the ACS staff member or volunteer to identify himself or herself only as a "concerned citizen," while the sample letters cast aspersions on organizations that compete with the ACS in fund-raising.[18] The idea, apparently, is for such letters to appear spontaneous and genuine rather than to be recognized for what they really are—a deliberate contrivance of the ACS's public-relations and propaganda machine.

The manual advises caution, for "there are certain dangers in an active campaign against look-alikes [and] we do not wish to be perceived as self-serving whistle blowers attempting to bully lesser organizations from the cancer arena" (which is, of course, exactly what the ACS is trying to do). Accordingly, affiliates are warned to avoid "direct confrontation, which could appear self-serving, by enlisting the support of third parties" such as "staff and volunteers from other major nonprofit organizations, like the American Heart Association."[19]

Isn't it odd that the central complaint against look-alikes raised by the Big Three is that the newcomers are self-serving rather than interested solely in public service? Despite such arguments, and without hesitation, the ACS also engages in self-serving practices, such as attempting to eliminate its competition through a smear campaign. Since the campaign apparently fizzled, the ACS and its allies attempted to enlist members of Congress to back a political solution to the "problem" of competition. In other words, the ACS's idea is to collude with the AHA and ALA in attacking look-alike organizations without revealing to the public that those involved are affiliated with the Big Three and engaged in anticompetitive activity.

With regard to one sample letter to the editor entitled "Look-Alike Nonprofit Organizations Cheating the Public," ACS affiliates are advised to label look-alikes as "cheaters": "When we were in school, there were always cheaters. . . . From school, the cheaters have moved on to business, politics, and sports. . . . Now it seems, the cheating element has taken another step downhill and entered the field of nonprofit organizations, particularly in the area of cancer research." These "cheaters," the manual continues, are "like the lady who took a short cut in the New York Marathon . . . or the athletes at the Olympics who used steroids." By entering the nonprofit fund-raising field, "the flimflam man has found another way to prey upon honest people."[20]

As far as actual evidence of "cheating" is concerned, sample letters in the ACS manual recommend accusing look-alikes of using "words like 'Foundation,' 'Research,' 'Society,' 'National,' or 'American' in their titles."[21] But since the ACS does not have a trademark on words like *research* or *foundation,* and since there are many legitimate cancer-research foundations, one wonders why such language is expected to produce shock and indignation among those who read the letter.

As further alleged evidence of cheating, the manual suggests that look-alikes be accused of placing some of the funds they raise "into their bank accounts instead of into cancer research."[22] As discussed in chapter 4, however, ACS affiliates also hold hundreds of millions of dollars in cash, securities, real estate, buildings, and fleets of automobiles, so funds that could have been used for cancer research or for assisting cancer patients and their families have been hoarded by the ACS. The ALA and AHA also have large asset holdings. For the ACS to accuse *other* cancer charities of cheating by keeping cash and other assets in reserve is hypocritical and deceptive.

Lobbying the States

The Big Three have not only attempted to enlist the aid of Congress in eliminating their fund-raising competition, they have also used their political clout at the state level of government. For example, the ACS recently persuaded the Pennsylvania attorney general, Ernie Preate, Jr., to sue a competing cancer charity, the Cancer Fund of America (CFA), for allegedly confusing the public. According to a letter to the editor signed by Paula J. Fritz, executive director of the McKean County, Pennsylvania, ACS, "what the Cancer Fund of America is doing is not illegal." But the attorney general's office has "received enough calls to warrant the filing of a lawsuit against CFA."[23]

Curiously, the attorney general does not accuse the CFA of illegality, but of confusing the public because "the door-to-door volunteer program described by CFA in its solicitation materials is very similar to that established and traditionally used by the American Cancer Society."[24] Apparently, the ACS and the Pennsylvania attorney general believe the ACS should enjoy a legal monopoly on door-to-door solicitation! One has to wonder: Can the Girl Scouts legally sell cookies door to door in the Keystone state?

Interestingly, when faced with public criticism over this nonsensical notion, the Pennsylvania attorney general's office contradicted itself. In a letter to a citizen who had inquired about the CFA, Mollie A. McCurdy, chief deputy attorney general, stated explicitly that "no charity has a monopoly on a method of solicitation, including door-to-door campaigns."[25] This letter was written three months *before the lawsuit was filed.* Apparently, the ACS persuaded the attorney general to reverse his position. In fact, Attorney General Preate admitted that the ACS came to him and lobbied him to file the lawsuit against its competitor: "I am delighted to be used by the American Cancer Society," he told the *Harrisburg Patriot.*[26]

Even though the attorney general of Pennsylvania never accused the CFA of doing anything illegal, and the accounting firm of Peat

Marwick concluded that the CFA's financial practices "are in conformity with generally accepted accounting principles," the state of Pennsylvania apparently forced the CFA and five other charities into a consent agreement that required each of them to pay more $50,000 to other charities in the state and to the attorney general's office. The CFA paid the fine rather than expend far greater resources in continued litigation with the state of Pennsylvania, which has seemingly unlimited legal resources. If "you can't fight city hall," fighting the much bigger and better-funded statehouse is out of the question.

What seems to have occurred in this case is that the ACS convinced a Pennsylvania public official to harass its competitors and to file a lawsuit that would threaten to bankrupt the defendants even if they won the suit. Realizing that a legal battle against the state of Pennsylvania is an impossible task for a small charity, the so-called look-alikes decided to cut their losses in a consent agreement. Then the attorney general gave much of the money collected from the fines not to the state treasury, but to the ACS! The ACS received thousands of dollars by getting a state official to attempt to drive its competitors out of existence.

All the newer health charities could do was to issue press releases protesting their treatment by the state. In one, James T. Reynolds, CFA's president, stated that the Pennsylvania attorney general "allowed his office to be used by the American Cancer Society in order to limit CFA's ability to serve its charitable purpose. They see CFA as a threat to their near monopolistic use of volunteers to solicit door-to-door."[27]

SHOOTING ONESELF IN THE FOOT

As strange as it might seem at first, the older, established health charities might be shooting themselves in the foot, so to speak, by trying to eliminate competition from newer charities. Simply put, the Big Three might receive more, rather than less, revenue because of the activities of the look-alikes. The established charities view the total amount of contributions to their causes as fixed and fund-raising as a zero-sum game: Each dollar collected by look-alikes is a dollar not collected by the Big Three. This view is erroneous for two reasons: First, the total donations "pot" is enlarged by the existence of look-alikes, and second, the older charities are likely to benefit more from the larger pot than the look-alikes whose efforts cause the pot to grow.

This reasoning, which at first glance might seem odd, can be illustrated by an analogy to the automobile market. Suppose that a new car maker, Lemon, tries to break into the market by running television ads that entice customers to purchase its new sedan. Millions of viewers see the Lemon ads, but most are loyal to *long-established* automakers, such as Ford, General Motors, Chrysler, Toyota, Nissan, Mercedes, and Honda.

The newcomer's ads may indeed persuade some viewers to buy a new car. But only a few will buy the Lemon sedan; most of those who catch the new-car "bug" as a result of Lemon's ads will not go to the newcomer's dealerships because of their allegiance to other brands. Thus, whether it intends to or not, by advertising its sedan the new firm increases the total number of new cars purchased from all makers. But due to consumer loyalty and brand recognition, the primary beneficiaries are the *other* automakers. The major automakers might well sell more cars with the competition and advertising from the newcomer than they would if the newcomer did not exist.

In the context of health charities, successful fund-raising requires all look-alikes to tout their diseases, thereby increasing public concern and awareness about disease in general. By enhancing donor interest in various diseases, which encourages additional contributions, the newly formed groups increase the total amount contributed for their particular diseases. But many contributors exhibit brand loyalty to various charities: They view the ACS as the primary cancer charity; the AHA as the primary heart fund; and the ALA as the primary lung-disease charity. The Big Three will thus get a disproportionately large share of any increase in total donations.

Taking the logic one step further, there's yet another reason why the Big Three could be much better off with competition from look-alikes, especially if the look-alikes actually *are* scams! Suppose a donor, who has for years been generous to the ACS and is totally committed to its goals and programs, receives a mail solicitation from the National Cancer Appeal (NCA) that states in microscopic print that "your donation will finance a 'conference' in Acapulco for us and our friends." Conscientious contributors who read the fine print will put the NCA's solicitation in the trash—the cause is not worthy of their support. But it is also quite possible that these donors will think along the following lines:

1. I received this appeal from this clearly fraudulent look-alike, and thousands of other people probably found it in their mailbox, too.

2. I checked the fine print, as I always do with mail solicitations, but most people probably don't bother to read the small print.
3. Other people will be taken in by this scam and will send money to the NCA rather than the ACS—the most deserving of all cancer charities.
4. I don't want to see the ACS hurt by these shysters, so I am going to *increase* my gift to the ACS this year and will encourage my family and friends to increase their donations also.

DECEPTION VERSUS COMPETITION

No one doubts that there have been instances of deceptive or fraudulent fund-raising by nonprofit organizations in the cancer field and elsewhere, just as there is a degree of fraud, misuse, and abuse of funds in business, government, religion, and every other institution in contemporary America. The American Association of Fund-Raising Counsel has estimated, however, that *less than 1 percent of more than $100 billion raised annually for charitable purposes constitutes fraud.*[28] One wouldn't guess that the figure was so low, however, by listening to the executives of the Big Three, who have done their best to insinuate that fund-raising fraud is rampant. In calling for nothing less than a legal prohibition of fund-raising by the newer health charities, these executives have implied that fund-raising fraud is closer to 20 percent than 1 percent of sums raised.

Without denying the significance of deceptive fund-raising and the need to stop it, it is important to distinguish carefully between deception and healthy competition. Many so-called look-alike fund-raising organizations provide valuable services that clearly benefit the public. Competition produces a larger overall volume of products or services, improves quality, and is as beneficial to the nonprofit sector as it is to business and politics.

Some of the major health charities have gone to the extreme of asking the federal government to ban look-alike charities that compete with them for donations. The old-line organizations have proposed that their activities be judged not in comparison with those of newer charities (which they think should be outlawed), but rather by information in their own annual reports and information provided by them to the National Charities Information Bureau. This would be akin to the domestic auto industry asking the government for a complete ban on foreign competition and suggesting that domestic autos be judged not according to consumer choice and comparison shopping, but according to self-serving information provided by the industry itself. This notion will not withstand even casual examination.

Although there are genuine concerns about deceptive or fraudulent fund-raising, much of the political activities by the major health charities seem to be nothing more than another example of powerful special interests using the powers of the state to thwart legitimate competition.

9

IS THERE A CURE FOR WHAT AILS HEALTH CHARITIES?

Of every thousand dollars spent in so-called charity today, it is possible that nine hundred and fifty dollars is unwisely spent—so spent, indeed, as to produce the very evil which it hopes to mitigate or cure.
—Andrew Carnegie, 1933

Andrew Carnegie, a founding father of the U.S. steel industry, was also one of America's most celebrated philanthropists. He contributed generously to educational and religious causes, establishing hundreds of free public libraries and providing organs for numerous churches. As a businessman, Carnegie's "efficiency and his thorough knowledge of the industry" earned him the reputation of a "terror" among his fellow steel producers. His business motto—"Watch the costs and the profits will take care of themselves"—personified his belief that success depended on detailed knowledge of business operations and costs.[1]

His business philosophy extended to his charitable endeavors, which is why his claim that 95 percent of all charity dollars was spent "unwisely" might not have been an exaggeration. Carnegie himself was committed to charity, but was convinced that the vast majority of charitable monies were wasted. Thus, the notion that charity programs are inefficient and that much more could be achieved with the contributions that they receive is not new. Questions about charitable operations have existed for more than a half-century.

All charities are susceptible to unwise spending because, as discussed in chapter 2, nonprofits are insulated from both market and political competition. Competition provides at least some incentives for efficiency and constrains the actions of for-profit and government organizations. Nonprofits are overseen by self-perpetuating boards of directors and no one—other than their executives and staffs and the interest groups that benefit from their operations—has a direct financial interest in their survival.

Health charities are particularly susceptible to inefficient operations for at least two reasons. First, the vast majority of their funds is obtained from millions of small contributions from the general public, and a donor who gives $5, $10, or even $50 has little incentive to investigate carefully how his or her donation is spent on the health charity's activities. In contrast, many nonprofit organizations, such as educational institutions and public-policy groups, receive most of their revenues not from individual donors but from foundations and corporations. Major donors have both the expertise and the motivation to monitor the programs they finance and, if they believe that their contributions were not well spent, future grants will not be provided. Thus, there are some checks and balances on nonprofits that depend on large grants from major donors, but these checks and balances do not apply to nonprofits that raise most of their funds from the general public.

Second, unlike most other charities—even those that seek funds from the general public—many health charity donations are motivated by emotions, such as grief over the loss of a loved one or a friend. Legacies and bequests from disease victims seeking to spare others from their fates are not uncommon, and it is obviously impossible for such donors to raise questions from the grave about how their contributions were spent.

Fewer external checks and balances on a nonprofit's activities increase the likelihood that the organization will be inefficient and will serve special interest groups—in the case of health charities, executives and staff and the medical establishment. Earlier chapters document that such behavior is not hypothetical, but has existed for decades. Recently, the United Way of America scandal highlighted clearly how loose external controls and the absence of effective internal oversight permitted its chief executive to misuse charitable donations on a grand scale over a period of years. Among hospitals, nursing homes, and insurance companies, there is ample evidence of exploitation of an organization's nonprofit status for personal benefit. It is not surprising, therefore, that there is ample potential for inefficiencies in the nation's voluntary health agencies. Because donors have virtually no incentive and little expertise to monitor how their donations are spent, health-charity managers have wide discretion, which permits them to pursue programs that often benefit managers and staffs and the medical profession more than patients, their families, and the public. As Senator Sam Nunn (D-Ga.) has observed, such behavior appears to be "prevalent" in the nonprofit health area.[2]

Our study is predicated on the belief that health charities accomplish a great deal of good—there is no doubt about the validity of this statement. If the health charities had for decades grossly abused the public trust by misusing their revenues, sooner or later that behavior would have been discovered and exposed. Thus, our objective is not to uncover scandal, but to address four simple questions that bear repeating here. These are questions that should be of central concern to every conscientious contributor:

1. Does the charity use its funds efficiently by producing services and programs at the lowest cost?
2. Does the charity use its funds for the purposes described in its fund-raising appeals?
3. Do those in need benefit from the charity's programs?
4. From the perspective of society and contributors, could better results be achieved by redirecting resources to other activities; in other words, are the charity's programs appropriate?

The health charities contend that the first three answers should each be yes and that the fourth answer should be no. According to the health charities, two independent watchdogs ensure that donations are spent appropriately: the health charities' auditors and charity-rating groups, especially the National Charities Information Bureau (NCIB) and the Philanthropic Advisory Service (PAS) of the Better Business Bureau. But neither auditors nor rating services have uncovered malfeasance in the past: Major scandals were revealed at United Way of America and at Covenant House *after* approval by both charity-rating services and their independent auditors. Clearly, something is amiss.

Both the rating services and the auditors use the same financial information in assessing a health charity's performance, but these data cannot be used to answer any of the four basic questions that we believe are essential to understanding whether a particular charity is good, bad, or indifferent. The crux of the difficulty is that the cost of providing a service is counted as part of the service itself. Thus, a charity that is very inefficient—that has high costs—may appear to be doing a great deal of good if one looks only at its financial statements.

Although many health charities describe themselves as voluntary organizations that rely heavily on volunteers who, by definition, are not paid or compensated for their services, the fact remains that as much as half of all revenues are spent on salaries, fringe benefits, and payroll taxes. By any standard, health-charity executives are well compensated;

one can do very well financially by purporting to do good. Thus, the efficiency of the health charities could be greatly enhanced if better use were made of the volunteer armies under their command, even if no other changes were made.

Readers may be surprised, if not shocked, to learn that the health charities have accumulated tens of millions of dollars in cash, certificates of deposit, stocks and bonds, fleets of automobiles, and land and buildings while claiming in fund-raising appeals that there is a desperate shortage of funds to finance programs. This wealth clearly benefits health-charity executives and staffs, but it raises questions about the ultimate goals of these organizations and the mind set of their executives.

The ultimate goal of every health charity should be to go out of existence—to find cures for its disease. Thus, one would expect every health-charity executive and staff member to start each year with the conviction that *this* is the year that cancer or heart or lung disease is conquered and that aid to disease victims will be better than ever. To maximize the probability that these goals are achieved, every dollar available must be spent on the health charity's mission and as effectively as possible. When donations are used to acquire assets, funds are diverted from programs—unless the assets are programs themselves, such as the American Cancer Society's Hope Lodges. Ownership of commercial property and land also diverts management attention away from the organization's central mission: the battle against disease. At the very least, if donations are used to purchase land, buildings, automobiles, and so forth, the health charities should inform donors that this is how their donations will be used.

HEALTH-CHARITY ACTIVITIES

To understand and evaluate what the Big Three (the American Cancer Society, the American Heart Association, and the American Lung Association) really do, it is necessary to analyze the content of their programs, not the financial data related to these programs. Most service activities are conducted by the state and local units of health charities rather than the national headquarters because most volunteers work in the communities where they live. In general terms, health charity programs consist of five activities, although not all health charities engage in all five: public education, professional education, research, patient services, and community services.

Public Education

We believe that health charities spend too much for public education, for three reasons. First, how is it possible to educate the public about diseases that the medical profession admits it does not understand? Second, much of the lifestyle advice offered by the health charities (see your doctor if you have heartburn, for you may actually have cancer) is so simplistic that it is not only worthless but it may also *disarm* the public, much like the boy who cried "Wolf!" did. Worse, much of the lifestyle advice is misleading, contradictory, and in some cases flat-out wrong, leading to adverse health consequences. In the one instance in which the health advice is undoubtedly sound (tobacco is harmful to health), the information has become such common knowledge that it is difficult to justify spending large sums to educate the public any further. Finally, the health charities' own statistics showing how many people are educated about disease each year, if valid, state that large proportions of the public have already gotten the messages. So why continue to spend tens of millions of dollars each year beating the same drum?

Professional Education

It is difficult to justify using charitable donations to pay for the continuing education of health professionals who, as a group, earn among the highest incomes in the nation. Clearly, professional education is important—everyone wants their physicians, dentists, and nurses to be up to date on the latest drugs and treatments—but this fact does not suggest that it is appropriate for the health charities to pay for or subsidize this education. Other professionals pay for their continuing education, and such fees are tax-deductible as a business expense. To ask donors—who, on average, undoubtedly earn less than medical professionals—to pay for the latters' continuing education is nothing less than Robin Hood in reverse. There are too many unmet needs for each of the Big Three to spend large sums annually for this purpose.

At the same time that substantial sums are available to educate medical professionals, little spending seems to be targeted to the poor—at least in the case of the American Cancer Society (ACS). In 1989, the ACS issued a report entitled *Cancer and the Poor,* which stated that the poor were not being adequately served by cancer programs; that cancer education for the poor was "insensitive and irrelevant"; and that the poor suffered disproportionately from cancer. The essence of charity is to help those who cannot help themselves. Donors expect their contributions to help those who are less fortunate than they are. In fact, the critical considerations for a prospective donor are not only how much of each dollar received actually provides services, but also *who is being served*. Conventional wisdom may hold that health-charity dollars are spent first and foremost on the poor, but the facts do not bear this out.

Before criticizing the ACS for its revelation that the poor do not receive adequate cancer services and education, it is important to recognize that the American Heart Association spends *nothing* on patient services and that the American Lung Association allocates less than 1 percent of its annual income to provide direct aid to lung-disease patients—despite fund-raising rhetoric suggesting otherwise. Many health charities do little to aid the poor, although they often allude to such programs in their appeals for contributions. A major problem that must be addressed is how to ensure that donations to charity reach the needy rather than the relatively well-off.

Research

The Big Three emphasize research in their fund-raising appeals to the public. Everyone hopes to see disease eradicated; the victories over polio and smallpox whetted the public's appetite for more successes. Although it is not widely known, health charities play at best a minor role in disease research. With regard to cancer, the taxpayer (via the federal National Cancer Institute) spends more each year on cancer research than the ACS has spent in its entire history. Also unrecognized is that the health charities often do not support researchers in their quest to learn the causes of and cures for disease. Rather, many health charities offer seed grants so that recipients can write proposals to obtain larger grants from the National Institutes of Health (NIH). By engaging in this practice, the health charities support the work of a small, tightly knit group of researchers and institutions. Through the latters' close links with the NIH, we assert, health charities may hinder research progress by discouraging innovative approaches. A small research clique exerts significant control over the disease-research agenda, a structure that may impede major breakthroughs. In other words, the likelihood of major breakthroughs might be greatly improved if health charities withdrew from the research arena entirely— a counterintuitive proposal that has also been advanced by other critics who claim that the medical establishment, in collaboration with the health charities, direct research to channels that maximize the likelihood of profit. Although we do not share the notion that profits drive the research agenda, we demonstrated that the same conclusion can be reached by assuming that the health charities are motivated only by the very best of intentions in the research arena. The problem, however, is that the best of intentions are not sufficient to guarantee good results. According to the old adage, the road to hell is paved with good intentions.

Patient and Community Services

Health charities have an important role to play in the battle against disease. We believe these organizations can accomplish a great deal more good with the resources they already have at their disposal simply by redirecting their funds and activities to those areas where they have a comparative advantage. What distinguishes charities from all other institutions in society is their ability to mobilize and direct the efforts of volunteers. Aside from their role in fund-raising campaigns, volunteers are ideally suited to carry out two activities: aid to disease victims (that is, patient services) and community services. Better use of volunteers through expanded patient and community services would provide major benefits to society. The funds used to support the expansion of patient and community services already exist: Vast sums would be made available if the health charities greatly reduced or eliminated subsidies for educating affluent medical professionals, drastically lowered spending on dubious or duplicative public education programs, and withdrew from the disease-research arena. Hundreds of millions of additional dollars could also be obtained by using accumulated wealth for patient and community programs. Indeed, we argue that a great deal could be done to alleviate the nation's health care crisis if the health charities cooperated with free community clinics to aid the medically indigent.

The programs offered by the American Cancer Society to cancer victims serve as models of what can be accomplished by voluntary efforts in local communities. The ACS organizes volunteers to transport cancer patients to their medical treatments; loans equipment; provides medicine and nutritional supplements; conducts a number of rehabilitative programs; sponsors cancer-patient support groups; provides information about cancer and its treatment; and aids patients in obtaining housing near medical centers when they travel from distant locations to receive medical care. Even though these programs are exemplary and provide a prototype for other health charities to follow, the ACS's own statistics pointedly reveal that many potential clients are not currently being served, so much more must be done.

The need for charitable assistance for disease victims is not only enormous, but is also rapidly growing. The elderly are the fastest-growing segment of the nation's population and, as a group, make the greatest demands on the nation's health care system. Even though the medical needs of the poor and uninsured are not currently being met, the Big Three convinced a congressional committee to hold hearings on look-alike organizations, newly formed entities in the health field that might compete with the long-established health charities for contributions. The goal of the Big Three was to use the power of government to ban these upstarts and to label them "frauds." To some degree, fraud exists everywhere—in the for-profit sector, in government, and in the nonprofit sector, including religious organizations—but there is no persuasive evidence that fraud is widespread among new health charities. Moreover, there are sound reasons to expect that existing health charities actually benefit financially from the newcomers' activities, even if some of the new groups are, in fact, pure scams. Rather than spend time, energy, and funds on an inquisition against so-called look-alikes, the established health charities would make better use of these resources by aiding needy disease victims.

R_x: LET THE SUNSHINE IN

Certainly, when an organization . . . enters the general marketplace in
seeking funds, it has an obligation to publicly account for the use of
these funds. —Carl Bakal, *Charity U.S.A.*

How can health charities be encouraged to spend their funds more efficiently and to direct their services to those in need? The health charities, like other organizations, have a built-in bureaucratic inertia that propels them along in their comfortable routines and discourages zero-based budgeting for programs. Once started, programs take on a life of their own, and the managers and staffs whose jobs and livelihoods depend on these activities become active lobbyists for not only the continuation but also the expansion of their roles in the organization. The external forces that limit, at least to some degree, the bureaucratic impulses in for-profit businesses and in government enterprises are largely absent in the nonprofit sector, and donors cannot count on auditors and watchdog groups to provide the necessary incentives for change.

This leaves two realistic alternatives for disciplining the management of health charities: ethics and public scrutiny. Promoting ethical behavior is certainly a worthwhile objective; social reformers of one sort or another have tried this approach for decades. There is a widely held belief, for example, that putting more ethical people in government will improve its efficiency. This seems to be the modus operandi of the politically active religious right. Most business schools now offer courses in business ethics, and many corporations offer seminars on the subject for their managers. But after decades of experimentation, such programs have produced few successes. It appears that ethical norms are not something that can be quickly or easily altered by university courses, seminars, or public policy.

So public scrutiny is the more likely tool for reforming health charities. We advocate states' adoption of "sunshine laws" that would make it easier for citizens to garner detailed information about the activities and expenditures of nonprofit organizations. This approach is especially appropriate for nonprofits that receive most of their funding from the general public. For example, many states already have freedom of information laws that apply to state agencies and even to their employees. In Virginia, for example, the salaries of state university faculty and administrators are easily obtained simply by requesting the listing, which is kept in university libraries. Any citizen—or, more importantly, any investigative journalist or interested scholar—can readily discover how much university employees are being paid.

Something akin to the federal Freedom of Information Act would also be useful at the state level, so that donors could obtain certain information about health charities' expenditures. Citizens should be able to examine these expenditures through access to the charities' detailed financial records, including expenditure receipts. This would permit interested parties to discover not just how much was spent in total on travel, but whether the traveler flew coach or first class (or on the Concorde), stayed at luxury hotels or at motel chains, ate at five-star or moderately priced restaurants, and hired a cab or a chauffeured limousine. If the funds are spent appropriately, why should a health charity have any reservations about letting anyone who asks look at its payment vouchers and receipts that are used to justify expenditures?

At first glance, this solution seems to accomplish little. After all, making information available on request does not provide any incentives for small donors to take the time and effort to ask for that information. The point, however, is that merely requiring the information to be readily available will, in and of itself, have a "chilling" effect on the activities and expenditures of the health charities. Would the executives of the Washington, D.C., Blue Cross–Blue Shield affiliate have spent tens of thousands of dollars flying on the Concorde or purchasing vintage wine and other perks if they knew that anyone could examine their expense accounts at any time? Would William Aramony of United Way of America have charged new golf clubs to his expense account if this were the case? Would he have spent huge sums on chauffeured limousines if the limousine invoices were open to public examination? We doubt it.

The important point is that sunshine laws make it easy for anyone to investigate in detail what's going on inside the health charities, and it only takes the effort of one enterprising journalist or researcher to blow the whistle on excesses and alert the public to questionable expenditures and activities. Even a small chance that an investigative journalist or a scholar would delve into payrolls, expense accounts, annual meeting expenses, lists of property acquisitions, and similar documents that chart how health charities and other nonprofits are spending donors' contributions would make board members and executives think twice about their programs and expenditures.

The revelations about the inefficient use or abuse of funds by charities that have been revealed to date are likely just the tip of a very large iceberg. Moreover, these surfaced only by chance. The United Way of America (UWA) scandal brewed for years while the UWA staff said nothing. If it weren't for disgruntled employees or former employees occasionally blowing the whistle, the UWA episode might never have surfaced and the abuses could have continued indefinitely. Thus, there is a need to provide better public access to information about the financing and activities of health and other charities that seek donations from the general public.

The value of enhanced access to information is illustrated by the aftermath of the UWA scandal. Once the story was published and the UWA's practices became public knowledge, many donors *and board members* awoke from their complacency and began doing what they should have been doing all along: asking questions about UWA expenditures. According to the *Washington Post*, after the scandal broke, "more donors [were] writing letters about pay levels while directors [were] more likely to raise questions and request data to set executive salaries." National Charities Information Bureau President Kenneth Albrecht added that "there is an awful lot of attention being paid to these salaries . . . and this kind of attention hasn't been there before. . . . You have board members now wondering how salaries will look in the papers." The UWA scandal created a ripple effect of concern about charities. "Until the United Way business," said Albrecht, "I don't believe I got any letters talking about salaries [of nonprofit managers]."[3]

The lessons from the UWA episode are straightforward. Substantial abuse can occur over long periods of time if information is withheld from the public. Revelations of wrongdoing at one charity can set off a chain reaction of interest in the activities and expenditures of others, any of which, if the information were accessible, could also be investigated. Most states require charities that solicit donations within their borders to file financial and other statements with the state attorney general or similar office, but in many cases the requirement is for only the most basic information. Moreover, because there is little oversight, much of the information can be false or misleading. According to the *Washington Post*, "Some charities operating in Maryland routinely file reports with the state that give consumers misleading or incomplete accounts of their spending practices, and dozens of others fail to comply with any official disclosure requirement." As Maryland regulator Winfield M. Kelly, Jr., told the *Post*, "Very little information is made available about the operation of charities. . . . If it's true in Maryland, it's probably true everywhere else in the country."[4]

Unlike other critics, whose proposals are undoubtedly well intentioned, we do not believe that the solution to charity problems lies in giving regulators more power to control and regulate charities. Government regulations have a tendency to create burdens—in terms of the time, effort, and resources required to comply with them—that often outweigh any social benefit. It would be unwise to increase the regulatory burden on nonprofits because the resources spent complying with regulations would not be available for charitable purposes.

Experience tells us that it would be far more effective to empower *donors* rather than regulators with the ability to monitor charities, just as it is almost always better to empower consumers rather than government bureaucracies to regulate for-profit firms. It is particularly telling that the United Way of America had turned its operations around (including the firing of William Aramony) because of pubic scrutiny, not because a new federal or state regulatory agency was created or a new set of regulations devised.

The ultimate responsibility for the operations of charities lies with their respective boards of directors. As discussed in earlier chapters, many of these directors are complacent and detached from the day-to-day operations, which gives the charity's management (usually with the help of a small clique of directors) wide discretion in the organization's operations. In far too many instances, the result is an organization that is operated primarily for the benefit of the managers of the charity, not patients, their families, donors, or the general public.

Sunshine laws granting greater public access to information about a charity's spending and operations will also influence the behavior of board members. The Hoover Institution scholar Martin Anderson illustrates this for the case of university boards of directors (universities are also nonprofit institutions). Most university trustees are complacent, says Anderson, as are most other nonprofit board members. An effective way to get them to become more concerned and active is "to turn the hot beam of the public spotlight on them. Trustees need, and deserve, a merciless scrutiny."[5] Anderson's advice is as applicable to health-charity board members as it is to university trustees, which are his special concern:

> We need to ask who they [the university board members] are, what their qualifications are for the job, what actions they have taken or not taken, how they voted on issues that came before their governing boards. We need to make them as accountable to us as the most public of public figures. We need photographs of them and stories about them in the newspapers; we need to hear them on radio and see them on television. We need to know them well enough so we can write them and telephone them, and personally tell them how we feel about their performance. We need to praise them when they do well, and we need to punish them when they are negligent.[6]

The one group in society with the power to bring trustees "out into the sunlight," says Anderson, are the press and the media. This is why we believe that sunshine laws and state-level Freedom of Information Acts are wise public policies. They would make it easier for the media and researchers to inform the public about the operations of both health charities and their boards of directors. Such a course of action would surely get the attention of board members, for, as Anderson relates, most of the people who serve on the boards of major corporations and universities and other nonprofit organizations are not only very accomplished people, they are also very private people who are not at all comfortable dealing with "inquisitive writers or reporters."[7]

REGULATION IS NOT THE CURE

The predictable response of government officials to charity misbehavior, as mentioned above, is to propose tighter government controls over charities. State attorneys general already have power to prosecute fraud and other criminal behavior, but regulators are also clamoring for more *regulatory* powers. State government controls over charities were substantially reduced by a series of court rulings in the 1980s, including one that barred governments from "telling charities how they should spend their money."[8] State charity regulators are unhappy with these rulings and many of them advocate legislation that would restore their powers.

But such legislation would greatly weaken the independence and integrity of charity as we know it. Giving regulators the ability to tell charities how they should spend their money would convert charities into little more than appendages of government. And enough exposés have been written about government mismanagement to indicate that these agencies are the last institutions anyone would want to direct charity expenditures and operations.[9] Bureaucrats are not known for their frugality, wisdom, or efficiency in spending other peoples' money—or in instructing other people about how to spend their own money. Nevertheless, many well-intentioned social reformers advocate the unrealistic goal of a regulatory agency that, for the first time ever, would eschew politics, ignore the perverse incentives inherent in all government enterprises, and regulate charities in a way that would truly serve the public interest—if such a concept could ever be defined.

Carl Bakal, for example, concluded his book, *Charity U.S.A.,* by asserting that

> what is needed is a newly created, independent, nonpolitical federal agency, comparable to the Securities and Exchange Commission (SEC), which would oversee charities and take action against abuses. To free what might be called the Charities Regulatory Commission (CRC) from political pressures, its board members, perhaps five in number, reflecting all elements of philanthropy from donors to donees, would be appointed by the president with the consent of the Senate.[10]

It is puzzling how a researcher as astute as Bakal, whose book is filled with insights, can be so naive about what can be accomplished by regulation. Bakal is not the only one with this shortsightedness; many well-intentioned social reformers seem forever determined to ignore political reality as they continue to recommend unworkable, unrealistic, and utopian solutions to the nation's economic and social problems.

It is illogical to believe that requiring members of a Charities Regulatory Commission to be appointed by the president and senators—all of whom are politicians whose every decision is politically motivated—would somehow render the agency "nonpolitical." A nonpolitical government agency is a contradiction in terms, regardless of whether it is part of the federal or state or local government. When charity is politicized, politics, not efficiency, will be the guiding force in resource-allocation decisions, often to the detriment of the recipients of charity and of the general public.

Political control of charities might also reduce donations, for potential donors would naturally suspect that their money would be spent more for political than charitable reasons. Charity would suffer if citizens thought of charity management in the same way that they think about the management of the Postal Service, the Department of Motor Vehicles, or the Pentagon.

If Bakal's prescription were followed, federal regulation of charities would create a blizzard of paperwork and divert energy and resources away from charitable programs. The abilities of existing charities to serve the public would be reduced; many smaller charities would likely go out of business; and the formation of new charities would be discouraged:

> Detailed reports, following specified accounting and financial guidelines, would have to be filed periodically with the CRC. These reports would provide certain basic information about an organization, including its purposes, programs, priorities, plans; receipts and expenditures; names, addresses, and salaries or expenses of its officers, directors, or trustees; possible conflicts of interest; financial arrangements with fund raisers; past difficulties with the law; and perhaps some evaluation of the organization's performance.[11]

If all this information were not promptly supplied to the regulators, says Bakal, the government could "refuse registration, and hence the right to solicit" donations.[12] Although well intentioned, such recommendations are ill conceived. Bakal's "cure" is worse than the "disease."

Advocates of more regulation of charities should be aware of the historical record of government regulation of for-profit firms. Nobel laureate Ronald Coase, who, as former editor of the *Journal of Law and Economics*, published numerous studies of the effects of government regulation, concluded that

> there have been more serious studies made of government regulation of industry in the last fifteen years or so, particularly in the United

States, than in the whole preceding period. These studies have been both quantitative and nonquantitative. . . . The main lesson to be drawn from these studies is clear: they all tend to suggest that the regulation is either ineffective or that when it has a noticeable impact, on balance the effect is bad, so that consumers obtain a worse product or a higher-priced product or both as a result of the regulation. Indeed, this result is found so uniformly as to create a puzzle: one would expect to find, in all these studies, at least some government programs that do more good than harm.[13]

More government control of health and other charities would also likely do more harm than good and should be avoided.

Health charities already make significant contributions to alleviating the nation's health care crisis. Much more could be done, however, if the health charities reduced their spending on public and professional education and on research and used these resources to aid disease victims and to provide community services. Accumulated wealth should be dramatically reduced, providing additional millions of dollars for programs. If such changes are not made, the question will remain about who benefits from the health charities: the public or the health charity's executives and staffs and the medical profession. Charities are unique institutions in American society because only they can mobilize volunteers. Thus, health charities should place much more emphasis on programs and activities that serve the needy and are carried out by volunteers.

NOTES

Chapter 1. Introduction: Are Health Charities Ailing?

1. Alexis de Tocqueville, *Democracy in America*, ed. Richard D. Heffner (New York: Mentor Books, 1956), p. 198.
2. Marvin Olasky, *The Tragedy of American Compassion* (Washington, D.C.: Regnery Gateway, 1992); idem, "Beyond the Stingy Welfare State," *Policy Review* 54 (Fall 1990), pp. 2–14.
3. U.S. Bureau of the Census, *Statistical Abstract of the United States, 1992* (Washington, D.C.: U.S. Government Printing Office, 1992), pp. 375–76.
4. Deborah M. Burek, Karin E. Koeck, and Annette Novallo, eds., *1990 Encyclopedia of Associations* (Detroit: Gale Research, 1989).
5. Senator Orrin Hatch, "Opening Statement," *Legal Services Corporation Act Amendments of 1983*, 98th Cong., 1st sess., 1983, p. 1.
6. For a detailed discussion, see Charles K. Rowley, *The Right to Justice: The Political Economy of Legal Services in the United States* (Brookfield, Vt.: Edward Elgar Publishing, 1992).
7. Senate Committee on Labor and Human Resources, *Oversight of the Legal Services Corporation, 1983: Hearings before the Committee on Labor and Human Resources*, 98th Cong., 1st sess., 1983, p. 506.
8. "Cancer Society Is the Best-Known Charity in U.S.," *NonProfit Times* (November 1989), p. 1.
9. American Cancer Society (ACS), *Cancer and the Poor: A Report to the Nation* (Atlanta: ACS, 1990).

Chapter 2. The Political Economy of Health Charities

1. Ludwig von Mises, *Human Action* (New Haven, Conn.: Yale University Press, 1949), p. 270.
2. Reason Foundation, *Privatization 1993* (Santa Monica, Calif.: Reason Foundation, 1993).
3. Ludwig von Mises, *Bureaucracy* (Westport, Conn.: Arlington House Publishers, 1944), p. 1.
4. James T. Bennett and Thomas J. DiLorenzo, *Official Lies: How Washington Misleads Us* (Alexandria, Va.: Groom Books, 1992), especially chapter 3.
5. Carl Bakal, *Charity, U.S.A.* (New York: Times Books, 1979), p. 130.
6. Ibid., p. 129.
7. Ibid., p. 131.
8. Ibid., p. 143.

9. U.S. General Accounting Office (GAO), *A Proposal for Disclosure of Contractual Arrangements between Hospitals and Members of Their Governing Boards and between Hospitals and Their Medical Specialists*, MWD-75-73 (Washington, D.C.: GAO, 1975), p. 2.

10. Amatai Etzioni and Pamela Doty, "Profit in Not-for-Profit Corporations: The Example of Health Care," *Political Science Quarterly* 91 (Fall 1976), p. 434.

11. Mary A. Mendelson, *Tender Loving Greed* (New York: Knopf, 1974), pp. 196–97.

12. Bennett and DiLorenzo, *Official Lies*, pp. 83–108.

13. Harvey Katz, *Give! Who Gets Your Charity Dollar?* (Garden City, N.Y.: Doubleday, 1974), pp. 89–90. (The other three members of the "big five" to which Katz refers are the American Cancer Society, the American Heart Association, and the American Lung Association.)

14. American Lung Association (ALA), "A Message from the Managing Director," *Annual Report, 1983* (New York: ALA, 1983), p. 5.

15. Major C. Wells, "Upper Cardozo Residents Get TB Skin Tests," *Washington Post*, October 22, 1972.

16. Major C. Wells, "District TB Tests Judged Ineffective," *Washington Post*, April 28, 1973.

17. Lynn Payer, *Disease-Mongers: How Doctors, Drug Companies, and Insurers Are Making You Feel Sick* (New York: Wiley, 1992).

18. Ibid., pp. 4–5.

19. George G. Kirstein, *Better Giving: The New Needs of American Philanthropy* (Boston: Houghton Mifflin, 1975), p. xvii.

20. Katz, *Give!*, pp. 156–57.

21. Bakal, *Charity, U.S.A.*, p. 127.

22. Ibid., p. 128.

23. Walter S. Ross, *Crusade: The Official History of the American Cancer Society* (New York: Arbor House, 1987), p. 245.

24. National Charities Information Bureau (NCIB), *American Heart Association* (New York: NCIB, 1989), p. 1.

25. Payer, *Disease-Mongers*, p. 82.

26. Ibid., p. 219.

27. Ralph W. Moss, *The Cancer Industry: Unravelling the Politics* (New York: Paragon House, 1989), p. 400.

28. Payer, *Disease-Mongers*, pp. 75–76.

29. Ibid., p. 176.

30. Moss, *The Cancer Industry*, p. 406.

31. Richard Carter, *The Gentle Legions* (Garden City, N.Y.: Doubleday, 1961), p. 142.

32. Ross, *Crusade*, p. 214.

33. Ward Sinclair, "Disease Lobbies: Where, How of NIH Spending," *Washington Post*, March 8, 1990.

34. Ibid.

35. National Institutes of Health (NIH), *NIH Advisory Committees: Authority, Structure, Function, Members* (Bethesda, Md.: NIH, 1989), p. iii.

36. Moss, *The Cancer Industry*, p. 433.

37. Ibid., p. 434.

38. Ibid., p. 97.

39. Ibid., p. 98.

40. Ibid., p. 99.
41. Ibid., p. 107.
42. Ibid., p. 108.
43. Ibid., p. 116.
44. Ibid., p. 118.

Chapter 3. Health Scams and Heart Scams

1. Carl Bakal, *Charity, U.S.A.* (New York: Times Books, 1979), p. 130–131.
2. Ibid., p. 143.
3. Ibid.
4. Ibid., p. 136.
5. Frank Ryan, *The Forgotten Plague: How the Battle against Tuberculosis Was Won— and Lost* (Boston: Little, Brown, 1993), p. 390.
6. Bakal, *Charity, U.S.A.,* p. 136.
7. Ibid.
8. Harvey Katz, *Give! Who Gets Your Charity Dollar?* (Garden City, N.Y.: Double-day, 1974), p. 78.
9. Ibid., p. 80.
10. Ibid., p. 81.
11. Ibid., p. 82–87.
12. United Way of America, *Report to the Board of Governors of United Way of America,* prepared by Verner, Liipfert, Bernhard, McPherson, and Hand (Washington, D.C.: UWA, 1992), p. 14 (hereinafter cited as *UWA Report*).
13. Charles E. Shepard, "Perks, Privileges and Power in a Nonprofit World," *Washington Post,* February 16, 1992.
14. UWA, *UWA Report,* p. 1.
15. Ibid., p. 3.
16. Shepard, "Perks, Privileges and Power," p. A-38.
17. UWA, *UWA Report,* p. 37.
18. Ibid.
19. Ibid.
20. Ibid.
21. Ibid, p. 37.
22. Ibid., p. 39.
23. Ibid., p. 4.
24. Ibid.
25. Ibid.
26. Alicia Mundy, "It Works for All of Them," *Regardie's* (February/March 1992), p. 21.
27. UWA, *UWA Report,* p. 11.
28. Shepard, "Perks, Privileges and Power," p. A-38.
29. Ibid.
30. Mundy, "It Works for All of Them," p. 24.
31. Charles Shepard, "United Way's For-Profit Offspring," *Washington Post,* February 24, 1992.
32. Charles Shepard, "Endowment Funds Bought Florida Condo," *Washington Post,* February 27, 1992.
33. Ibid.

34. UWA, *UWA Report,* p. 40.
35. Mundy, "It Works for All of Them," p. 24.
36. Shepard, "United Way's For-Profit Offspring."
37. Ibid.
38. Ibid.
39. UWA, *UWA Report,* p. 18.
40. Ibid., p. 19.
41. Shepard, "United Way's For-Profit Offspring."
42. Charles Shepard, "A Year Later, United Way Still Faces Investigations, Morale Problems," *Washington Post,* March 10, 1993.
43. Laura Lippman, "United Way Struggles Amid Slump," *Baltimore Sun,* March 21, 1993.
44. Karen Riley, "Putting a Premium on Lifestyle," *Washington Times,* January 27, 1993.
45. The source for all but the last of these list items is Riley, "Putting a Premium on Lifestyle."
46. Thomas Heath and Albert Crenshaw, "Blue Cross Spent Freely on Perks," *Washington Post,* November 15, 1992.
47. Barbara Rose, "Spending Abuses at Heart Fund," *Crain's Chicago Business* (March 23, 1992), p. 1.
48. Ibid.
49. Ibid., p. 34.
50. American Hospital Association, *Hospital Statistics, 1985 Edition* (Chicago: American Hospital Association, 1985), pp. 8–11.
51. James T. Bennett and Thomas J. DiLorenzo, *Unfair Competition: The Profits of Nonprofits* (Lanham, Md.: Hamilton Press, 1988).
52. Judith R. Lave and Lester B. Lave, *The Hospital Construction Act: An Evaluation of the Hill-Burton Program, 1948–1973* (Washington, D.C.: American Enterprise Institute, 1974), p. 14.
53. Laura Sanders, "Profits? Who, Me?" *Forbes* (March 23, 1987), p. 79.
54. P.L. 79-725, Title VI, Section 622(f), 60 Stat. 1042–43.
55. Michael S. Balter, "Broken Promises," *The Nation* (June 12, 1985), p. 16.
56. Ibid.
57. Regina E. Herzlinger and William S. Krasker, "Who Profits From Nonprofits?" *Harvard Business Review* 65 (January/February 1987), pp. 93–107.
58. Ibid.
59. Ibid., p. 104.
60. Ronald Kessler, "Pathologists: More Profits, More Pay," *Washington Post,* November 1, 1972.
61. Ibid.
62. Ronald Kessler, "Hospital Center Officials Used Connection to Reap Profits," *Washington Post,* October 31, 1972. See also William Stockton, "Bank with Officers on Blue Cross and Blue Shield Boards Use Their Funds," *New York Times,* August 5, 1987.
63. Ibid.
64. Ibid.
65. Milton Friedman, *Input and Output in Medical Care,* Hoover Institution Public Policy Essay (Stanford, Calif.: Hoover Institution Press, 1992), p. 1.

66. Ibid., p. 3.
67. Ibid.
68. Ibid., p. 4.
69. Ibid., p. 5.
70. Ibid., p. 12.
71. Ibid.

Chapter 4. The Business of Health Charities

1. National Health Council (NHC), *Report on Voluntary Health Agency Revenue and Expenses, Fiscal Year 1990* (Washington, D.C.: NHC, 1992), pp. 1–2 (hereinafter cited as *1990 Report*).
2. National Health Council, *Report on Voluntary Health Agency Revenue and Expenses, Fiscal Year 1989* (Washington, D.C.: NHC, 1991), pp. 6–10.
3. Ibid., p. 4.
4. NHC, *1990 Report*, p. 6.
5. Ibid., p. 12.
6. Walter S. Ross, *Crusade: The Official History of the American Cancer Society* (New York: Arbor House, 1987), p. v.
7. American Heart Association (AHA), *Annual Report, 1991* (Dallas: AHA, 1991), p. 1.
8. American Cancer Society (ACS), *Annual Report, 1991* (Atlanta: ACS, 1992), p. 2.
9. These percentages were computed from the financial statements in each of the three charities' annual reports for fiscal year 1991. Total compensation was computed by adding all salaries, fringe benefits, and payroll taxes from the consolidated financial statements. See AHA, *Annual Report, 1991*, pp. 13–14; ACS, *Annual Report, 1991*, p. 20; and American Lung Association (ALA), *Annual Report, 1991* (New York: ALA, 1992), p. 22. It is interesting that the NHC reports do not include any information on compensation.
10. ACS, *Annual Report, 1991*, p. 2.
11. For each fiscal year, Arthur Andersen & Company prepares audited financial statements for each of the ACS's fifty-seven divisions and for its national headquarters, as well as a consolidated financial statement. The audited financial statement contains a table entitled "Statement of Functional Expenses," which shows the amount spent on each expense item for each of the five program services and for fund-raising expenses and management and general expenses. The salaries, benefits, and payroll taxes were obtained from this table. The audited financial reports are for fiscal year 1989 or 1990, depending on the state.
12. Henry C. Suhrke, "The Aramony Affair," *Philanthropy Monthly* 91 (November 1991), p. 5.
13. For more information on this matter, see Stephen G. Greene, "Compliance with Salary Rules: Often Grudging," *Chronicle of Philanthropy* (March 24, 1992). In this article, Edward H. Able, Jr., executive director of the American Association of Museums, complained, "Because you work for a charitable organization, you now have no right to privacy.... This is one more straw on the camel's back that makes attracting the best and the brightest to the charitable community even more difficult." Such overblown, self-serving statements do not deserve rebuttal. At many state colleges and universities, salary information is a matter of public

record. At George Mason University, where one of the authors teaches, the current salary of everyone from the institution's president to the part-time groundskeeper is reported on a computer printout available on request at the library's reference desk. This disclosure has not yet caused the sky to fall.

14. Kurt Loft, "Cancer Industry Thrives on Disease," *Tampa Tribune,* March 17, 1992.

15. Greene, "Compliance with Salary Rules," p. 30.

16. Joan M. Mazzolini, "Cancer Society Criticized on How It Spends Its Money," *Cleveland Plain Dealer,* April 26, 1992.

17. Gregory Flannery, "Giving to the Cancer Society: Good Deed or Rip-Off?" *Claremont County Review,* April 15, 1992.

18. Many other state divisions have highly paid executives; the list here is suggestive, not exhaustive. According to ACS tax returns, the head of the Minnesota division earned $109,526 in 1987; in that year, the executive vice-presidents of the Connecticut and Illinois divisions made $97,285 and $95,066, respectively. See also Patricia Anstett ("Economist Criticizes State Cancer Society," *Detroit Free Press,* November 2, 1992), who reports that the head of the Michigan division made $102,000 in 1992 (plus generous fringe benefits) and that "six other [ACS-Michigan executives] earn between $55,000 and $75,000 a year."

19. Salary information for California was obtained from the ACS's federal tax return (IRS Form 990, Schedule A, Part I) for 1990 for the fifty-seven consolidated divisions, and from ACS-California's CT-2 filing with the Office of the Attorney General of California for the year ending August 31, 1991.

20. The number of employees earning more than $30,000 was taken from the ACS's IRS Form 990 (Schedule A, Part I) for national headquarters and from the return filed for the consolidated organization (national headquarters plus the fifty-seven divisions) for fiscal year ended August 31, 1990.

21. Mazzolini, "Cancer Society Criticized."

22. Arthur F. Stocks, letter to author James T. Bennett, September 19, 1991.

23. ACS, *Annual Report, 1991,* p. 21, n. 1.

24. ALA, *Annual Report, 1991,* p. 23, n. 9.

25. Cynthia Crossen, "Organized Charities Pass Off Mailing Costs as 'Public Education,'" *Wall Street Journal,* October 29, 1990.

26. Alison Leigh Cowan, "New Accounting Proposals Create Nonprofit Anxiety," *New York Times,* July 29, 1990.

27. Stocks, letter to Bennett (emphasis in original).

28. "IRS Will Change Focus of Auditing Charities," *Insight* (January 14, 1991), p. 43.

29. Crossen, "Organized Charities."

30. Ross, *Crusade,* p. 194.

31. Ibid., p. 195.

32. Stocks, letter to Bennett.

33. Photocopies of these bills were sent to the authors by an anonymous source, presumably a staff member at ACS-California's office in Oakland. Since word of this research became public, both authors have been inundated with information about the American Cancer Society provided by anonymous sources and by other insiders who identified themselves. All of this material has been interesting, but much of it deals with issues that are beyond the scope of our analysis.

34. NHC, *1990 Report,* p. 6.

35. Figures for 1981 were taken from James T. Bennett, *Health Research Charities: Image and Reality* (Washington, D.C.: Capital Research Center, 1990), p. 19, table II-2. Figures for fiscal year 1991 were obtained from the consolidated balance sheets; see ACS, *Annual Report, 1991,* p. 20; AHA, *Annual Report, 1991,* pp. 13–14; and ALA, *Annual Report, 1991,* p. 22.

36. ACS, *Annual Report, 1991,* p. 18 and p. 21, n. 4.

37. ALA, *Annual Report, 1991,* p. 22, n. 3.

38. ACS, *Annual Report, 1991,* p. 22, n. 8.

39. John Henderson, interview by Lee Kirk, Lee Kirk Show, radio station WWEE, Cleveland, April 14, 1992.

40. Arthur Andersen & Company, *American Cancer Society—Colorado Division, Inc., Financial Statements as of August 31, 1990, Together with Auditors' Report,* n. 4.

41. Holly Hall and Grant Williams, "Professor vs. Cancer Society," *Chronicle of Philanthropy* 4 (January 28, 1992), p. 27.

42. Ibid.

43. Much of the discussion in this section is taken from James T. Bennett, "Caveat Contributor," *Alternatives in Philanthropy* (Washington, D.C.: Capital Research Center, 1991).

44. For example, see David Steitfeld, "What Gives? Before Writing Out Your Check, Check Out the Charity," *Washington Post,* December 13, 1990; Lynn Simross, "Priority for the '90s Should Be the Big Payoff," *Los Angeles Times,* December 27, 1989; Abigail Van Buren, "Dear Abby," *San Francisco Chronicle,* February 1, 1989; Barry Meier, "Seeking Charities That Actually Help," *New York Times,* December 2, 1989; and Sylvia Porter, "Some Charities Post Excessive Expenses," United Press International, December 13, 1989.

45. Anne L. New, *Service for Givers: The Story of the National Information Bureau* (New York: National Information Bureau, 1983), pp. 8–11, p. 31. Prior to the early 1980s, the National Charities Information Bureau (NCIB) was known as the National Information Bureau. New's book provides an excellent historical perspective for interested readers.

46. Alison Leigh Cowan, "The Gadfly Who Audits Philanthropy," *New York Times,* October 7, 1990. The NCIB's approved 1990 operating budget shows total expenses of only $760,000; see National Charities Information Bureau, *1989 Annual Report* (New York: NCIB, 1989), p. 11.

47. NCIB, *1989 Annual Report,* p. 5.

48. Meier, "Seeking Charities That Actually Help."

49. Pamela Bayless, "Covenant's Woes Peril Board, Sites," *Crain's New York Business* (March 12, 1990), p. 1; "Ritter Got $140,000 from Trust for Runaway Youths," United Press International, March 7, 1990.

50. Rosalie Crowe, "Be Wary: Not All Causes Worthy," *Phoenix Gazette,* December 15, 1989.

51. Alison Leigh Cowan, "The Gadfly Who Audits Philanthropy."

52. Philanthropic Advisory Service, *Give . . . But Give Wisely,* December 1990 (brochure).

53. National Charities Information Bureau (NCIB), *Wise Giving Guide,* October 1990, p. 6.

54. The audited financial statements in the ALA's *Annual Report, 1991,* state that

"each constituent and/or affiliate Lung Association is required to remit 10 percent of its sharable revenue to American Lung Association [national headquarters]. In return, American Lung Association provides national leadership and certain services and supplies to its constituent and affiliate Lung Associations. Supplies provided by American Lung Association include Christmas Seals and other fundraising materials and health education materials, all provided at a price which approximates cost." See ALA, *Annual Report, 1991,* p. 26, n. 1B.

55. NCIB, *Wise Giving Guide,* p. 6.
56. Ibid.
57. Hall and Williams, "Professor vs. Cancer Society," p. 27.
58. Sandra Evans, "Charities Receive Little from Virginia Fund-Raiser: Bulk of Donations Covers Company's Costs," *Washington Post,* May 1, 1989.
59. NCIB, *1989 Annual Report,* p. 5.
60. NCIB, *Wise Giving Guide,* p. 2.

Chapter 5. Public Education or Public Confusion?

1. National Health Council (NHC), *Report on Voluntary Health Agency Revenue and Expenses, Fiscal Year 1990* (Washington, D.C.: NHC, 1992), p. 13.
2. American Cancer Society (ACS), *Annual Report, 1988; Annual Report, 1989; Annual Report, 1990;* and *Annual Report, 1991* (Atlanta: ACS, 1988, 1989, 1990, and 1991, respectively), pp. 10–11, p. 11, p. 11, p. 11, respectively.
3. American Cancer Society, *Cancer Facts and Figures, 1988* (Atlanta: ACS, 1988), p. 7; idem, *Cancer Facts and Figures, 1992* (Atlanta: ACS, 1992), p. 7
4. Karen G. Packer, letter to author James T. Bennett, December 19, 1990.
5. "Great American Smokeout," *Times Republican,* November 17, 1989.
6. Opal A. Fagle, letter to Jan Newell, April 17, 1986.
7. Philip Rubin, *Clinical Oncology for Medical Students and Physicians: A Multidisciplinary Approach,* 6th ed. (New York and Rochester, N.Y.: American Cancer Society and the University of Rochester School of Medicine and Dentistry, 1983), p. 20; Ralph W. Moss, *The Cancer Industry: Unravelling the Politics* (New York: Paragon House, 1989), p. 9.
8. Abigail Trafford, "A Bold Crusade," *Washington Post,* December 3, 1991.
9. Steven A. Rosenberg and John M. Barry, *The Transformed Cell: Unlocking the Mysteries of Cancer* (New York: G. P. Putnam's Sons, 1992).
10. National Charities Information Bureau (NCIB), *American Cancer Society* (New York: NCIB, 1990), p. 2.
11. Richard Carter, *The Gentle Legions* (Garden City, N.Y.: Doubleday, 1961), p. 145.
12. Sandy Rovner, "Heartburn—'Tis the Season," *Washington Post,* December 26, 1989.
13. Lynn Payer, *Disease-Mongers: How Doctors, Drug Companies, and Insurers Are Making You Feel Sick* (New York: Wiley, 1992), pp. 105–6. On page 65, Payer cites a survey showing that 17 million Americans took over-the-counter antacids twice a week or more in the spring of 1991.
14. Carter, *The Gentle Legions,* p. 146.
15. Edith Efron, *The Apocalyptics: Cancer and the Big Lie* (New York: Simon and Schuster, 1984), p. 478.
16. Robert D. Tollison and Richard E. Wagner, "Self-Interest, Public Interest, and

Public Health," *Public Choice* 69 (1991), p. 335. The latest cancer scare involves cellular telephones. See John Burgess, "Cancer Scare Leaves Cellular Phone Owners, Firms with Frayed Nerves," *Washington Post,* January 26, 1993.

17. Moss, *The Cancer Industry,* p. 232.

18. American Heart Association (AHA), *Annual Report, 1988* (Dallas: AHA, 1988), p. 2.

19. American Heart Association, *Think Heart Disease Only Strikes Men? Think Again* (n.d.). This brochure was distributed in March 1991 as part of the AHA's annual fund-raising campaign. Although oriented toward women, in most cases the same lifestyle advice would, with obvious exceptions, apply to men as well.

20. For a detailed discussion of the HeartGuide Seal, see James T. Bennett, *Health Research Charities: Image and Reality* (Washington, D.C.: Capital Research Center, 1990), chapter 6.

21. "Heart Association Withdraws Plan to Endorse Foods," *Washington Post,* April 3, 1990.

22. Marian Burros, "Heart Group Begins Food Labeling amid Outcry," *New York Times,* February 1, 1990.

23. "Foodbusters," *New York Times,* February 2, 1990.

24. "Who Should Label Food?" *Washington Post,* January 29, 1990.

25. AHA, *Annual Report, 1988,* p. 10.

26. Steven Waldman, "How Lobbyists Play the Numbers Game," *Newsweek* (February 12, 1990).

27. See, for example, George Lobsenz, "Auto Pollution Blamed for up to 120,000 'Excess Deaths,'" United Press International, January 19, 1990, and Brooks Boliek, "Lung," States News Service, January 19, 1990.

28. W. Dale Nelson, "Lung Association Asks $91 Million for Tuberculosis 'Looming Epidemic,'" Associated Press, January 30, 1992. For additional information on the new TB epidemic, see Don Colburn, "TB: The Scourge Strikes Again," *Washington Post,* January 12, 1993.

29. Bruce D. Charash, *Heart Myths: Common Fallacies about Prevention, Diagnosis, and Treatment* (New York: Viking Penguin, 1991), p. 20. The ACS nutritional guidelines are reported in John Laslo, *Understanding Cancer* (New York: Harper & Row, 1987), pp. 131–36. Much of the material in this section is taken from James T. Bennett and Thomas J. DiLorenzo, *Health Research Charities II: The Politics of Fear* (Washington, D.C.: Capital Research Center, 1991).

30. See Ruthe Eshleman, *The American Heart Association Cookbook,* 4th ed. (New York: David McKay, 1984); Rodman D. Starke and Mary Winston, eds., *The American Heart Association Low-Salt Cookbook: A Complete Guide to Reducing Sodium and Fat in the Diet* (New York: Times Books/Random House, 1990); and Scott M. Grundy and Mary Winston, eds., *The American Heart Association Low-Fat, Low Cholesterol Cookbook* (New York: Times Books/Random House, 1989).

31. Eshleman, *The American Heart Association Cookbook,* p. v.

32. "Reducing the Risk of Heart Attacks," *San Francisco Chronicle,* November 15, 1989.

33. Jon Van, "Heart Association Prepares for Fight over Cholesterol," *Chicago Tribune,* November 11, 1989.

34. Mark Bloom, "Controversy Continues over Food Labeling," *Washington Post,* January 17, 1989.

244 *Notes to Pages 113–18*

35. Starke and Winston, *The American Heart Association Low-Salt Cookbook,* dust-jacket.
36. Ibid., p. vii.
37. "Health Warning Can Be Taken with a Grain of Salt," *Rocky Mountain News,* November 14, 1990.
38. Richard Saltus, "A Second Look at Salt," *Boston Globe,* October 8, 1989.
39. "Health: Too Little Salt Can Pose Peril, Study Says," *Rocky Mountain News,* November 17, 1989.
40. Charash, *Heart Myths,* pp. 37–41.
41. Thomas J. Moore, *Heart Failure: A Critical Inquiry into American Medicine and the Revolution in Heart Care* (New York: Simon and Schuster, 1989), p. 76.
42. "The Salty Truth: A Low-Salt Diet Doesn't Benefit Everyone, Michigan Study Finds," *Orange County Register,* December 7, 1989.
43. Saltus, "A Second Look at Salt."
44. Starke and Winston, *The American Heart Association Low-Salt Cookbook,* pp. 272–73.
45. Eshleman, *The American Heart Association Cookbook,* p. iv.
46. Karola Saekel, "Alcohol Can Take the Heat," *San Francisco Chronicle,* May 2, 1990.
47. Edward Dolnick, "The Mystery of the Healthy French Heart," *San Francisco Chronicle,* May 27, 1990.
48. "Burger Chains Told to Trim the Fat," *St. Louis Post Dispatch,* April 12, 1990; and "Trim Use of Beef Fat, Chains Told," *Chicago Tribune,* April 12, 1990.
49. Alix F. Freedman, "Heart Association to Put Seal of Approval on Foods—But Will Consumers Benefit?" *Wall Street Journal,* December 13, 1988.
50. "Cancer Risk Factor Challenged: Study Disputes Diet Advice for Averting Breast Disease," *Washington Post,* October 21, 1992.
51. Steven Morris, "First Fat Substitute Heads for Your Table," *Chicago Tribune,* February 23, 1990.
52. Joe Crea, "Eat Your Veggies—But Forget the Meat," *Orange County Register,* September 12, 1990.
53. Gina Kolata, "Red Meat, Fat Tied to Colon Cancer: Study Says Diet Key Factor in Who Gets Disease," *Orange County Register,* December 13, 1990. See also Denise Webb, "Nutritionists Differ on Vegetarianism," *New York Times,* September 12, 1990; and Joe Crea, "Vegetarianism Is in Vogue for Health and Ecology," *Sacramento Bee,* October 3, 1990.
54. Sandra Blakeless, "New Habits Can Reverse Heart Blockage; Reduction of Stress Deemed Important," *Orange County Register,* July 21, 1990. See also Marian Burros, "Very Low-Fat Diet Really Does Unplug Arteries, Study Shows," *Orange County Register,* October 10, 1990.
55. "Feeding Frenzy," *Newsweek* (May 27, 1991), pp. 46–53.
56. Ibid., p. 50.
57. Jeremy Rifkin, *Beyond Beef: The Rise and Fall of the Cattle Culture* (New York: Dutton, 1992), pp. 1–2.
58. Brenda C. Coleman, "Cholesterol Confusion: Some Call Cholesterol the 'Fourth Horseman of Heart Disease,' but Critics Say Hype Has Caused Fear of Food," *St. Louis Post Dispatch,* December 30, 1989.
59. Sally Squires, "Cholesterol Guessing Game: Consistent Results Are Hard to

Obtain When People Try to Check Their Blood Fat," *Washington Post*, March 6, 1990.

60. Dolores Kong, "Anticholesterol Drugs Cut Heart Disease Sharply," *Boston Globe*, November 8, 1990.
61. Charash, *Heart Myths*, pp. 4–5.
62. Art Ulene, *Count Out Cholesterol: American Medical Association Campaign against Cholesterol* (New York: Knopf, 1989), pp. xi-xii.
63. Payer, *Disease-Mongers*, pp. 171–87.
64. Charash, *Heart Myths*, p. 11.
65. Ibid., pp. 14, 18, and 20.
66. Thomas J. Moore, "The Cholesterol Myth," *Atlantic Monthly* (September 1989), p. 37.
67. Dolnick, "The Mystery of the Healthy French Heart."
68. Squires, "Cholesterol Guessing Game."
69. Payer, *Disease-Mongers*, p. 183.
70. Marian Burros, "Cholesterol Matters, but How Much?" *New York Times*, October 4, 1989.
71. Erin Marcus, "Studies Suggest a Violent Side of Lower Cholesterol," *Washington Post*, September 4, 1990.
72. Christopher J. Georges, "Studies Find a Link between Aggressiveness and Cholesterol Levels," *New York Times*, September 11, 1990.
73. "Chronic Anger Called Real Killer," *Sacramento Bee*, December 16, 1990.
74. Barbara Roessner, "Caution: Joy Is Dangerous—New Research Says Control Is Key to Longevity," *San Francisco Chronicle*, December 5, 1990.
75. "Styles of Anger Studies," *San Francisco Chronicle*, October 9, 1989.
76. Lisa Scott, "Radical Doctor Will Run Local Cancer Program," *Orange County Register*, September 2, 1990.
77. "Study Links Women, Cholesterol Levels," *St. Louis Post Dispatch*, January 15, 1990.
78. Charash, *Heart Myths*, p. 7.
79. Joyce Price, "Old Men's Depression Tied to Low Cholesterol," *Washington Times*, January 9, 1993.
80. "Heart Groups Reaffirm the Health Benefits of Lower Cholesterol," *New York Times*, November 16, 1989.
81. Carole Sugarman, "Solid Margarine: Heart Disease Risk Linked to Certain Types of Fat," *Washington Post*, August 28, 1990.
82. "Margarine May Cause Heart Disease," *Washington Post*, October 8, 1992.
83. Malcolm Gladwell, "Oat Bran's Claims Weakened: No Major Role Found in Curbing Cholesterol," *Washington Post*, January 18, 1990.
84. Stephanie Turner, "Interpreting What the Experts Say about Fat, " *San Francisco Chronicle*, August 22, 1990.
85. Malcolm Gladwell, "Olive Oil's Benefits Don't Pan Out; No Evidence Found That Mono-Unsaturated Fats Cut Cholesterol Levels," *Washington Post*, March 1, 1990.
86. Starke and Winston, *The American Heart Association Low-Salt Cookbook*, p. 14.
87. John Tanasaychuk, "You've Got to Break a Lot of Shells to Find the Truth," *Orange County Register*, May 30, 1990.
88. Marty Meitus, "Now, Egg Lovers Can Take Heart," *Rocky Mountain News*, Janu-

ary 3, 1990. See also Stephanie Turner, "Setting the Limits on What We Can Eat," *San Francisco Chronicle,* September 19, 1990; Gerald Etter, "Here's Where the Yellow Went," *Chicago Tribune,* June 21, 1990; and "Measuring Eggs' Cholesterol Gets a Fine Tuning," *Chicago Tribune,* October 19, 1989.

89. "Decaffeinated Coffee May Raise Cholesterol," *St. Louis Post Dispatch,* November 15, 1989. See also David Perlman, "Decaffeinated Coffee Linked to Cholesterol," *San Francisco Chronicle,* November 14, 1989; and Betsy A. Lehman, "A Tempest in a Coffee Pot," *Boston Globe,* November 27, 1989.

90. "Coffee Filter Appears to Be Vital to Keeping Cholesterol Down," *Chicago Tribune,* November 23, 1989. Also, see "Cholesterol Tests Brewing Coffee—New Health Study," *San Francisco Chronicle,* November 23, 1989.

91. "Feeling Frisky after That Morning Cup of Coffee," *Sacramento Bee,* January 19, 1990.

92. Gina Kolata, "Study Seeks No Link of Coffee, Heart Disease, but Experts Remain Divided on Risk," *Sacramento Bee,* October 11, 1990.

93. Carole Sugarman, "Nutritional Flip-Flops: What to Do about Milk and Margarine," *Washington Post,* October 13, 1992.

94. "Baldness Seen as a Link to Risk Factors in Heart Disease," *New York Times,* May 31, 1990; Jon Van, "Cholesterol High in Kids Glued to TV," *Chicago Tribune,* November 14, 1990.

95. Beatrice Trum Hunter, "Food Health Claims: Fact vs. Fiction," *Consumers' Research* (May 1990), p. 14. In passing, we note that even the tabloids have covered the diet craze. A story in the May 14, 1991, *National Examiner* is headlined "Pizza Sensation Prevents Cancer and Heart Attacks." The recipe that appears on p. 29 omits both pepperoni and anchovies.

96. See Thomas Szasz, *Sex: Facts, Frauds and Follies* (Oxford, England: Basil Blackwell, 1980).

97. Kenneth H. Cooper, *Aerobics* (New York: M. Evans, 1968).

98. Carol Drucoff, "Has Fitness Fizzled? While Many Workout, Most Prefer the Couch," *Washington Post,* January 30, 1990.

99. "What Can We Do with Our Hearts?" *San Francisco Chronicle,* November 19, 1989.

100. Daniel Q. Haney, "Dreams Could Be a Nightmare for the Heart," *Washington Times,* February 4, 1993.

101. Sally Squires, "Exercise Is Defense against Hypertension," *Washington Post,* December 1, 1992.

102. The interested reader may consult Harold L. Karpman, *Preventing Silent Heart Disease* (New York: Crown Publishers, 1989).

103. "The Risk in Getting out of Bed at Night," *San Francisco Chronicle,* November 14, 1989.

104. J. R. Johnstone and Chris Ulyatt, *Health Scare: The Misuse of Science in Public Health Policy,* Critical Issues no. 14 (Perth, Australia: Australian Institute for Public Policy, 1991), p. 52.

105. Trum Hunter, "Food Health Claims," p. 14.

106. See Payer, *Disease-Mongers,* especially pp. 172–78.

107. Ibid., p. x.

108. For a fascinating discussion of how medical practices and definitions of diseases vary across nations, see Lynn Payer, *Medicine and Culture* (New York: Penguin Books, 1988).

109. Payer, *Disease-Mongers,* pp. 180–81.
110. "Interview of Surgeon General C. Everett Koop," *New York Times,* December 13, 1985.
111. U.S. Congress, House, Committee on Energy and Commerce, *Cigarettes: Advertising, Testing, and Liability, Hearings before the Subcommittee on Transportation, Tourism, and Hazardous Materials, House of Representatives,* on H.R. 4543, 100th Cong., 2d sess., 1988, pp. 441–42 (emphasis added).
112. Ibid., p. 442.
113. American Lung Association, *Annual Report, 1987* (New York: ALA, 1987), p. 5.
114. American Cancer Society, *Cancer and the Poor: A Report to the Nation* (Atlanta: ACS, 1989), p. 5. This statement is made in virtually all ACS publications, including its annual reports.
115. Ibid.
116. Ibid.
117. Ibid., p. 1.
118. Ibid., p. 8.
119. Ibid., p. 1
120. Ibid., p. 7
121. Ibid. See "St. Louis Hearing Testifier Profiles" in appendix.
122. Ibid., p. 27.
123. Ibid. (Emphasis added).
124. Ibid., p. 3.
125. Ibid. (Emphasis added).
126. Ibid. (Emphasis added).
127. Sandra G. Boodman, "Fear of Breast Cancer," *Washington Post,* January 5, 1993.

Chapter 6. Subsidizing Professional Education and Research

1. "Most People Want More Medical Research," *Washington Post,* July 14, 1992.
2. M. L. Brown, "The National Economic Burden of Cancer: An Update," *Journal of the National Cancer Institute* 82 (1990), pp. 1811–14.
3. "American Lung CEO Sees Communications as One of the Keys to Success of Nonprofits," *NonProfit Times* 5 (May 1991), p. 10.
4. American Heart Association (AHA), *Annual Report, 1991* (Dallas: AHA, 1991), p. 4.
5. American Cancer Society (ACS)-Ohio, *Annual Report, 1991* (Dublin, Ohio: ACS-Ohio, 1991), p. 4.
6. See James T. Bennett, *Salaries and Wealth or Cancer Services? A Study of the American Cancer Society—Wisconsin Division* (Milwaukee: Heartland Institute of Wisconsin, 1991), p. 4.
7. James T. Bennett, *American Cancer Society—Colorado Division: Health or Wealth?* (Golden, Colo.: Independence Institute, 1991), p. 4.
8. ACS-Ohio, *Annual Report, 1988–89* (Dublin, Ohio: ACS-Ohio, 1989), p. 6.
9. Spencer Rich, "Doctor's Average Income $164,300," *Washington Post,* May 21, 1992.
10. Spencer Rich, "Average Staff Doctor Said to Earn $139,700," *Washington Post,* February 24, 1993.
11. Robin Herman, "Salaries Up, Supply Down in Family Practice," *Washington Post,* September 3, 1991.
12. "Nurses' Incomes on the Rise," *Washington Post,* December 15, 1992.

13. Rich, "Average Staff Doctor Said to Earn $139,700."

14. "American Lung CEO Sees Communications as One of the Keys to Success for Nonprofits," p. 10.

15. Mike Feinsilber, "The Charitable Impulse: Even the Professionals Have Trouble Deciding Where to Give," Associated Press, February 2, 1992.

16. American Heart Association, *Annual Report, 1991* (Dallas: AHA, 1991), pp. 11–12. At the end of 1991, the AHA discontinued publication of two monthly publications, *Modern Concepts of Cardiovascular Disease* and *Current Concepts of Cardiovascular Disease and Stroke*. See *Ulrich's International Periodicals Directory, 1992–93*, 31st ed., vol. 3 (New Providence, N.J.: R. R. Bowker, 1992), pp. 5238, 5175.

17. American Lung Association (ALA), *Annual Report, 1991* (New York: ALA, 1991), pp. 13, 21.

18. Ibid, p. 21.

19. AHA, *Annual Report, 1991,* pp. 11–12 (emphasis added).

20. See James T. Bennett and Thomas J. DiLorenzo, *Unfair Competition: The Profits of Nonprofits* (Lanham, Md.: Hamilton Press, 1989).

21. American Heart Association, *Annual Report, 1991* (Dallas: AHA, 1991), pp. 1–2.

22. ACS, *Cancer Facts and Figures, 1992,* p. 21.

23. For a discussion of health charities lobbying Congress for research funds for the National Institutes of Health (NIH), see James T. Bennett, *Health Research Charities: Image and Reality* (Washington, D.C.: Capital Research Center, 1990), pp. 59–67.

24. W. Virgil Brown, letter to *National Review* editor John O'Sullivan, October 8, 1991 (emphasis added).

25. AHA, *Annual Report, 1991,* pp. 2, 13.

26. American Lung Association, *Annual Report, 1990* (New York: ALA, 1990), p. 2.

27. American Lung Association, *Annual Report, 1987* (New York: ALA, 1987), p. 11.

28. American Lung Association, *Annual Report, 1981–1982* (New York: ALA, 1982), p. 15.

29. Damon Runyon–Walter Winchell Cancer Research Fund (DRWWCRF), *Annual Report, 1990* (New York: DRWWCRF, 1990), p. 5.

30. Ralph W. Moss, *The Cancer Industry: Unravelling the Politics* (New York: Paragon House, 1989), p. 3.

31. "Mr. Nixon: You Can Cure Cancer," advertisement in the *New York Times*, December 9, 1969.

32. Ibid.

33. Victor Cohn, "New Agency on Cancer Opposed," *Washington Post*, March 10, 1971.

34. A sampling of the articles of interest might include the following: "A Clarification on Cancer Funds," *Washington Post*, March 3, 1971; Stuart Auerbach, "Cancer Fight Set by Nixon," *Washington Post*, May 12, 1971; "Playing Politics with Cancer Research," *Washington Post*, May 13, 1971; Stuart Auerbach, "Cancer Unit Approved by Senate," *Washington Post*, July 8, 1971; "Can 79 Senators Be Wrong?" *Washington Post*, July 18, 1971; Stuart Auerbach, "Argument on Hill: How to Cure Cancer," *Washington Post*, September 16, 1971; "A New Opportunity to Fight Cancer," *Washington Post*, October 6, 1971; Stuart Auerbach, "Nixon Plan on Cancer Discarded," *Washington Post*, October 16, 1971; "The

Conquest of Cancer," *Washington Post*, October 19, 1971; "More on the Cancer Bill," *Washington Post*, October 26, 1971; Richard L. Lyons, "Expanded Cancer Research, Within NIH, Voted by House," November 16, 1971; Cristine Russell, "The Politics of Cancer," *Washington Post*, November 28, 1971; "Nixon Help Sought in Cancer Impasse," *Washington Post*, December 4, 1971; Stuart Auerbach, "Conferees Agree on Cancer Effort," *Washington Post*, December 8, 1971; "Wider Study of Cancer Approved by House," *Washington Post*, December 10, 1971; Stuart Auerbach, "Debate on Cancer Legislation Will Resume in House Today," *Washington Post*, September 15, 1971; and "The Conquest of Cancer," *Washington Post*, September 23, 1971.

35. Abigail Trafford, "A Bold Crusade," *Washington Post*, December 3, 1991.
36. Ibid.
37. U.S. General Accounting Office (GAO), *Cancer Patient Survival: What Progress Has Been Made?* GAO/PEMD-87-13 (Washington, D.C.: GAO, March 1987), pp. 2–3.
38. U.S. General Accounting Office, *Breast Cancer: Patient's Survival*, GAO/PEMD-89-9 (Washington, D.C.: GAO, February 1989), p. 2.
39. Ibid., p. 3.
40. Ibid., pp. 2–3.
41. ACS, *Cancer Facts and Figures, 1992*, pp. 25–26.
42. Moss, *The Cancer Industry*, pp. xii–xiii.
43. Ibid.; see chapter 11 for a discussion of vitamin C and chapter 10 for one of hydrazine sulfate.
44. Ibid., p. 417.
45. Samuel S. Epstein, *The Politics of Cancer* (San Francisco: Sierra Club Books, 1978), p. 1.
46. David Brown, "Cancer Research Groups' Efforts Called Misdirected," *Washington Post*, February 5, 1992.
47. Samuel S. Epstein, "The Cancer Establishment," *Washington Post*, March 10, 1992.
48. Not everyone shares Epstein's views. Largely in response to Epstein's claim that carcinogens in the environment are the primary cause of various cancers, Edith Efron wrote *The Apocalyptics: Cancer and the Big Lie* (New York: Simon and Schuster, 1984), which challenged Epstein's central thesis. No one doubts that some cancers can be traced to carcinogens—for example, exposure to radiation can cause leukemia—but whether *most* cancers can be traced to this source is a much more complex issue.
49. E. H. Johnson, "Kepler and Mysticism," in History of Science Society series, *Johann Kepler: 1571–1630* (Baltimore: Williams & Wilkins, 1931), p. 72.
50. Arthur Koestler, *The Watershed: A Biography of Johannes Kepler* (Garden City, N.Y.: Doubleday, 1960), pp. 218–19.
51. Arthur Koestler, *The Act of Creation* (New York: Macmillan, 1964), p. 129.
52. Richard S. Westfall, *Essays on the Trial of Galileo*, Vatican Observatory Publications, Special Series: Studi Galileiani (Notre Dame, Ind.: University of Notre Dame Press, 1989), p. v. See also Ludovico Geymonat, *Galileo Galilei: A Biography and Inquiry into His Philosophy of Science* (New York: McGraw-Hill, 1965).
53. See Arthur Koestler, *The Sleepwalkers: A History of Man's Changing Vision of the Universe* (New York: Macmillan, 1959).

54. Ibid., p. 15.
55. Reed Merrill and Thomas Frazier, *Arthur Koestler: An International Biography* (Ann Arbor, Mich.: Ardis, 1979), p. 18 (emphasis added).
56. James D. Watson, *The Double Helix* (New York: Atheneum, 1968), pp. xi–xii.
57. Steven A. Rosenberg and John M. Barry, *The Transformed Cell: Unlocking the Mysteries of Cancer* (New York: G. P. Putnam's Sons, 1992), p. 262.
58. Arthur Koestler, *Insight and Outlook: An Inquiry into the Common Foundations of Science, Art, and Social Ethics* (New York: Macmillan, 1949), p. 257, n. 5.
59. The interested reader should consult Moss, *The Cancer Industry*, chaps. 8 and 9.
60. American Cancer Society, *Cancer Facts and Figures, 1991* (Atlanta: ACS, 1991), p. 2.
61. Moss, *The Cancer Industry*, chapter 11.
62. American Cancer Society, *Cancer Facts and Figures, 1989* (Atlanta: ACS, 1989), p. 27 (emphasis added).
63. Moss, *The Cancer Industry*, p. 216.
64. "Diving for Drugs: Scientists Search the Sea," *Journal of the National Cancer Institute* 84 (July 15, 1992), p. 1602.
65. Ibid.
66. Albert Rothenberg, *Creativity and Madness: New Findings and Old Stereotypes* (Baltimore: Johns Hopkins University Press, 1990), p. 6.
67. Moss, *The Cancer Industry*, p. 433.
68. Ibid., p. 405.
69. American Cancer Society, *Annual Report, 1976* (Atlanta: ACS, 1976), p. 26, n. 9.
70. Michael F. Heron, letter to author James T. Bennett, July 8, 1992.
71. American Cancer Society, "Policy on Conflict of Interest," adopted February 13, 1976, and amended November 17, 1990, p. 1.
72. Walter S. Ross, *Crusade: The Official History of the American Cancer Society* (New York: Arbor House, 1987), pp. 4–5.
73. Scott McCartney and Fred Bayles, "Farm Aid Program of '88: 'Drought' Payments Even in Wet Areas," *Los Angeles Times*, December 31, 1989.
74. The payments were approved on January 27, 1992, and October 9, 1992. Interested readers can request copies of the payment documents from the Virginia Department of Health by citing control numbers 65929003 and 65929004 for those dates, respectively.
75. David M. Raup, *The Nemesis Factor* (New York: W. W. Norton, 1986), pp. 202–203.
76. Epstein, *The Politics of Cancer*, p. 323–24.
77. See, for example, James T. Bennett, *Health Research Charities*, pp. 55–56.
78. Epstein, *The Politics of Cancer*, p. 426.
79. House Subcommittee on Intergovernmental Relations and Human Resources, Committee on Government Operations, *The National Cancer Program (Part 1, Overview of Program Administration), Hearings before the Subcommittee on Intergovernmental Relations and Human Resources*, 95th Cong., 1st sess., 1977, p. 399.
80. Ibid., pp. 407–408, 418.
81. Ross, *Crusade*, p. 5.
82. U.S. Congress, House, *Hearings on the National Cancer Program*, p. 118 (emphasis added).
83. Ibid., p. 447.

84. Moss, *The Cancer Industry*, p. 355. Chapter 17 is devoted to the cancer establishment.

85. Ibid., pp. 389–90.

86. House of Representatives, *Are Scientific Misconduct and Conflicts of Interest Hazardous to Our Health?* H. Rept. 101-688, 101st Cong., 2d sess., 1990, p. 65. Also, see Frank Kuznik, "Fraudbusters," *Washington Post Magazine* (April 14, 1991), p. 22.

87. House of Representatives, *Are Scientific Misconduct and Conflicts of Interest Hazardous to Our Health?* p. 23.

88. Rosenberg and Barry, *The Transformed Cell*, p. 151.

89. Stephen Goode, "Trying to Declaw the Campus Copycats," *Insight* 9 (April 18, 1993), pp. 10, 28–29.

90. Epstein, *The Politics of Cancer*, p. 425.

91. AHA, *Annual Report, 1991*, p. 4.

92. House Subcommittee on Intergovernmental Relations and Human Resources, *The National Cancer Program*, pp. 398–99 (emphasis added).

93. House Subcommittee on Intergovernmental Relations and Human Resources, *The National Cancer Program*, p. 399.

94. Stephen Klaidman, *Health in the Headlines: The Stories Behind the Stories* (New York: Oxford University Press, 1991), book jacket.

Chapter 7. Sweet Charity: Patient and Community Services

1. Charity begins at home—and stays there, for the most part. In many parts of the world, people who are considered poor in the United States would be considered relatively well-off. Hunger and homelessness are many times more severe in India than in the United States. Yet most Americans are concerned with social problems where they live, even though the problems are much worse elsewhere. "Out of sight, out of mind" is one explanation for the parochial (in contrast to world) views most Americans have about the needy. Another explanation is that donors know that the problems elsewhere are so widespread that they seem intractable and beyond aid. A small contribution may do a great deal if the need is not overwhelming, but it would amount to only a drop in the ocean in the world's poorest nations. Problems in foreign countries are left to international agencies or to the government.

2. Walter S. Ross, *Crusade: The Official History of the American Cancer Society* (New York: Arbor House, 1987), p. v.

3. American Heart Association (AHA), *Annual Report, 1991* (Dallas: AHA, 1991), p. 1.

4. American Cancer Society (ACS), *Annual Report, 1991* (Atlanta: ACS, 1991), p. 2.

5. National Health Council (NHC), *Report on Voluntary Health Agency Revenue and Expenses, Fiscal Year 1989* (Washington, D.C.: NHC, 1991), pp. 8, 10.

6. Ibid., p. 15.

7. Ibid., p. 17.

8. Constance Engelking, "American Cancer Society Patient Service Programs: An Update," in *Continuing Care, Proceedings of the Sixth National Conference on Cancer Nursing, Seattle, Wash., July 25–27, 1991* (Atlanta: ACS, 1992), p. 11.

9. American Cancer Society, *Cancer Facts and Figures, 1992* (Atlanta: ACS, 1992), p. 26.

10. ACS, *Annual Report, 1991,* p. 13.

11. Engelking, "American Cancer Society Patient Service Programs," p. 17.

12. Ibid., p. 17.

13. Ibid.

14. ACS, *Annual Report, 1991,* p. 13. For a survey national in scope, the sample sizes seem very small. Age and occupational characteristics are based on a sample of 164 Road to Recovery program recipients; marital status, on 161 recipients; and household income, on 135 recipients.

15. ACS, *Annual Report 1991,* p. 13.

16. Harriet Zoller, "Look Good . . . Feel Better: Coming of Age," *Cancer News* 45 (Spring 1991), pp. 6–8.

17. Lina Calandra, *Look Good . . . Feel Better Fact Sheet* (Washington, D.C.: Cosmetic, Toiletry, and Fragrance Association [CTFA] Foundation, n.d.).

18. Lina Calandra, "Look Good . . . Feel Better Restores Cancer Patients' Self-Image and Appearance," (Washington, D.C.: CTFA Foundation, n.d.).

19. ACS, *Annual Report, 1991,* p. 13. For the record, Look Good . . . Feel Better is a "product-neutral" program. No product line or manufacturer is promoted or endorsed.

20. Harriet Zoller, "Reach to Recovery: A Woman-to-Woman Success Story," *Cancer News* 43 (Autumn 1989), p. 15.

21. Ibid.

22. ACS, *Cancer Facts and Figures, 1992,* p. 26.

23. ACS, *Annual Report, 1991,* p. 13.

24. Zoller, "Reach to Recovery," p. 17.

25. American Cancer Society, *CanSurmount Program Manual* (Atlanta: ACS, 1985), foreword.

26. ACS, *Cancer Facts and Figures, 1992,* p. 26.

27. American Cancer Society, *CanSurmount* (Atlanta: ACS, 1985).

28. Examples of materials provided by the national headquarters include American Cancer Society, *CanSurmount Promotion Kit Patient Visitor Program* (Atlanta: ACS, 1985); idem, *CanSurmount Patient Visitor Program Training Manual* (Atlanta: ACS, 1985); and idem, *CanSurmount Patient Visitor Program Volunteer's Handbook* (Atlanta: ACS, 1985). The authors thank Michael F. Heron, senior vice-president for communications of the American Cancer Society, for providing copies of these materials.

29. Engelking, "American Cancer Society Patient Service Programs," p. 13.

30. Ibid., pp. 13–14.

31. ACS, *Annual Report, 1991,* p. 13.

32. *Rehabilitating Laryngectomees: The Program of the International Association of Laryngectomees* (Atlanta: ACS, n.d.), pp. 3–4.

33. Ibid., p. 10.

34. *First Steps: Helping Words for the Laryngectomee* (Atlanta: ACS, n.d.).

35. Engelking, "American Cancer Society Patient Service Programs," pp. 13–14.

36. We gratefully acknowledge the assistance of Michael F. Heron for providing this overview of the I Can Cope program as well as materials describing ACS programs cited elsewhere in this chapter.

37. Engelking, "American Cancer Society Patient Service Programs," p. 18.

38. Bill Moyers, *Healing and the Mind* (New York: Doubleday, 1993), p. 67.

39. Lynn Payer, *Medicine and Culture* (New York: Penguin Books, 1988), p. 24.

40. In case the reader is surprised by wide differences in medical care across countries, consider how much variation there is across states in surgery for prostate cancer in the United States. "In Rhode Island, the operation was performed on about 20 of every 100,000 men on Medicare, but in Alaska, it was done on 429 of every 100,000 [a 21.5-fold discrepancy!]." In addition, there are huge changes over time: "The rate of radical prostatectomy was 5.75 times higher in 1990 than in 1984." Despite all this, there is little evidence that this surgery measurably lengthens life expectancy. See David Brown, "Little Benefit Seen in Prostate Surgery," *Washington Post*, May 26, 1993.

41. The "Hawthorne effect" refers to experimental studies on how work groups affect productivity. The studies were conducted in the late 1920s in Chicago by Harvard University researchers at the Hawthorne Works of the Western Electric Company. The researchers found that groups develop norms of behavior and use social pressure on group members to enforce conformity with these norms. Thus, participation in a group can change an individual's attitudes and, if there is a link between healing and the mind, disease victims may benefit from participation in a support group. For an in-depth treatment of these early sociological studies and their findings, see F. J. Roethlisberger and William J. Dickinson, *Management and the Worker: An Account of a Research Program Conducted by the Western Electric Company, Hawthorne Works, Chicago* (Cambridge, Mass.: Harvard University Press, 1949).

42. Payer, *Medicine and Culture*, pp. 9–10.

43. Moyers, *Healing and the Mind*, p. 331.

44. Ibid., p. xii.

45. Joyce Price, "Alternative-Medicine Unit Told to Get Busy," *Washington Times*, June 25, 1993.

46. ACS, *Annual Report, 1991*, p. 13.

47. Readers who consult Engelking's article, the source for the information shown in table 7.1, should be warned that due to mechanical and proofreading errors, her figures are misnumbered. Her figure 2 is for the laryngectomee program, not the CanSurmount program; figure 3 is for the ostomy program, not the laryngectomee program; and figure 4 is for the CanSurmount program, not the ostomy program. These errors have been confirmed by the Patient Services Department of the ACS.

48. Samples of American Lung Association (ALA) fund-raising letters and appeals were provided by the ALA of Northern Virginia. Some of these messages are still in use in the annual Christmas Seals campaign.

49. The ALA's *Annual Report, 1991*, shows total revenues of $123,485,000 for 1991 and that $542,799 was spent on "assistance to individuals." See American Lung Association, *Annual Report, 1991* (New York: ALA, 1991), pp. 21–22.

50. AHA, *Annual Report, 1991*, p. 4.

51. ALA, *Annual Report, 1991*, p. 26. To conform to the NHC's method of reporting spending, the ALA's expenditures must be "restated."

52. Lynn Payer, *Disease-Mongers: How Doctors, Drug Companies, and Insurers Are Making You Feel Sick* (New York: Wiley, 1992), pp. 174–75.

53. Ibid., p. 14.

54. Louise B. Russell, *Is Prevention Better Than Cure?* (Washington, D.C.: Brookings Institution, 1986), p. vii (emphasis added).

55. Russell, *Is Prevention Better Than Cure?*, pp. 2–3.

56. Milton C. Weinstein and William B. Stason, *Hypertension: A Policy Perspective* (Cambridge, Mass.: Harvard University Press, 1976), p. 60; see also idem, "Economic Considerations in the Management of Mild Hypertension," *Annals of the New York Academy of Sciences* 304 (March 30, 1978), pp. 424–40.

57. In 1990, health care cost Americans $665 billion, about $2,600 per capita; these expenditures are expected to exceed $800 billion in 1992. In 1960, aggregate health care expenditures accounted for less than 6 percent of gross national output; by 1990, however, this figure had risen to 12.2 percent—the highest of any nation in the developed world. If current trends continue, in little more than a decade almost one-fourth of the nation's output will be produced by the health care sector. See Rexford E. Santerre, Stephen G. Grubaugh, and Andres J. Stollar, "Government Intervention in Health Care Markets and Health Care Outcomes: Some International Evidence," *Cato Journal* 11 (Spring/Summer 1991), pp. 1–12; Victor Cohn, "Moving on Health Care Reform," *Washington Post*, January 21, 1992; Paul Taylor, "Tying Choices to Health Coverage," *Washington Post*, January 26, 1992; and Malcolm Gladwell, "Reforming the Health Care System: An American Paradox," *Washington Post*, February 6, 1992.

58. Kevin C. Kelleher, "Free Clinics: A Solution That Can Work . . . Now!" *Journal of the American Medical Association* 266 (August 14, 1991), pp. 838–39.

59. John M. Garvin, "Voluntarism in Health: A Forgotten Solution," *Philanthropy* 6 (Spring 1992), p. 1.

60. Michael E. Teller, *The Tuberculosis Movement: A Public Health Campaign in the Progressive Era* (New York: Greenwood Press, 1988), p. 48. See also Richard Carter, *The Gentle Legions* (Garden City, N.Y.: Doubleday, 1961), p. 71.

Chapter 8. Health-Charity Look-Alikes

1. S. David Young, *The Rule of Experts: Occupational Licensing in America* (Washington, D.C.: Cato Institute, 1987), p. 1.

2. Milton Friedman and Simon Kuznets, *Income from Independent Professional Practice* (New York: National Bureau for Economic Research, 1945).

3. William D. White, "Dynamic Elements of Regulation: The Case of Occupational Licensure," *Research in Law and Economics* 1 (1979), pp. 15–33.

4. Lawrence Shephard, "Licensing Restrictions and the Cost of Dental Care," *Journal of Law and Economics* 21 (April 1978), pp. 187–201.

5. Timothy R. Muzondo and Bohumir Pazderka, "Occupational Licensing and Professional Incomes in Canada," *Canadian Journal of Economics* 13 (November 1980), pp. 69–77.

6. Mancur Olson, "Supply Side Economics, Industrial Policy, and Rational Ignorance," in C. E. Barfield and W. A. Schambra, eds., *Politics of Industrial Policy* (Washington, D.C.: American Enterprise Institute, 1986), p. 66.

7. David Boaz, *Liberating Schools* (Washington, D.C.: Cato Institute, 1991).

8. Thomas J. DiLorenzo, "Why Free Trade Works," *Readers Digest* (February 1989), p. 92.

9. House Subcommittee on Transportation and Hazardous Materials, Committee on Energy and Commerce, *Deceptive Fund-Raising by Charities, Hearings before the Subcommittee on Transportation and Hazardous Materials*, 101st Cong., 1st sess., 1989.

10. Ibid., p. 105.

11. Ibid., p. 104.

12. Ibid.

13. Ibid., p. 103.

14. Ibid., p. 154.

15. Cited in Cynthia Crossen, "Organized Charities Pass Off Mailing Costs as 'Public Education,'" *Wall Street Journal*, October 29, 1990. See also James T. Bennett, "Caveat Contributor," *Alternatives in Philanthropy* (March 1991).

16. House Subcommittee on Transportation and Hazardous Materials, *Deceptive Fund-Raising by Charities*, p. 158.

17. Ibid., p. 155.

18. Ibid., p. 204.

19. Ibid., p. 183–84.

20. Ibid., p. 201–2.

21. Ibid.

22. Ibid.

23. Paula J. Fritz, letter to the editor, *Kane Republican*, June 29, 1992.

24. *Commonwealth of Pennsylvania v. Cancer Fund of America*, case no. 277, 1992, p. 33.

25. Mollie A. McCurdy, letter to Mrs. Henry S. Williams, December 16, 1991 (made public during 1992 hearings on charitable fund-raising in Pennsylvania).

26. Carmen Brutte, "4 National Charities Accused of Misdirecting Funds," *Harrisburg Patriot*, August 4, 1992.

27. Cancer Fund of America news release, November 2, 1992.

28. House Subcommittee on Transportation and Hazardous Materials, *Deceptive Fund-Raising by Charities*, p. 105.

Chapter 9. Is There a Cure for *What Ails Health Charities?*

1. Burton W. Fulson, Jr., *Entrepreneurs vs. the State: A New Look at the Rise of Big Business in America, 1840–1920* (Herndon, Va.: Young America's Foundation, 1987), p. 65–66.

2. Cited in Karen Riley, "Putting a Premium on Lifestyle," *Washington Times*, January 27, 1993.

3. Michelle Singletary, "Probing the Pay at Nonprofits," *Washington Post*, May 3, 1993.

4. Thomas Heath, "Some Charities in Md. File Misleading Accounts," *Washington Post*, April 26, 1992.

5. Martin Anderson, *Imposters in the Temple* (New York: Simon and Schuster, 1992), p. 202.

6. Ibid.

7. Ibid., p. 203.

8. Heath, "Some Charities in Md. File Misleading Accounts."

9. See, for example, Martin L. Gross, *The Government Racket: Washington Waste from A to Z* (New York: Bantam Books, 1992).

10. Carl Bakal, *Charity, U.S.A.* (New York: Times Books, 1979), p. 456.

11. Ibid.

12. Ibid.

13. Ronald Coase, "Economists and Public Policy," in J. F. Weston, ed., *Large Corporations in a Changing Society* (New York: New York University Press, 1975), pp. 182–84.

INDEX

257